HENRY COOPER

HENRY COOPER

THE AUTHORISED BIOGRAPHY OF BRITAIN'S GREATEST BOXING HERO

Robert Edwards

Acknowledgments

The author wishes to thank Sir Henry and Lady Cooper, Lord and Lady Teviot and in particular, for his diligent research and enthusiasm, Tony Gee. Thanks also to Andrew Lownie (the architect of this), Susan Dowdall at the *Daily Mail* and all at BBC Worldwide.

Picture credits

SECTION ONE: 1 & 4 Courtesy of Sir Henry Cooper; 2 © Allsport; 3 & 8 © Empics; 5 © Popperfoto; 6, 13 & 14 © *Daily Mail*; 7 & 12 © Allsport; 9–11 © Popperfoto.
SECTION TWO: 1, 2, 4–6 & 9 Courtesy of Sir Henry Cooper; 3, 5, 6, 8, 10–12 © *Daily Mail*; 7 © PA News.
SECTION THREE: 1–4 © *Daily Mail*; 5 © Popperfoto; 6 Courtesy of Sir Henry Cooper; 7 & 8 © Hulton Getty Picture Collection; 9 & 10, 12 © *Daily Mail*; 11 © Empics; 13 © Syndication International.

Published by BBC Worldwide Limited, Woodlands, 80 Wood Lane, London W12 0TT

First published 2002
Copyright © Robert Edwards 2002
The moral right of the author has been asserted.

ISBN 0 563 48831 X

Commissioning Editor: Ben Dunn · Project Editor: Julia Charles
Copy-editor: Judith Scott · Designers: Linda Blakemore and Kathy Gammon
Picture Researcher: Miriam Hyman · Production Controller: Christopher Tinker

Set in Garamond
Printed and bound in Great Britain by Butler & Tanner Limited, Frome
Colour separations by Radstock Reproductions Limited, Midsomer Norton
Jacket and plate sections printed by Lawrence-Allen Limited, Weston-super-Mare

Contents

For my mother

Introduction

THERE CAN BE VERY FEW SPORTSMEN whose career and reputation mark them out as instantly recognizable to a public outside their sport but there is one figure whose extraordinary popularity, by virtue of the traits he exhibits, marks him out as belonging to that select band, the 'national treasures'. He is Henry Cooper.

Before television, such figures were rare; they would be seen on newsreels, perhaps heard on the radio, and we would read of them in the press, but the advent of mass visual broadcasting allowed them an audience that would have been unheard-of even a few years before. The development of satellite broadcasting multiplied their audiences again by many times, and so as the 1950s gave way to the next decade, sports were considered to be a global activity, and participants had to be of a global standard. If they were not, they would fall by the wayside, and indeed many, particularly boxers, went the way of musical-hall comedians. A sportsman's character became important, too, as a mass audience could be quick to spot a personality who did not seem to deliver a certain character with which they were comfortable. It is different today, of course – Mike Tyson still has a huge following, despite his obvious character traits.

Henry Cooper survived the transition from private parochialism to public globalism. His fans spanned Europe and America once he had proved that he was a world-class heavyweight. He did this in 1958 when he beat the formidable Zora Folley, then ranked second in the world, behind the great Floyd Patterson.

And Henry's personality shone through: relaxed, modest, realistic and hugely skilled. At the time he won the British and Common-wealth heavyweight title in 1959, he was still living with his parents on an equally modest council estate in southeast London, sharing a room with his twin brother, George. He only moved out when he married in 1960. Unsurprisingly, George went, too.

As he rose to prominence (and stayed there), the nation came to identify with him. On the occasion of his first encounter with Cassius Clay in 1963 in a world title eliminator, when he put the American on the canvas, the country was heartbroken when he lost the fight. That he lost it by chicanery was clear, but he said nothing. When, on the occasion of his last fight against Joe Bugner in 1971 he lost through what can be only described as suspicious refereeing, Britain was doubly saddened, as the event triggered his retirement. In between, when he fought Muhammad Ali for the world title in 1966, it was a more important sporting occasion to many, particularly this author, than the World Cup Final of the same year.

All in all, Henry Cooper fought 55 professional bouts as a heavy-weight; he won 40, lost 14 and drew one. He successfully defended his British and Commonwealth title a record number of times and won three Lonsdale belts while doing it. That he had to sell these a few years ago in order to meet his liabilities as a Lloyd's name touched the nation as deeply as anything that had happened to him professionally.

His post-retirement career kept him in the public eye like no other man; he seemed ageless. In fact, he looks very similar now to the Henry Cooper of 30 years ago, when the last biography was published.

But time has moved on; there are things he can say now that he could only hint at then. The woes that befell him as a Lloyd's under-writer are, while well known, still something of a mystery which we can explore, as one venerable British institution is cynically ripped off by another.

I first started discussing this project with Sir Henry after the pub-lication of my biography of Stirling Moss; in many ways Sir Stirling brokered the introduction as the pair are not only good friends but also share a manager for certain events. Stirling is also a boxing fan. Although I had met Henry (very briefly) at a boxing evening some years before, I had no real acquaintance with him whatsoever, so when the familiar figure strolled into the London Golf Club in Sevenoaks, Kent, which was our agreed rendezvous, and simply shoved out a huge hand in greeting, I confess to being quite charmed.

Such is the demeanour of the man that the prospect of working with him on this project was, professionally as well as personally, a compelling one. As he leaned forward to explain some of the niceties of professional boxing (as opposed to mere violence) I realized that he is probably one of the most articulate and relaxed men I have ever met. The difference between the amateur and the professional, expressed in terms of career, was fascinating, as was his description of the 1963 Clay fight, which he famously lost. The rigours of the training camp, the dirty tricks of the ring, all is there, expressed lucidly, honestly and with the assurance that only a man with a career such as his can offer.

Some of the bad guys of the period are interesting, too, particularly now that many of them are dead, and we can breathe more easily. With so much money about, we should not be too surprised at the people we find lurking in the shadows – we meet the odd gangster, some truly terrifying businessmen and promoters, as well as a host of fighters, many of them obscure and forgotten now, but in their day, men who struck fear into a prudent heart. There are boxers Henry wishes he could have fought (Joe Louis, his childhood inspiration), there are boxers he is glad he managed to avoid (Rocky Marciano, Sonny Liston) and those he knew he could beat (Cassius Clay). There are men he wishes he could have hurt more (Piero Tomasoni) and those, particularly the three who knocked him out (Patterson, Johansson, and Folley) all of whom he recalls he rather liked. Being knocked out, he assures me, is entirely painless if an expert such as Patterson does it.

The sociology of boxing in these years 1954–1971 is interesting. The double life that he unavoidably led, living on a council estate while lunching in the West End as British heavyweight champion, was one with which he dealt very well indeed, and I have the impression that if he had to start again, he would change very little about himself. He does regret that his twin brother, George, did not progress further as a boxer, but George had recurrent fitness difficulties that frankly held him back. The pair made a good team at fights, though, with George acting more or less as Henry's trainer when he himself retired. There is some suspicion that of the two men George might have been a touch more aggressive when their paths were parallel, not out of sibling rivalry, but merely temperament. Interestingly, although the pair are identical, they are 'symmetrical' or 'mirror' twins – Henry is left-handed, George right. They live a few miles from each other in Kent and are as close now as they ever were.

Henry and George enjoyed a unique relationship with manager Jim Wicks that was brokered by a journalist after the brothers had finished their National Service with the 4th Battalion, Royal Army Ordnance Corps, in 1954. They had both fought in the Army as amateurs and turned professional under Wicks as soon as they were released. Wicks was a totally honest but deceptively hard man, who managed the twins' careers with great integrity. This is not always the case, as critics of the sport are quick to point out. The Wicks/Cooper relationship was very much *in loco parentis*. It was also the envy of fighters managed by lesser men, and there were plenty of those.

Wicks had started out life as a bookmaker and progressed to management rather as a second career. He was a heavy gambler and, by all accounts, a successful one. His headquarters, the gym above the *Thomas à Becket* pub in the Old Kent Road became, under his management, a mecca for British boxing and something of a social hub for the fans of the sport. Celebrities made sure they were seen there, watching the fighters train. All very gladiatorial.

Henry is quite straightforward as to motivation: he fought because it was his business to fight and not for reasons of some misty-eyed sentimentality. Wicks identified this and as a result theirs was a strong partnership. Boxing is a brutally Darwinian sport and there is a professional 'sudden death' element to it. A fighter who is over-matched and loses serially will stand little chance of recovering in order to take on worthier opponents. Conversely, a fighter who is constantly under-matched, fighting relative midgets and achieving a series of easy victories will not be considered a draw by promoters. It is a fine balance and Wicks found it; Henry was British champion for longer than any other man.

Awareness of boxing is deep in our collective psyche, whether we follow it, or approve of it, or not. The very terminology, the lexicon of boxing, is all around us and we use it quite unconsciously every day:

'coming up to scratch', 'throwing in the towel', 'making a fair fist', 'out for the count', 'saved by the bell', 'on the ropes' and so on.

This book is not intended to be a history of the prize ring, and not only because I am not particularly qualified to write that book. I am not, unlike others, steeped in the history of boxing, but I do regard its traditions as being of great significance to my story, as I see in Henry Cooper a man who has inherited the mantle of so many men in the past, champions of Britain, or at least England, whose popularity at the time was very similar to that enjoyed by him now.

The evolution from accomplished sportsman to national treasure is not an easy process to follow; one day we find that it has simply happened. In Britain, it is not always a status conferred purely by statistical success, either. There is a further quality that is required – that of character, as if the British believe that only the man who has so little to prove can be acceptably humble, and not in a Uriah Heep sense, either. Many men who achieved a great deal less than Henry did are far from that, of course, and are as a result far less popular and sought after.

Boxers can have something of an uphill struggle in this particular, purely because of the nature of their sport. It is not one that many understand (indeed, many people even refuse to accept even that it is a sport), save that it has a very dark side to it. It can be difficult to reconcile what our popular boxers such as Henry Cooper actually did for a living with the fact that we also like them so much; for they do and did what the vast majority of us simply cannot conceive of doing: climbing into a ring with another man, under formal and old-established rules, and beating him, fair and square, with frequently bloody results.

The association of the observer with what is actually happening in a boxing ring is quite unlike other sports. Many feel that they could drive a Grand Prix car, or manage their way around a golf course with some credit, or even serve an ace at a major tennis tournament (and they are probably wrong in all those assumptions) but climb into a ring with Ingemar Johansson, or even Brian London? No; it would be quite unthinkable.

Given the very shadowy nature of boxing, particularly when Sir Henry Cooper was Britain's senior exponent of it, his public started to identify with the simple fact that his involvement in it seemed to have left him morally untouched, unlike, perhaps, Sonny Liston, who while he was a tremendous hero to some, would probably not have included the late Queen Elizabeth the Queen Mother among his fans.

Some sportsmen are so competitive, so aggressive, that their state borders on that of a kind of autism. The public realizes this and often feels distanced, even repelled, as a result. I have met racing drivers, for example, who have never won a race, nor even achieved a podium position, but some of them have exhibited such a swaggering self-regard that I feared – not much, I must confess – for their sanity. I have never met a boxer like this; to be sure, there are those who rise to a certain tongue-in-cheek level of *performance*, but the suggestion is always there that this is so close to self-parody as to be considered an entertainment: merely perhaps, the hobby of easily bored men. The boxer's pride is generally a quiet thing, and we like and admire them for that.

No one who reads this book will be remotely surprised when I say that I like boxing rather a lot. It is an interesting sport and I admire what fighters do very much. The fact that it has been, literally and metaphorically, 'on its back foot' for some time is a matter of great regret to me. I have also had a go at it myself; in the 1960s, when I was at school, it was considered morally compulsory to lace on the huge, ancient and iron-hard 'mauleys' (around the back of the bike sheds, usually) and square up in some grotesque and ill-supervised mismatch. I got soundly thumped, of course, and it hurt, rather a lot, as I recall. There is nothing quite like a good whack in the solar plexus before Latin to quite put you right off the subject. So, my admiration for most of the men who do this for a living knows few bounds.

Although I well remember so many of Henry's fights, it has been interesting for me to cross-refer to so many contemporary accounts of them from more seasoned observers than me who were at the ringside. By and large, but not exclusively, I have used broadsheet and special-ist press coverage, for the simple reason that it is generally well written and concise, and lacks that ghastly sentimentality that seems to infest the tabloid world, although the opinion of that most accomplished writer, Peter Wilson of the *Daily Mirror*, is always illuminating.

Similarly, the veteran observer Harry Carpenter's insightful pieces, which he wrote so well for the *Daily Mail,* have been invaluable.

Viewing contemporary footage of some of Henry's encounters has also been revealing, if only because the flawed nature of some of my own recollections are revealed, but it is important to stress that the perspective of television or video is strictly two-dimensional and can be highly misleading; the view of a boxing match offered by being seated near the ringside is far removed from that offered by being seated on a sofa and watching from a distance, if only because the spectator at a live match can see (and hear) how hard these men actually hit each other. Television denies us this.

Interestingly, even broadsheet coverage differed radically in its *reportage* of a given fight, even down to the details of times elapsed and relative points. This is not necessarily for reasons of professional sloppiness, merely an aspect of history. No two writers will ever see things in exactly the same way, which is why it is important to compare and contrast consistently. After reading the bulk of the broadsheet press, it seemed to me that the *Daily Telegraph*'s Donald Saunders and *The Times*'s Neil Allen seem to have been the most consistent, particularly in their pre-match assessments, which are a useful litmus test of the informed opinion of the day.

It is not, of course, for me to make light of the efforts of any of the men in this book, no matter now they engaged with their subject, Henry Cooper. No man who boxed at this level for a living deserves anything but the total respect of any writer on the subject. Thus in drawing conclusions as to the relative abilities of certain fighters – putting them into context – I have relied either on Henry, the informed press, or what I think to be a workable consensus of contemporary opinion. But one thing I have learned is that statistics are seldom the measure of any man.

For this aspect of sport is important: sportsmen operate strictly in their own context. We cannot evaluate any sportsman on an absolute basis, although we are always trying to do it, for the simple reason that conditions, most obviously the quality of opposition, are such a huge historical variable. With motor racing, or any sport that depends upon technology as much as nerve to take it forward, a driver can only be measured in his own time and this crucial aspect applies even to other more individual sports, such as mountaineering. What could Edward Whymper have accomplished with modern equipment? Boxing, however, is more fundamental, more basic. A fight staged sixty years ago, or even a hundred, would be quite recognizable now, and Tom Cribb would no doubt certainly appreciate the skills of Henry Cooper; whereas I cannot imagine what that brave driver Christian Lautenschlager would make of a modern Grand Prix car; he would probably love it, once it had been explained to him what it actually was.

The years fall away, and I stand face to face with Sir Henry Cooper in his drawing room, deep in rural Kent. Patiently, he is demonstrating to me why it is that southpaws are so difficult to fight; why it is that they should all be 'strangled at birth', as he only semi-humorously puts it. In fact, I can see his point exactly. Southpaws, for a boxer of Henry's polarity, are clearly very hard to hit properly if you engage with them conventionally and can be counted inconvenient at best, but when he switches to a regular stance and we are engaged normally, almost as if for a waltz, I glance down and see that huge, waiting left fist, its biggest knuckle almost the size and texture of a damaged golf ball. I realize that it is less than a foot away from my chin and that if that was what we were about, he could hit me before I could even consider blinking. I even know through which wall of his house I would probably travel. It is sobering. I begin to realize what the game is really about and hope that his well-honed instincts do not kick in; basically, I hope he likes me. A little homework has already revealed to me that it is this fist, which delivered the finest punch of its kind for a generation, could accelerate faster than a Saturn V rocket at full chat and, after travelling such a short distance, would connect with an impact of over four tons per square inch; the physics involved are quite ridiculous. I glance up at him, bathed in the light of final comprehension. The famous Cooper grin is followed by what I perceive to be a quick, knowing nod. He knows I understand. No words are really necessary.

What is startling, I suppose, is the sheer intimacy which two fighters must share; there must be constant, 100 per cent eye contact, as Henry puts it: 'It's all in the eyes; you can tell everything from the eyes.

If a man is going to throw a punch, he telegraphs it with his eyes, and if you've hurt him, you just know it by looking at him.'

*

Boxing is a sport driven by opportunity and is, perhaps more than any other sporting activity, a real mirror of life. The toe-to-toe opportunism of the fight itself, echoed by the deft opportunism of the promoters (and in some cases the managers) produces a rich cultural stew, which invites sampling with a very large spoon indeed. There have been many tragedies in the fight game – boxers who died in the ring – Benny Paret, beaten to death by Emile Griffith; Johnny Owen, who lingered six weeks in a coma before succumbing to the assault he had received from Lupe Pintor, and Jimmy Garcia, who died in 1995 following a brutal fight with Gabriel Ruelas. Then, of course, Gerald McClennan and Michael Watson, both damaged badly, McClennan sadly beyond repair. Also, consider the other casualties – Randolph Turpin and Freddie Mills, both suicides – not to mention so many others, their dreams of glory shattered as they died before their time in lonely rented rooms, unremembered. But I am afraid I still love it, or at least I love the *idea* of it.

There are not many fighters whose reputations grow after they retire. I can think of Jack Dempsey, Max Schmeling Joe Louis, Muhammad Ali and Henry Cooper. All, bar Henry, were world champions, but that is not the point. When a genuinely confused Max Baer asked, after Henry had entered the rankings in 1958, 'Tell me, doesn't that guy ever get mean?' he meant it quite seriously. Baer, a playboy by his own confession, was world heavyweight champion for 364 days after dropping the giant Primo Carnera and he simply could not understand why Henry Cooper seemed so placid.

There is a powerful lobby that argues that boxing is primarily a matter of economics and Henry Cooper is actually one of them. There is a very ancient joke, which I suspect re-emerges from generation to generation, of the landed earl, who, while riding the bounds of his estate, discovers a trespassing vagrant, taking his ease in the shade of a tree:

'What are you doing on my land?' cries the toff.

'Who says it's your land?' responds the tramp.

'Well, I inherited it.'

'From whom?'

'From my father'

'And where did he get it?'

'From his father.'

Well, it all goes further back in similar fashion to some era near the third crusade:

'And where did *he* get it?'

'Well, he fought for it, actually.'

'Right, you bugger,' says the tramp, taking off his tattered coat, 'I'll fight you for it now.'

So, who are we to deny Sonny Liston, from his shoeless and unlettered childhood, his fine house in Las Vegas?

*

Henry Cooper occupies a unique and enviable place in the contemporary British consciousness. The clear contrast between his public (and private) nature and the often grim business of prizefighting does not sit uncomfortably with anyone, even those who admire him as a man but detest what he did for a living – and there are, it must be said, many of those.

The sheer inaccessibility of boxing rather defines it to most people; one can stage a pro-celebrity event in most sports after all, except these martial arts. It is sometimes tempting to suggest it, of course, and many of us might imagine that Mike Tyson vs Paul Daniels would be an entertaining event to watch, but that simple reality, that boxing is actually about hurting people, sometimes very badly, and sometimes with quite disastrous results, makes many turn away from it. How can one like a man who does this for a living? Quite easily, in fact.

So, Henry Cooper is different. Different also from other fighters in terms of the perception with which he has long been regarded. Those who admire Henry, what he did, what he became, are a different group perhaps from those who admire Chris Eubank, although to a fighter, all are one – as intelligent men (and boxers by and large are highly intelligent, they have to be) they share both a living and a vast mutual respect and seldom really despise each other, whatever they may say in public.

His reputation is undimmed. For his fans, knowledgeable or not, he remains the man who asked Muhammad Ali, then called Cassius Clay, some questions to which the American (who seems now to be a *global* treasure) did not necessarily have a ready answer. To others, those whose interests occupy purely the British sport, he was the holder of no fewer than three Lonsdale belts, a record that cannot ever be beaten under current regulations, and when Henry was forced to sell them, the nation felt deeply for him, for they knew him to be a man who had started off in life with few material possessions, that these treasures, going under the hammer (or 'ammer, I suppose) at an obscure country auction, these trophies were objects for which he had fought, won for himself, literally taken with his own hands. He had not been born to them. This sorry spectacle was not that of some dissolute chinless wonder selling off his unearned and mortgaged inheritance, rather there was something almost biblical about it.

But boxing audiences are also more fickle and more merciless than the wider public. It is almost impossible to believe it now, but on the evening of 5 December 1961, over 40 years ago, Henry Cooper, the man we revere so much now, was actually booed out of Wembley Arena after being dropped by a carthorse kick of a right from that same Zora Folley whom he had outpointed three years before. As one commentator, Robert Daley of the *New York Times,* put it sympathetically at the time: 'Mercifully, he was probably too dazed to notice.' How times change ...

In his professional career Henry Cooper fought 44 men on 55 separate occasions. He won 40 fights (27 of them inside the distance), drew one and lost the other 14. These are mere numbers, of course, but they make up, by my calculation, 371 rounds, or 18½ hours of competition (and punishment) at the highest level. Like many fighters, he would have been willing to do more, but unlike so many who sadly did just that, he has come through the process completely unaltered.

But that is surely what boxing is about. It is a bilateral interrogation. How fast, strong, clever or brave? What have you *got* in there? It lifts a very few men to heights of confidence quite unknown to most and the majority of fighters thus remain forgotten. Henry Cooper has been retired from boxing for over 30 years, but he will not, I submit, be forgotten, because he quite simply survived the process. For this he thanks the quality of his management, for which read Jim Wicks, that avuncular but perhaps slightly sinister *maestro* from Bermondsey. The relationship between these two men is an exemplar of trust and understanding that is rare in any human activity, let alone sport, and well-nigh unique in boxing.

That he has survived so well, and that he demonstrates this so regularly by being such a public figure (and a knight, to boot) has been the cause of much appreciation, both public and private. When I set out to explore the life of this professional fighter – this prizefighter, I did so with the knowledge that Henry's personal appeal cuts across anything so trivial as social class or, even more importantly, whether or not the Cooper fan is even a fan of the sport at which he excelled. No, it is simpler than that. People love Henry Cooper because he came unscathed through a process that would quite terrify any imaginative person. He put himself in harm's way and came out on the far side of that quite unspoiled and clearly uncorrupted by a sport and a business that, by the time of his retirement, was becoming a byword for sleaze, a cipher for corruption. One can describe Sonny Liston (or Mike Tyson, for that matter) as a truly terrifying man, but that adjective comes nowhere near doing justice to some of those men who handled them and ran and damaged or destroyed their lives.

The British sport was not, of course, quite as grimy as its American counterpart, mainly because of a more monolithic regime of regulation. The British Boxing Board of Control (BBBC) has had many criticisms fired at it, and indeed many of them are entirely justified, and it is an organization that certainly has its detractors now, but it is true to say, no irony intended, that by and large they made a fair fist of it, however shabbily they occasionally treated Henry. Of course, they were up against rather less than the fragmented American regulators, who were often taking on (and occasionally in the pockets of) the Mob – seriously unpleasant people. The British underworld is happily a pallid and feeble thing by comparison with the likes of the Mafia; in the

USA, there were truly dreadful men like Frankie Carbo – here, we had those dismal fantasists, the Krays. Enough said.

Boxing, for very good reasons, has always had a whiff of corruption about it, whether justified or not, but despite the distaste with which it is often regarded, for a multitude of reasons, people actually rather like boxers. There is no particular paradox to this, no inconsistency; it is, I maintain, quite obvious. In spite of the fact that many of Sir Henry's fans would really rather prefer him to have done something else for a living, they also realize full well that if he had, he would simply not be the straightforward, proud man whom they admire so much. Henry Cooper, nice guy plasterer, is not the same thing at all as Sir Henry Cooper, KSG, OBE, – prizefighter. The man who beat Brian London to a confused and bloody pulp and broke the brave Gawie de Klerk's jaw in two places before the fight was stopped is the very same man who has also raised many, many millions for handicapped children and other good causes. That this fact may place the politically correct or the woolly-minded, bleeding-hearted liberal on the horns of a vast moral dilemma is, of course, less than dust to me – a mere rounding.

But it is interesting …

Robert Edwards, W. Sussex, 2002

PART ONE

THE BOXING TWINS

Prologue

'Pride still is aiming at the blest abodes,
Men would be angels, angels would be gods.'
ALEXANDER POPE, *Essay on Man*, (1733).

THE PRIDE OF EURYDAMUS THE ARGONAUT AND BOXER, it is said, is so great that it compels him to swallow his broken teeth rather than spit them out and therefore show his pain. It is quite possible that he has been clobbered by his co-adventurer, Polydeukes, who is a useful middleweight.

Polydeukes and his brother Kastor, who is also an Argonaut, are, according to mythology, the twin sons of Leda and Zeus. Unfairly, Polydeukes was (is, I suppose) immortal, whereas poor Kastor is not. Their sister is Helen of Troy. According to a vase purporting to show Polydeukes at work (literally, putting up his dukes), his opponent is his twin, although Kastor, it must be said, enjoys more fame as a horseman. This pair, the *Dioskuri*, later become the *Castori*, the Gemini twins of Roman mythology and modern astrology, Castor and Pollux, so in a sense both achieve immortality.

Although there is evidence of fist-fighting from all over antiquity, it is generally accepted that it is fundamentally a Greek sport, a pastime that bored soldiery use to maintain both their martial skills and their aggression. It is quite distinct from wrestling. To save their hands and allow them to hit harder, Greek fighters wrapped them in *Himantes*, soft thongs of kid or ox hide, which protect the knuckle of the clenched fist (*pugme*, from *puxos*, a box), leaving the fingers free. The later (c400 BC) *Oxeis Himantes*, literally 'sharp thongs', are preformed mitts of cured leather, which give a harder edge to a blow. They are padded with an inner layer of wool to spread the force of a punch and protect the fist and are quite recognizable as boxing gloves, albeit cruel ones. Even later, studs (*myrmekes*) are added, but never, apparently, at the Olympic Games.

So not only do the Greeks invent the boxing glove (and indeed the bandages), they also seem to have developed the penalty tiebreaker. If a bout goes on too long, presumably when the audience become bored and start to throw things (it was ever thus), then a process known as a *klimax* is ordered, whereby one fighter will accept, quite undefended, a blow from his opponent and the favour will then be returned until the inevitable happens. Presumably this implies that there is no formal points system, as the strategy is clearly intended to create a knockout.

Low punches are expressly forbidden and rest periods are by mutual consent. There are no formal divisions by weight, so presumably there is a common-sense matchmaker in there somewhere, as well as a referee. There are certainly promoters; Homer refers to a fight, staged by that heroic thug Achilles during the siege of Troy, that takes place between Epeus and Euryalus. Euryalus comes second but he still wins himself a drinking-cup for his efforts; for the winner, Epeus (appropriately enough for the man who designed, road-tested and built the Trojan horse), the prize is a mule.

Philostratus, writing much later, in AD 230, describes the ideal virtues of the good boxer, who should have 'long and powerful arms, strong shoulders, a high neck and powerful and flexible wrists'. Handicaps are a thick shin (preventing agility) and a large stomach (preventing supple movements). In addition, the boxer should possess perseverance, patience, great willpower and strength. It is a fair description, this, and represents possibly the longest continuum of any sporting ideal. Fat is clearly a bad thing but, aside from the physical attributes to be treasured, Philostratus is also describing intelligence – the perfect bloke, in fact. He only neglects to mention the one element that is important to this book – durable eyebrows.

Predictably enough, the Roman version of boxing is even crueller and more gladiatorial than the Greek. The Romans, forever pushing outward the envelope of public decency, see a huge potential in boxing. The Latin equivalent of the Greek *pugme* is *pugilatus*. From the recognizable encounters of the ancient Greeks at the 23rd

Olympiad in 688 BC, the sport has now become a fight to the death, not as an exercise of arms or skill, but simply an event to please the mob: organized murder. The *Oxeis Himantes* are now *Caesti* (from *Caedare* – the Latin verb 'to hack down') – metal-studded straps wrapped tight around the fist. The damage they can do is quite awful. They are in effect little more than crude knuckledusters. The loser earns no drinking-cup now – he dies, and the winner merely survives. In short, it is little more than a slave's activity.

After the abolition of the Olympic Games in AD 393, and shortly before the final collapse of Rome, we do not hear about boxing for nearly a millennium and a half. There are passing references to it from time to time, mainly as a pastime for soldiers, but culturally and socially boxing virtually drops from sight, a completely lost art, if art it could be called.

*

Unsurprisingly, it is in libertarian England, under the restored monarchy of Charles II, where we meet it again. It has not changed much from the free-for-all of the arena. The *Caestes* have gone; it is now a simple bare-knuckle affair, with kicking, holding, throttling and throwing all allowed. It resembles a degraded and hybrid oriental martial art (but entirely free of those ritual courtesies) crossed with a tap-room brawl as much as anything else, and one of the earliest recorded post-Cromwell bouts takes place in August 1681, when the Duke of Albemarle's unfortunate footman is stopped by a butcher's boy.

This encounter rather sets the tone of the development of the sport as a series of bored and dissolute aristocrats send their long-suffering servants out simply to beat each other up. The fighters are paid little but some of the side-bets are vast. It is a chaotic series of unregulated brawls. In 1719, though, it all changes when the terrifying James Figg, born in 1695 in Thame in Oxfordshire, declares himself 'Champion of England'. Figg has certainly done enough work; he is a curiously contemporary and disturbingly familiar figure to us now. Figg is illiterate, swaggering and shaven-headed and his modern equivalent can be found today in the cheap seats of any football ground, probably clutching a tin of high-octane lager. There is something faintly feral about him and he exhibits some distinctly criminal tendencies in matters fiscal. He will fight with anything, from cudgel to quarterstaff via fists and swords, and for anything – desiderata defined by him in 1727 as being 'money, love or a bellyful'. Perhaps Figg reminds us, professionally at least, more than a little of Jack Dempsey. But he is also a first-class showman.

Figg makes friends and sponsors quickly, in fact. As a prototypical curiosity, who clearly generates a dreadful fascination, he is celebrated by the literary and artistic figures of the day. His career, brief as it is, creates a popular reverence for fighters that has never really left us. William Hogarth engraves his trade-cards for him* and both Alexander Pope (still the best translator of the *Iliad*, where we first encounter boxing) and Jonathan Swift count him amongst their close acquaintances, possibly even writing his letters for him. His patron is the Earl of Peterborough, who funds and founds 'Figg's Amphitheatre' in the Tottenham Court Road, an ambitious project that is part duelling academy, part venue, part betting shop – it is London's first gym. It flourishes and will accommodate over 1,000 spectators.

These earliest prizefights are chaotic, full-blooded tear-ups of quite astonishing violence, totally in the Roman tradition. Kicking, eye-gouging, biting, butting and throwing are all permitted, indeed encouraged. Blood, teeth, sweat and snot, we can imagine, thicken the already smoky atmosphere in Figg's Amphitheatre. A favourite manoeuvre is the cross-buttock throw, similar to the *O Goshi* hip-throw from judo, with the added refinement that the thrower lands – as hard as he can – on top of his opponent's gut. Only a throw-down or a knockdown can end a round. The audience want blood and they usually get it. Deaths are frequent and Figg, unsurprisingly, does not live long. In 1727, for example, he fights – inconclusively – Ned Sutton, first with his fists, followed by a decider with cudgels – and he dies after a short, violent life in around 1734 (by some accounts 1740). His torch is taken up by a pupil and protégé, Jack Broughton,

---

* Hogarth had clearly done better work than this, as Figg's PR material is, by the standards of Hogarth's more famous output, quite dreadful, which rather suggests that it was a favour, or even the work of a pupil.

who apes Figg's skinhead tonsorial style. Both men are shaven-headed purely from a practical point of view because being grabbed by the hair was an occupational hazard.

Broughton is from Bristol and has been spotted as a likely lad by the master as he completely savages some hapless foe (later fistic mythology terms this opponent, with commendable loyalty to Broughton, as a 'bully') in a welter of blood, snot and pain at a West Country fair. Figg, who I think we can safely assume is not a man to be easily impressed, has seen in Broughton a kindred spirit and the Bristolian is quickly taken up by the Duke of Cumberland, who does for Broughton what the Earl of Peterborough has done for Figg, and builds him a fine academy of his own. It abuts the late Figg's Amphitheatre.

Broughton, though, is rather different. He affects disdain for the crudity of mere fighting and becomes perhaps the first *scientific* boxer, developing and teaching techniques such as blocking and slipping, which are still recognizable today. In 1741 a seminal fight takes place – the encounter between Broughton and a coach driver from Yorkshire, George Stevenson. Unfortunately, Broughton kills him, breaking three of his ribs and probably puncturing a lung in the process. Poor Stevenson lingers on for an agonizing month, during which the somewhat guilt-ridden Broughton develops a great affection for him. By now lionized by an adoring public, the victor starts to consider his position.

On 16 August 1743, The 'Broughton Rules' are published, '*As agreed by Several Gentlemen at Broughton's Amphitheatre*'. They represent the first serious effort at codifying the rules of engagement of boxing since the original Olympic Games. The seven rules have a limited set of objectives, and they are clearly intended to apply only to Broughton's own establishment, but they are relatively enlightened and humane by the standards of the time. By their very introduction, Broughton writes himself into the history books as the father of English, and therefore world, boxing. Here they are in more or less modern English:

1. That a square of a yard be chalked into the middle of the stage; and on every fresh set-to after a fall, or being parted from the rails, each second is to bring his man to the side of the square, and place him opposite to the other, and till they are fairly set-to at the lines, it shall not be lawful for one to strike at the other.

2. That, in order to prevent any disputes, the time a man lies after a fall, if the second does not bring his man to the side of the square within the space of half a minute, he shall be deemed a beaten man.

3. That in every main battle, no person whatever shall be upon the stage, except the principals and their seconds; the same rule to be observed in bye-battles, except that in the latter, Mr. Broughton is allowed to be upon the stage to keep decorum, and to assist gentlemen in getting to their places; provided always he does not interfere in the Battle, and whoever pretends to infringe these rules to be turned immediately out of the house. Everybody is to quit the stage as soon as the champions are stripped, before the set-to.

4. That no champion be deemed beaten, unless he fails coming up to the line in the limited time, or that his own second declares him beaten. No second is to be allowed to ask his man's adversary any questions, or advise him to give out.

5. That in bye-battles, the winning man to have two-thirds of the money given, which shall be publicly divided upon the stage, notwithstanding any private agreements to the contrary.

6. That to prevent disputes, in every main battle the principals shall, on coming on the stage, choose from among the gentlemen present two umpires, who shall absolutely decide all disputes that may arise about the battle; and if the two Umpires cannot agree, the said umpires to choose a third, who is to determine it.

7. That no person shall hit an adversary when he is down, or seize him by the ham, the breeches, or any part below the waist: a man on his knees to be reckoned down.

But as well as attempting a proper set of rules, Broughton makes another contribution, which will prove significant. He develops the modern boxing glove, the 'muffler', for use in sparring and more lily-livered amateur competition. His concern is purely cosmetic, to save his aristocratic students, who were his bread and butter, from: 'The inconveniency of black eyes, broken jaws and bloody noses.' Broughton's rules survive for nearly a century, in fact, and it is only in 1838, perhaps in deference to the new Queen, that they are revised.

Broughton, unlike his mentor Figg, lives to a great age, possibly due to a relatively early and controversial retirement. The Duke of Cumberland, clearly still flushed with his success in the wake of the Battle of Culloden, wagers £10,000, at odds reputed to have been 10–1, that Broughton will beat a new challenger, the disreputable Jack Slack. Slack, 'The first knight of the Cleaver', is the classic bruiser (actually a butcher from Norwich), who insults Broughton one day at a race meeting. Broughton offers to horsewhip him but is prevailed upon instead to accept a formal challenge for his championship. The fight takes place on 10 April 1750 and, after a rather one-sided start, Slack lands a lucky blow, which (temporarily) blinds the champion. Cumberland, though, seeing his £10,000 – a truly colossal amount of money – rapidly disappearing, accuses Broughton of selling ('swallowing') the fight and, after the ex-champion's seconds throw in the towel, he withdraws his backing and even goes so far as to have Broughton's academy closed down later on. It is a distressing end to a quite glorious career – Broughton has held the title for over ten years and his departure leaves something of a vacuum at the top of the sport. As Slack, seeing opportunities of a more commercial nature in prize-fighting, reverts to his previous trade in Covent Garden with a sideline in training, fixing and bribing. He prospers.

After Broughton, the champions come and go, some of them more or less reputable than others, but clearly prizefighting is soon becoming a very seamy business indeed. Thrown fights, crooked betting, more deaths and severe injuries all combine to focus the attention of the law upon it very closely indeed and the organization of boxing matches develops into an art itself and coaching inns, on well-known roads and turnpikes, become a favoured venue. Advertising is largely by word of mouth or covertly distributed handbills. Boxing thrived as the worst-kept secret in Britain.

Promoters and matchmakers, many of them connected with the turf, ensure that prizefighting remains firmly in the gutter where Slack put it. One of the most influential is Colonel Dennis O'Kelly, whose other claim to sporting immortality is that he is the owner of one of the greatest racehorses of all time – *Eclipse*. O'Kelly is responsible for the careers of several celebrated Irish fighters who dominate the sport from 1770 until a new crop of English fighters arrive upon the scene, of whom the most well known is Tom Jackling, who fights, for reasons best known to himself, as Tom Johnson.

But the first successor to Broughton of any historical importance is Daniel Mendoza, 'The Light of Israel'. Born of Spanish Sephardic Jewish ancestry in Aldgate in the East End of London, Mendoza is a small man, 5ft 7in, and he swiftly rises up the rankings, cannily promoting his own fights and beating a succession of proven opponents. One in particular, a young toff by the name of Richard Humphries, becomes a particular bugbear; the pair fight three times, and Humphries wins the first bout, reporting to his (unnamed) sponsor: 'Sir, I have done the Jew and am in good health.'

Mendoza battles on, clearly fighting against rather more than mere opponents – he wins both times against Humphries at their subsequent rematches – before becoming acknowledged champion of England in 1792. He himself is toppled three years later by one 'Gentleman John' Jackson, who has clearly read the rules and spotted a gap in them, for his tactic is simple: he grabs Mendoza, perfectly legally, by his luxuriant locks with one hand and hammers him in the face with the other until he drops, after 11 minutes. If anything, Mendoza is an even more technically skilled fighter than Broughton had been but against such exploitation of Broughton's clearly rather naive rules, he stands little chance. But by his cleverness, even in the teeth of the establishment opposition, Mendoza succeeds in giving prizefighting a better name than anyone in 50 years.

In 1814, Jackson, who wisely retires after only a handful of fights, forms the Pugilistic Club, operated from his academy at No 13 Bond Street, London, which attempts to exert some discipline upon boxing.

At one level it is successful, and counts among its members both the Prince of Wales and the Duke of Clarence, but it fails to achieve its purpose. It breaks up in 1825.

Despite the opposition of the law there is still a huge amount of popular support for boxing. It is, along with horse racing, basically the national spectator sport, and similar types of crowds follow both activities. Interestingly, although duelling is legal, as a matter of honour between, it is assumed, two gentlemen who are apparently quite prepared (and allowed) to kill each other, prizefighting is not. But by the nineteenth century, the prizefighters are men of truly national importance and enthusiasm for the 'noble art' cuts right through society, from the royal family downwards. The patronage of rich men is naturally important to the activity and retired boxers are often to be seen in the employ of their aristocratic supporters and sponsors, as bodyguards, messengers and, frequently, leg-breakers. But the prize ring also produces figures of astonishing social import. One (of whom much more later) is John Gully, briefly champion of England, who retires from the ring in 1808 and becomes the Member of Parliament for Pontefract. As a colliery boss, Gully becomes a wealthy man and highly successful racehorse owner. A Liberal, naturally.

More deaths in the ring, caused mainly by the custom of seconds being allowed to physically carry their man into the centre of the square, only to see him immediately flattened, cause a generally agreed revision to Broughton's original rules in 1838. The square yard is replaced by a simple line scratched in the soil or chalked in the centre of the ring, so that if a fighter cannot reach it unaided – 'come up to scratch' – he is declared beaten.

So the first half of the nineteenth century, building on the work of Mendoza, has also seen a slight improvement in professional standards over the second half of the eighteenth. Perhaps it is remarkable that the sport survived the eighteenth century at all given the philosophical tenets of that period, which culminated in the intellectual glories of the Enlightenment; but there was conflict in plenty as well, from the American Revolution, as well as the French Revolutionary and Napoleonic wars, so there was no shortage of martial ardour, and violent and risky sports generally prosper in the wake of military conflicts.

The early nineteenth-century champions, men such as Henry 'Hen' Pierce 'the Game Chicken', John Gully and the three Toms – Cribb, Spring and Cannon – are feted wherever they appear; they enjoy total social mobility in a much more rigidly stratified era than ours. At the coronation of George IV in 1821, no fewer than 18 prize-fighters are hired to keep order, more specifically to bar the entry of his estranged and unhygienic wife, Caroline of Brunswick, who is banned from the occasion, which must have been a distressing encounter for her. Indeed, 19 days after that, she died, un-mourned by George, who loathed her, but rather missed by the mob in front of whom she liked to cavort. A year before that, the Irish fighter Daniel Donnelly was knighted at the instigation of George IV when he is still the Prince of Wales. Donnelly was in fact the first boxing knight and would remain so for over 180 years.

The late Georgian, Regency and early Victorian periods produce further notabilities as well as the odd bad boy. Ben Caunt, twice champion, is apparently a national treasure, whereas William Abednigo Thompson – 'Bad Bold Bendigo' – is in prison 28 times, mainly for being drunk and disorderly. Thompson is one of a trio of triplets born to a quite extraordinary harridan, who also has 18 other children. It is she who teaches him to box (she is recorded as having fought as a prizefighter – against male opponents – herself) and launches his career. The rivalry between Caunt and Thompson rather serves to define this era of the prize ring; the two men meet each other for the last time in 1845. The fight lasts 93 rounds, with a time elapsed of two hours and ten minutes. Thompson wins the encounter under controversial circumstances and retires. Later, he forswears drink to become an evangelistic preacher. There is a persistent story that the thirteen-ton bell in the clocktower of the Houses of Parliament is named 'Big Ben' in honour of Caunt, but research suggests that it was actually Sir Benjamin Hall, a particularly fat government minister, who was the inspiration for the name.

The popularity of the senior exponents of prizefighting, against the illegality of what made them so famous, put the authorities in some-thing of a quandary. It is a matter of record that very few of the top drawer of the English ring ever went to prison – at least, not for fighting – although several lesser fighters were scooped up by magistrates, rather as a gesture than anything else. Anyone who arrested the national champion for assault was liable to have a riot on their hands very quickly, and the magistrates realized that, so the most popular prizefighters were tolerated by the law purely on sufferance. Their popularity (and their wealthy patrons) granted them effective immunity from the law. It was a bizarre situation.

But the high public regard in which these prizefighters are held in the eighteenth and nineteenth centuries is of itself not paradoxical, for they represent something that is quite inaccessible to the general public, particularly after the demise of duelling. These men fight for their living, a career that puts them firmly on the margins of the law, and thus they are by definition outsiders, and the general public rather likes outsiders, particularly when they exhibit characteristics away from their work that are quite removed from what they do professionally. This contrast is to be seen throughout the evolution of the sport; the general popularity of fighters such as James Broughton, Ben Caunt, John Gully, Tom Cribb, Max Schmeling, Joe Louis and indeed Henry Cooper has as much to do with their work outside the ring as it does with their efforts within it. They are themselves men of apparent but pleasing contradictions; they seem to have a self-determination denied to most of us and we like, admire and even envy them for that. That public response to certain boxers remains unchanged. Others, we find on closer inspection to be flawed and we quickly turn away from them.

But aside from all that, a subject to which we can revert, another prizefighter is now coming up fast: he is Tom Sayers. He challenges for the championship of England in June 1857, the year our story begins...

CHAPTER ONE

Hard Times

'It is a most miserable thing to feel ashamed of home.'
CHARLES DICKENS, *Great Expectations*, (1861).

1857 WAS A BUSY AND DISTRESSING YEAR for London, indeed the whole country, for it was the year of the Great Indian Mutiny, which had swept through the north of the subcontinent with unimagined ferocity, and was, in the late autumn and early winter, suppressed with equal brutality. The mutiny was the single dominant event of the period, perhaps the most savage military encounter of the imperial epoch.

The London of 1857 would, to a twenty-first century time traveller, be physically recognizable, but rather strange. The Irish peer Lord Palmerston was Prime Minister and while he was no particular democrat, he was, despite the disaster of the mutiny, popular (except with the Queen) and ruled the empire not from No 10 Downing Street, which he regarded with disdain, but rather from his own fine town house in Piccadilly, far superior, and from where he could admire the streetwalkers, or from his grand country estate in Hertfordshire, Brocket Hall. Among his leisure interests (mainly carnal, it must be said), he was a strong supporter and defender of prizefighting.

On 16 June of that year, Tom Sayers, a compact but sturdy bricklayer from Sussex, challenged William Perry, 'The Tipton Slasher' for the English prizefighting championship title. The fight took place – eventually, after several hurried relocations – on the Isle of Grain, in Kent, and Sayers won it. It was a famous encounter, lasting ten rounds. Wince when you realize that the time elapsed was one hour and forty-two minutes. At 5ft 8in, Sayers gave away (four inches) in height and no fewer than 40lbs in weight to his opponent. Technically, he was not actually champion yet; he still had to beat Tom Paddock, who had been the previous title-holder, but who had been too ill to fight before. Unsurprisingly, Sayers was to beat him, too.

Historic encounters though they were, great fights indeed, they were to be eclipsed by the dire news from India, which took six weeks to arrive, that ten days after Sayer's victory over Perry, the massacre at Cawnpore had taken place. No event in nineteenth-century history, not even the previous disaster at Balaklava (1854) nor the greater one to come at Isandlwhana (1879) made for a greater impact on Victorian English consciousness than Cawnpore. It was a seminal moment for the average Brit and rather served to set the tone, not only of public approval of the vengeance that would be wrought upon the mutineers but also the general tone of colonial military policy until the end of the century. It was events such as this that made it clear that an aggressive spirit was perhaps no bad thing.

These matters may or may not have mattered much to William Cooper, 24, from Bishopstoke, Hampshire, as the East India Company Army recruitment drive heated up to unparalleled levels of intensity, for his mind was probably more focused on his fiancée, Bedana Keenen, a year younger than himself, who had moved, with her father Edward, a labourer, and her mother and sister (both named Bridget), from County Kildare, probably in the wake of the series of potato famines that had swept through Ireland a decade before the mutiny in India. They might well, like so many others, have chosen America, but had they done so (they could almost certainly not afford the passage) this book would not have been written.

A cooper, of course, is a barrel-maker, but William Cooper was a farm labourer. In 1857 there was little difference between the Hampshire countryside where he had been born and raised and that of Essex, where, by the time of his marriage to Bedana on 6 September 1857, he lived and worked. The newly married couple settled in a house (which may possibly have then been a tied cottage) where they had already been living together, at 1 North Street, in the parish of West Ham, near Plaistow. Bedana's mother, Bridget Keenen, moved in too, which rather suggests that she was a widow by now. Bridget senior appears to have given birth to Bedana quite late, at the age of 46, as she gives her age in the 1861 census as 72, against Bedana's 26. A

Catherine Tatum, 50, also from Ireland, who lists her occupation as laundress, is staying with them as a visitor.

William's new mother-in-law would have been old enough to witness that extraordinary event in Irish sporting history, the Donnelly–Cooper prizefight, which had taken place, allegedly in front of 20,000 spectators, in the year of the Battle of Waterloo, 1815. The two men fought at the Curragh, just outside Dublin, and it was an encounter that both passed into legend and was immortalized in song. It is entirely possible that a young Palmerston was present.

In April 1860, three years after William Cooper's marriage, the English version of the prizefight of the century took place at Farnborough, on the far side of Hampshire from William's birthplace. It was between Tom Sayers and an American, John C. Heenan of California. Heenan was the 'US champion'. Although the fight was quite illegal, that little detail failed to prevent both Palmerston, current Prime Minister and also ex-local MP, as well as Charles Dickens and William Thackeray from turning up to watch, and neither did it prevent special trains being laid on to transport the avid punters to the match, to a resigned acceptance by the forces of law and order.

In truth, it was a justifiable nervousness on the part of the authorities concerning the size and nature of the crowds who would attend these fights that really governed the attitude of the authorities to them. After all, there had been a serious risk of massive and violent civil disobedience since the 1848 Chartist riots. Boxing, as a violent sport, was considered to be a serious risk to law and order, given that the spectators, frequently drunk and energized by what they had seen, might decide to extend the spirit of the conflict out into the wider countryside. There had emerged an unwritten understanding, though, that prizefighting was an undesirable (but probably unavoidable) social necessity since the abolition of bear-baiting in 1803 and cock-fighting in 1849. Any activity that drew large numbers of unruly spectators to a given place was considered to be of dubious social value, and this state of affairs would last several decades. But given the interest shown in it by the upper echelons of society, it made strict enforcement of boxing's illegal status quite difficult; it was *de facto* protected, but remained firmly in the twilight.

But, illegal or not, this fight was an epic; after 2 hours and 20 minutes and totalling 42 rounds, the last five of which were total chaos, the result was a declared draw as the two contestants, who as a result of this encounter later became the best of friends, took to their heels. The unseemly riot that followed at least allowed the Prime Minister and his cronies to beat a dignified retreat.

The fight was hardly a secret (every major paper including the *New York Times* had a reporter present) and questions were asked in the House, which triggered a debate later on, in 1862 in the Lords. Palmerston, who carried the instincts of the Regency sporting gent well into the high Victorian period, argued strongly against Lord Lovaine, who argued, as a Whig would (most still do) that the sport was barbaric. A 'motion of censure' was passed, which, while it was neither one thing nor another, did not help the cause of prizefighting. In truth, it was a trivial matter by comparison with the demands placed upon parliament in the field of foreign affairs – there was by now a civil war in America, after all.

*

The great campaign to rebuild London's dire and unhealthy drainage system started in the 1860s and the requirements for labour were huge. This enterprise was one of the biggest public works programmes of the era and it went hand in hand with great swathes of public housing for the poor, led by the American philanthropist George Peabody and the English heiress Angela Burdett-Coutts. By 1864, we find that William Cooper has left the land and is now applying his skills working as a digger on one of Joseph Bazalguette's great enterprises, the Abbey Mills pumping station in West Ham. His life has moved on and, sadly, Bedana appears to have died, as his wife is now named as Bridget (also née Keenen), whom we might assume to be Bedana's sister. Interestingly, her age is given as the same as Bedana's would have been, so the two were probably twins, a characteristic that often runs in families and would certainly run in this one.

As William changed his job, so he changed his address, for by the time his third child (and second son), George, is born on 1 August 1864, the growing family (a daughter, Harriet, had arrived in 1862) are to be found at 5 Brooks Road, West Ham, which must have been rather handy for William's work. The new birth is registered on 9 September and we can see from the entry on the certificate that, alas, Bridget is illiterate, for she signs her name with a simple X.

But unlettered or not, Bridget is a true communicator. With her from Ireland she has brought her family's stories and songs, and one in particular is to have an important influence on the family's later life. It is the epic account of the Daniel Donnelly fight from all those years before and handed down in the oral tradition; it was to become a favourite of little George's, and thus rather important to this book. It is certainly not great verse – we will hear far worse before this book is finished, I assure you – but it is evocative:

> *Come all you true bred Irishmen*
> *I hope you will draw near,*
> *And likewise pay attention*
> *To those few lines I have here.*
> *It is as true a story*
> *As ever you did hear,*
> *Of how Donnelly fought Cooper*
> *On the Curragh of Kildare.**

One important spin-off of the Sayers/Heenan encounter was that amateur boxers started to consider their position. The Corinthian tradition, as exemplified by men like Palmerston, was alive and well (if creaking, slightly) and living within the Amateur Athletic Club (AAC), a new organization whose members viewed with dismay the increasing socio-legal pressure to impose an absolute ban on boxing in all its forms, amateur or professional.

A founder member of the AAC was John Graham Chambers, not long down from Magdalene College, Cambridge, where he had

---

* What the song does not say, of course, is what happened to brave Daniel Donnelly. Despite all the glory (as well as a knighthood), he died in 1820, a hapless drunk with not a penny to his name. But the story of Donnelly would fire little George Cooper's imagination before long.

befriended John Sholto Douglas, the eighth Marquess of Queensberry. Chambers determined that a set of rules that might serve to legitimize boxing was now mandatory, as the pressure mounting on the sport was huge, and those who were proponents of it were justifiably nervous.

In 1865, Chambers set to work. What he came up with was in effect the invention of twentieth-century boxing: a sport we would recognize now. The Chambers rules, which passed into history as the Queensberry Rules (their noble sponsor) are relatively simple. There are 12 of them:

1. To be a fair stand-up boxing match in a 24 foot ring, or as near that size as practicable.

2. No wrestling or hugging allowed.

3. The rounds to be of three minute's duration, and one minute's time between rounds.

4. If either man falls through weakness or otherwise, he must get up unassisted, ten seconds to be allowed for him to do so; the other man meanwhile to return to his corner, and when the fallen man is on his legs the round is to be resumed and continued until the three minutes are expired. If one man fails to come to the scratch in the ten seconds allowed, it shall be in the power of the referee to give his award in the favour of the other man.

5. A man hanging on the ropes in a helpless state, with his toes off the ground, shall be considered down.

6. No seconds or any other person to be allowed in the ring during the rounds.

7. Should the contest be stopped by any unavoidable interference, the referee to name the time and place as soon as possible for finishing the contest; so the match must be won and lost, unless the backers of both men agree to draw the stakes.

8. The gloves to be fair-sized boxing gloves of the best quality and new.

9. Should a glove burst, or come off, it must be replaced to the referee's satisfaction.

10. A man on one knee is considered down, and if struck is entitled to the stakes.

11. No shoes or boots with springs allowed.

12. The contest in all other respects to be governed by the revised rules of the London Prize Ring.

These rules impose upon boxing a code that puts it firmly within a type of moral framework that is both humane and perhaps even legally defensible. They mark a turning point as the sport finally starts to put its house in order. There can be little doubt that their mere existence ensured the survival of the sport in any form. The most important aspect of them was their clear intention in attempting to ensure that the art of pugilism would be allowed to dominate the ring. A secondary effect was that the sport of wrestling could now develop on its own. Whether we should be particularly grateful to Chambers and Queensberry for that is quite another question.

There was another Chambers involved in drafting these rules. He was Arthur Chambers (no relation) a professional boxer and a friend of Queensberry's. The pair had toured America together shortly after the Civil War. It is likely that his contribution was to add to and modify the original proposals to include several new elements, which result in an activity that is clearly recognizable today; indeed, a fight fought under these regulations would still be perfectly legal. I list them on the following pages, as it is interesting to note the effect of the input of a professional boxer.

The rules were finally published by a committee of the Pugilist's Benevolent Association in 1866.

1. All contests to be decided in a roped ring not less than 15 feet and not more than 24 feet square.

2. Contestants to box in light boots or shoes or in socks.

3. In all contests the number and duration of rounds must be specified. The limit of rounds shall be twenty three-minute rounds; the interval between the rounds shall be 1 minute. All championship contests shall be of twenty three-minute rounds. The gloves to be a minimum weight of 6 ozs. and shall be provided by the promoter.

4. The contestants shall be entitled to the assistance of not more than four seconds who are to be approved by the promoter, and no advice can be given by the seconds during the progress of a round. In all contests the decision shall be given in favour of the contestant who attains the greatest number of points. The points shall be for:
ATTACK – direct or clean hits with the knuckle part of the glove on any part of the front or sides of the head or body above the belt.
DEFENCE – guarding, slipping, ducking or betting away
(Where points are otherwise equal, the preference to be given to the contestant who does most of the leading off, or who displays the best style.)

6. The referee may disqualify a contestant for delivering a foul blow, intentionally or otherwise, for holding, butting, palming, shouldering, falling without receiving a blow, wrestling or for boxing unfairly by hitting with the open glove, the inside or the butt of the hand, with the wrist or elbow, or for roughing.

7. If in the opinion of the referee a deliberate foul is committed by a contestant, such contestant shall not be entitled to a prize. The referee shall have the power to stop a contest if, in his opinion a man is unfit to continue, and that man shall be deemed to have lost the contest.

8. No seconds of any other person to be allowed in the ring during the rounds. Each contestant shall be entitled to the assistance of not more than four seconds, who must take up positions outside the ring during the rounds and who must not, under pain of disqualification of their principal by the referee, coach, assist in any manner or advise their principal during the rounds, or enter the ring during the progress of a contest. A second refusing to obey the order of the referee shall be removed from his position and replaced by another approved by the referee.

9. The contestant failing to come up when time is called or refusing to obey the referee, shall lose the contest. A man on one knee, or when on the ropes with both feet off the ground, shall be considered down.

10. If a contestant slips down, he must get up again immediately. His opponent must stand back out of distance until the fallen man is on his feet, when the contest shall be resumed. A contestant who has knocked down his opponent must immediately walk to his own corner, but should the fallen man be knocked down in that corner, the contestant delivering the knockdown shall retire to the farthest corner. A man knocked down must rise unassisted in ten seconds or lose the contest.

11. Should a glove burst or come off, it must be replaced to the satisfaction of the referee. The time thus lost shall be considered as no part of the stipulated period of the round.

12. The contestants shall not hit while in a clinch. A clinch shall be constituted by both men holding, either with one or both hands.

13. The referee shall decide (a) any question not provided in these rules; (b) the interpretation of these rules.

Modern boxing had arrived. These rules effectively transferred control of the boxing match from the mob to a single nominated individual who, it was made clear, was in total command of proceedings. It was to become a tradition of the English ring, directly as a result of the work done by Chambers and his circle, that the ultimate authority in any organized fight be the referee. In a narrow sense, the boxing ref was an extraordinarily powerful figure, particularly because the level of betting on boxing matches was huge, even if punts the size of the one which the Duke of Cumberland had lost a century before were now rare.

*

By 1868 the West Ham pumping station project is completed and William, Bridget and their growing family are on the move again, still in West Ham, but now to 21 Greengate Street. William continues as a general labourer and fathers twins, Maria and William, who arrive in 1869, to be followed four years later by Emily. The family is now as large, with five children, as it is going to get.

At around the time of Emily's birth in 1873, it seems that Bridget Cooper dies, quite possibly in childbirth; she would have been 40 at the time. William remarries a local Plaistow girl, Mary, whose maiden name we cannot discover. As significant as his remarriage is the fact that William and his brood decide to relocate completely; they head south of the Thames to 19 Williams Place, near the Elephant & Castle in Newington. By that time, the relentless urbanization and gentrification of the Plaistow district had reduced the differences between the teeming anthill of humanity that characterizes the south bank of the Thames and the urban sprawl which replaces the once rural Essex borders to almost nil. It is quite likely that the Coopers have been priced out of their neighbourhood.

South of the river, it is all rather different. In nearby Bermondsey there are regular riots and marches by disaffected (and hungry) dockers and their families that regularly spill over into Westminster and the City of London. More than once the Army is called out to disperse them. There is disease, too, which rips through the crowded tenements with blinding speed. Cholera is the most common, but despite the heroic efforts of men like Bazalguette, the state of public health is still quite dire and infant mortality is at levels that are found today in the third world. Dysentery is a particular killer.

Interestingly, all three men of working age in the Cooper family are now involved with horses, which suggests, but does not confirm, that William Cooper's own rural origins possibly had an equestrian flavour to them before he moved to London. William, who is now 49, is by no means too old to wield a pick or shovel, but he has forsaken jobbing labouring and is now described as a 'Horse Keeper to a bakery'. Eldest son Charles has done even better: he is described as a 'Riding-Master', and little George Cooper, by now only 17, is following a similar career, but without notable success yet – he is a 'Horse Keeper out of employ'.

But George has also discovered boxing, as the echoes of 'Donnelly and Cooper' ring down the years. Unfortunately, the forces of law and order have it under the microscope, in a last ditch effort to stamp it out. In 1882, Mr Justice Hawkins in the case of *Regina versus Coney* (Coney is clearly a prizefighter) handed down a landmark decision:

> *Every fight in which the object and intent of each of the combatants is to subdue the other by violent blows is a breach of the peace and it matters not, in my opinion, whether such a fight be a hostile fight begun in anger, or a prizefight for money or other advantage. In each case the object is the same and in each case some amount of personal injury to one or both of the combatants is a probable consequence; and although a prizefight may not commence in anger, it is unquestionably calculated to rouse the angry feelings of both before its conclusion. I have no doubt, then, that every such fight is illegal and the parties to it may be prosecuted for assaults upon each other. Many authorities support this view.*

Indeed they did. Hawkins's pronouncement was one of a long line of negative verdicts as to the suitability of boxing as either sport or spectacle; for this reason, some subtle practices were to emerge that would attempt to redefine the aims of boxing and they would be codified as a list of do's and don'ts of the most extraordinary priggishness.

Despite the fact that the Queensberry Rules have (except in the higher reaches of the sport) taken root, the bare-knuckle tradition is obstinately embedded in the noble art. Certainly, there is evidence that prizefights under the Queensberry Rules take place as early as 1872, but the sea change in the sport only comes in 1891, when the first world championship is fought under the new regime. Until then, bouts took place both with the 'raw 'uns' and the 'mauleys' in equal measure.

Boxing and drinking also went hand in hand and with the rapid development of railways the coaching inn was becoming a thing of the past. This simple fact liberated useful spaces where clandestine fights could be held and the innkeepers became, in effect, the first promoters and matchmakers of the sport. They also established another dubious tradition: they also became the first bookmakers. In short, the sport of illegal boxing, if we can call it that, fell into the effective control of the country's pub landlords.

For George Cooper, this was a pity, as it seems that he was becoming something of a black sheep of the family. To say that he was a scamp would be something of an understatement. Perhaps the loss of his mother affected him; certainly he would until his death lose no opportunity to produce, at the drop of a hat, any or all of the songs and verses which stepmother Bridget had patiently taught him and it became clear that he had also inherited an extremely fine voice.

He became (like his stepbrother Charles) a fine judge of horseflesh but these passions of his – singing, fighting and horses – all served to ensure that he was never far from a pub. He seems to have been a bright and quick-witted man, as he certainly had an ability to make plenty of money as a horse-coper, and was able to earn useful sums as a fighter and minder, a furniture porter and even as a semi-professional singer–songwriter, but it also seems that money rather burned a hole in his pocket. After a successful deal, commission or bout he would quite often drop from sight for days on end on a series of giant benders. He was not, it must be said, much of a saver.

But he had some interesting adventures. Family tradition has it that in 1883, one of his first jobs as a horse-keeper arrived, and it was an important one, to accompany a string of thoroughbred horses on their delivery to, ultimately, St Petersburg. In the days when men of his background went abroad only on military service, it must have been quite an experience. Naturally, he managed to become involved in a fight along the way.

Fighting was part of the fabric of society in nineteenth-century London, as it was in most metropolitan areas. Disputes would be settled face to face, man to man, without the services of the law in any form, neither attorney nor police. The level of street violence was colossal and it had become bone-deep in the culture, but there was never any suggestion that George was anything but a law-abiding citizen, save for the fact that he boxed, which, as we have seen, was technically illegal. Certainly, he appears not to have attracted the attention of the authorities.

But he comes down to us as an interesting man. He married, at an undetermined date, but certainly by the end of the century, a formidable Walworth lady by the name of Elizabeth Lindo, who had been born in 1862 and was thus two years older. She needed to be formidable, in fact, simply to put up with him, as he did not change his bachelor habits one iota. In her way, she was as tough as he was and the pair of them would cheerfully fight shoulder to shoulder against all comers; an unorthodox way of bonding, but clearly successful, as they stayed together until George's death. Her grandson recalled some of the family tales handed down to him: 'In those days if any family had a row they went out and had a stand-up fight. Granddad used to fight like a man and my Gran wasn't like most women, scratching and pulling hair; she could punch like a man. She used to roll up her sleeves and stand up and box. If two families had a row my Granddad would fight the other old man and my Gran would go and fight his wife. They were hard times.'

George's stamping ground rather depended upon which aspect of his portfolio career was currently to the forefront. He would fight, or sing, anywhere, and as a middleweight, he fought in and with some good company, fighters of the quality of Ted Pritchard, middleweight champion of England, for example, as well as less well-known figures like 'Pudney' Sullivan (whom he actually trained) and Ben 'Barney' Hyams. He certainly fought Pritchard on the evening of Thursday 15 March 1888 at a benefit evening for Hyams. Held at the Equestrian Tavern Music Hall, Blackfriars, the evening also included burlesque, as well as singing and dancing, and the boxers provided interesting exhibition interludes for the obviously mixed crowd. Possibly George sang as well, although he is only mentioned as a boxer in the *Sporting Life*'s enthusiastic account of the evening.

It is this redefinition of gloved boxing, as a music-hall entertainment from the late 1860s onwards as a result of decisions such as Hawkins's, as well as earlier case law, that buys the sport valuable time by effectively pulling its own teeth; nobody gets killed, perhaps a little blood flows, and much posturing is done. It is a crowd-pleaser but, thanks to the Queensberry initiative, it is now quite outside the legal definition of assault or battery. It is an entertainment, albeit a fairly bloody one. In this context, figures such as Pritchard flit in and out of the boundaries of the law as they alternate exhibition bouts with much more serious stuff, for two years later, Pritchard wins the English middleweight title – interestingly, on a referee's decision. That match, definitely not a burlesque side-show, takes place at Robert Habbijam's boxing rooms on Newman Street (between Goodge Street and Oxford Street), under conditions of total secrecy: only 15 high-paying observers from each side were permitted to attend. The purse was £400 – the price just over a century ago of a decent house.

Pritchard seems to have been a fairly close friend of George Cooper and, as we shall see, it is clear that George is not merely a brawler but is a fighter of some quality. Pritchard, it is said, thought that he was a fair match for his own talents, which, coming from a national champion, was high praise indeed. But it is also clear that honourable man though George is, he finds it difficult to take life seriously. He is not blessed by particularly good luck, as his grandson told me: 'It was at the *Flying Horse*, near the Elephant & Castle. Apparently he saw a hunchback there, playing a barrel organ. Suddenly the hunchback turned on a girl and started belting her – well, he wasn't having that and he tries to break it up, and the girl ups and sticks a bloody great hat-pin straight through his buttocks – literally pinning them together – they said he had to eat standing for a fortnight.'

*

A year after Pritchard's middleweight title fight in 1891, the National Sporting Club was established. It was this event that did more to reverse the fortunes of boxing than any other, for now the sport had an organizing body that could (and would) fight hard for its interests. Immediately, it took up the cudgels against any court that attempted to treat boxers or promoters as criminals and quite soon in its existence it started to achieve hard results. The Club, under its most active member, the wealthy Lord Lonsdale, managed to get decisions overturned and, as importantly, reversed. For the first time in its chequered history, prizefighting had a well-funded and organized lobby and was making headway. By the end of the Century, boxing was hugely popular, partly because of some of the extraordinary characters who were appearing in it now, and would appear in it later. There was one in particular: James Wicks. He was born in Bermondsey in 1895 and was, like George Cooper, of Anglo–Irish descent.

George and Elizabeth Cooper produced a son, Henry William, on 23 May 1901. George was 37 by then, which was relatively late to start a family. But, given what would happen within 13 years, it was a happy coincidence that the child would be spared the horrors of the Great War. By that time, George and Elizabeth were living in Elsted Street in Walworth.

Less than a mile to the north, at 39 Queen's Buildings, Collinson Street, just off Borough High Street, on 9 October 1906, a little girl, Lily Nutkins, was born. She was to have a very hard early life. Her mother, Maria, had been born Maria Bishop, and had married Henry Harvey Nutkins, a general dealer, at some day prior to 1886. It seems that Lily was a very late arrival, as she was the second of two children, the first, Henry Harvey junior, having arrived twenty years before. Clearly this was too much for Henry Harvey senior, as, aged 50, after having fathered yet another child, he soon fled the nest and simply disappeared, leaving Maria to bring up Lily and her little brother Tom on her own. She may have had some help from her son Henry junior, but it would be unlikely to have been substantial, as Maria worked extraordinarily hard. Condemned by her illiteracy to a life of hard labour, she rose at 4 a.m. and walked to work across London Bridge to clean out the fireplaces at the Bank of England.

*

George Cooper was still fighting at the age of 40. His bailiwick was as extensive as ever, and his son Henry William recalled that, just before the Great War, his proud father returned home with half a sovereign in loose change, which he had won in a brawl in a pub yard in Denmark Hill. The chances are that it had been a bare-knuckle fight, as George's hands were so swollen and sore that the young Henry William had to extract the *specie* from his father's pocket. That handful of change would keep the family in food and rent for over a week, but it was a hard way to earn a living.

Less stressful was singing. George had a fine voice, and clearly realized it, as he would use any excuse to demonstrate his vocal skills or, failing that, to tell stories. At the drop of a hat he would wheel out 'Donnelly and Cooper', irrespective of who was listening. Henry William recalled the memory of a slightly befuddled George telling stories to an empty kitchen in the small hours.

George was fighting professionally as well, and as a measure of the quality of his efforts he too is to be found at Habbijam's gym. Habbijam, fighter, promoter, matchmaker and referee, ran probably the tightest ship in London; any fighter not punching his weight was unceremoniously thrown out and denied his purse. Habbijam, from Birmingham, and clearly operating on the model laid down by Broughton, was probably the most significant figure in the English (or at least the London) ring.

George's skills were also highly sought after by such organizers as both a bodyguard and bouncer. He 'looked after' Bombardier Billy Wells, and was present on the door when Jack Johnson was shamefully barred from the National Sporting Club – an event which took place in 1908.

*

Henry William Cooper just missed fighting in the Great War. He enlisted at the end of 1918 in the Royal Horse Artillery and was awaiting his posting to go to France when the Armistice was signed in November. He became a lead rider in the King's troop of the Royal Horse Artillery (RHA), whose role then was rather more than ceremonial.

While he may have missed the war in France, he did not, unfortunately, miss the one in Ireland. He was, of course, of partly Irish ancestry, but then so was almost half the British Army by then, so there was little unusual in that. He was stationed first at Dublin Castle and recalled later that such was the appalling security offered to off-duty troops that as a rule they would buy their own side arms as, astonishingly, the Army did not provide them.

Almost inevitably, Henry William boxed. He was a useful welterweight, in fact, and made it to the semi-finals of his brigade championships, which he won. In the final, a man who turned out to be a professional in civilian life beat him. Remarkably, Henry William fought both contests on the same night, which might go some way to explaining the result. His consolation was £1, so technically at least he was a now a professional.

Henry William served in the RHA for seven years before rejoining civilian life in the year of the General Strike, 1926, which was also the year that his father died suddenly. George had been suffering from an undiagnosed gastric ulcer since 1922, so the medical report tells us, but it was a burst blood vessel, perhaps connected with the ulcer, perhaps with his liver, which would have been curling up at the edges by now, an event which occurred at the end of February. He was, typically, singing at a wedding at the time. He died on 13 May at the home they shared with many others at 19 Ash Street, after a recurrence of the same symptom. Elizabeth was at his bedside when he died.

Henry William, rather than stay with his mother, settled as a relieved civilian into lodgings at 33 Bedford Street, Newington. Next door at number 31 lived the Nutkins family. After a relatively brief courtship, Henry William Cooper and Lily Nutkins were married at St John's Church, Newington on 8 May 1927.

The couple moved to Daneville Road, Camberwell Green, where their first son, Bernard, arrived in 1930. The economic situation was dire, but not quite as bad as it was going to get. The stock market had crashed, but the full effects of this were yet to be felt, not that this would particularly bother either Henry William or Lily unduly, as life was always going to be hard for them, whatever the economic conditions; boom, bust, recession or depression, it made little or no difference to them. When times were really hard (and they would get really hard), it was more a matter of tightening an already constricting belt yet one more notch.

When Lily became pregnant in the late summer of 1933, neither she nor Henry had any inkling about their new baby. When asked what she would call it if it was another boy she said she rather liked the idea of Walter, not that there were any Walters in her particular family tree, but then there weren't any Bernards, either. The birth was due to take place in late April or early May at the Westminster lying-in (maternity) hospital. Lily had received a hint of what was to come, but failed to grasp it; she was even shown X-rays of herself. There had been an occasional example of twins in Henry William's family, but not, so far as she knew, in her own.

So, when healthy twin boys arrived on 3 May 1934, no one was more surprised than Lily. Any dismay she may have felt at the prospect of another mouth to feed (she was always, with good reason, a worrier) was quickly offset as she held the two new arrivals for the first time. The first baby out weighed in at 6lbs, the second, born 20 minutes later, was a little more hefty, a difference that would in fact persist.

As for naming these two, Lily recalled later that it was a maternity nurse, or perhaps a midwife who, as a matter of complete coincidence, thought of Henry and George, in that order. Both were Cooper family names, and they seemed appropriate, so Henry and George they became – neither was given a middle name.

Daneville Road was clearly going to become quite crowded, the proud parents realized, but not perhaps immediately. Much would depend on how fast these new arrivals started growing. Another nurse had noted that they looked to be likely lads. 'You mark my words,' she said, 'these two will be six-footers.' As things transpired, this was clearly the voice of experience.

CHAPTER TWO

A Wartime Childhood

'The childhood shows the man, as morning shows the day.'
JOHN MILTON, *Paradise Regained*, (1671).

THE COOPER FAMILY was as dislocated by the war as anyone could be. Almost as soon as their council house on the Bellingham Estate at 120 Farmstead Road was ready for them, they moved in and the order came that all three children were to be evacuated.

This was a depressingly common transaction during the war and entirely as a result of the pessimism which governed policy concerning the likely outcome of a war with Germany. Estimates concerning the probable level of casualties had resulted in some fairly dismal arithmetic. Gloomily, the Committee of Imperial Defence had predicted, in September 1939, that the first German air attacks would last 60 days and result in 600,000 casualties. An appropriate number of *papier mâché* coffins had been prepared and stacked ready, a million burial forms had been printed and issued and plans had been made, upon the outbreak of war, to simply evacuate more than one and a quarter million women and children from the major inner cities into rural or suburban areas before the *Luftwaffe* did to London, Liverpool and Glasgow what it had done to Guernica during the Spanish Civil War. The evacuation policy had some interesting outcomes, in fact, as the two economic nations really met each other for the first time. For the Cooper twins, aged six, it was to prove a bruising encounter.

The attitude of many households, almost invariably better off than their unwilling guests, was frankly hostile in many cases. Stories had begun circulating at the end of 1939, of unspeakable, unwashed children, both verminous and feral, pouring out of the inner cities, completely unfamiliar with such social imperatives as flushing loos or even underwear. One Glasgow mother was reputed to have scolded her six-year-old when it chose to relieve itself in someone else's home: 'You dirty thing, messing up the lady's carpet; go and do it in the corner.'

Given that the Cooper family was scooped up and redistributed rather late in the overall process, Bernard, Henry and George (who were most certainly not in that category, as Lily had worked as hard as she could to ensure that her sons were a credit to her) were on the receiving end of a certain inbuilt prejudice when they arrived in Lancing on the Sussex coast in early 1940. Bernard went to one house, the twins to another. It was the England of *Dad's Army*, even down to the location, but sadly devoid of humour.

The twins' new landlady, a Mrs Holland, seemed to take the view that if their presence was an inconvenience, then it was probably their fault rather than Adolf Hitler's. She had up to six other guests at times, including, inexplicably, a three-month-old baby. As custodian of the collective ration cards she could be expected to feed the children quite decently.

But, alas, not as well as Lily had. A seemingly endless diet of jam sandwiches was the usual fare, and while all three boys attended the local school, the only other attraction of a seaside town, the beach, was strictly off-limits, being both mined and festooned with barbed wire. Should a German invasion arrive, the Cooper boys, along with the rest of the population of Lancing, would have a ringside seat.

They would certainly witness the aftermath of Dunkirk as well as have a grandstand view of the Battle of Britain, but Henry's recollections are mainly concerned with the sheer misery of it. 'We all had to sleep across the same bed; this little baby would wake us up at some ungodly hour and I'll never forget the smell of that stuff they bring up – it would throw up all over the sheet, and she'd just wipe it down and turn the sheet over! I can still smell it now,' he related to me, with some disgust.

Henry senior and Lily, for economic reasons, were unable to see their children more than once or twice, which was torture for all concerned, albeit probably just as well for the fastidious Lily. There was worse to come, though, as Farmstead Road was also an early casualty of German night bombing and suddenly became clearly uninhabitable.

The house was hit by a German parachute mine on a Saturday night while Henry senior was working a late shift on his tram, and it was only by pure luck that Lily was not inside either. When the house was hit, she was visiting a near neighbour and nattering with her in her Anderson shelter. Altogether, 25 people were killed in that raid, and it took four days' work to find them all, or what was left of them. Effectively now the Cooper family was homeless, and given that the house would clearly not be repaired for at least 18 months, they were rather stuck.

A dubious and rather speculative solution arrived in the form of a colleague of Henry's who had relatives near Stroud in Gloucestershire. There was both work and accommodation – of a kind – available there. They chose to evacuate there.

When they saw the accommodation, it must have crossed their minds that Farmstead Road might after all have done for them very well, with or without its roof. Their new home was in fact a derelict and abandoned venison abattoir that was technically condemned. They were able to find work nearby, though, Henry William at an asbestos plant, Lily at a shadow factory making aeroplane parts. For the hard-working and houseproud Lily, this ordeal must have been terrible, even if drawing water from a well might have been a novelty. The couple, even further away from their sons than before, were well and truly miserable with this medieval existence.

This state was further compounded when Henry senior crushed three of his fingers in a rolling mill. Unable to work, but having to watch his wife work, was a further ordeal for him. He received £2 a week sick pay, and eventually some modest compensation. The pair's first thought was to liberate their children back into their own care, which they promptly did.

For the Cooper boys, anything would have been better than Lancing, and at least living in a semi-derelict country wreck was an adventure. Naturally, being so close to the shadow factory made it a restricted area, so for the brief time that they were there, they had to play hide and seek with the security services, which certainly added to the novelty, whatever it did to Lily's nerves. A great treat, though, was the vast pile of discarded deer antlers with which the ground floor of this dismal establishment was liberally scattered; the children had never seen such things before and they made fine toys.

Finally, Farmstead Road was ready for re-occupation in the late autumn of 1941 and a relieved family returned to it, after a brief stay in a requisitioned flat. Most of their possessions had been destroyed or stolen (looting, sadly seems to have been rife during the Blitz) and although there was a small amount of financial compensation for the loss of their home, they were forced to lead a rather basic life, but one which was tolerable now that the family was finally reunited. That state, however, would not persist for long.

It is a characteristic of the ill luck of the Cooper family that they always seemed to get caught out by changes in regulation. Henry senior, with six years of service behind him already, qualified for call-up only by virtue of a matter of days. He was called up in 1942, at 41 years of age, right on the limit of the age restriction after it was modified; despite his previous service in the Royal Horse Artillery and his clear knowledge of both guns and stroppy quadrupeds, he was rather illogically drafted into the Royal Army Medical Corps and, after initial preliminary training in Edinburgh, was dispatched as an orderly to the XIV Army in Calcutta from where he would join the rest of the forgotten army in Burma. His family would not see him for nearly three years.

At Farmstead Road, life went on, after a fashion. The weekly rent was a guinea, let alone household utilities, and Lily's income, including government supplementary payments to compensate for Henry senior's absence was only £3.10s. A scandalised correspondent reported to *The Times* in early 1940 that there were newly created single mothers whose husbands were serving with the forces, with two children to raise, who were being asked to live on less than £1 a week.

So, in the tradition of her forebears, Lily worked. At one stage she was holding down up to three jobs and the simple strain of it all, fretting over the task of feeding her children, not to mention dreading the arrival of the telegram from the War Office, which would be the only way of knowing the state of her husband, wore her down. Never a bulky woman, her weight plummeted as she denied herself food in order to feed her hungry trio. 'Mum would queue up at the butcher's and buy a sheep's head for ten pence, and out of that she could feed us all,' recalled Henry. 'It was amazing what she could do with it.' Clearly, Lily like most women who lived through the war, was an inventive cook. Nothing that could be used was thrown away. Unheard-of dishes today, like brawn and shinbone soup, made from the cheapest cuts of meat, were made to stretch a very long way.

The wartime diet, with all its rationing restrictions, actually produced an extraordinarily healthy generation of children. Henry and George grew quickly and were clearly two of the largest attendees at Athelney Road School. The fact that they were identical twins was a novelty, but one that also rather served to draw attention to them. They were neither bullied nor did they bully, but they learned quickly that the numerous scraps and incidents in the school playground would often be attributed to them simply because of their very high profiles and they learned very quickly to look after themselves. They were quick to respond.

Henry achieved his first knockout in the playground at Athelney Road School, during a handball game: 'Suddenly a little fellow called Bridges jumped on my back and started throwing punches. I got a bit of a temper on and dragged him over to me and punched him in the eye. I knocked him out. Another fellow rushed over but George held him off.' This would rather serve to define the later relationship between the Cooper twins: absolute and unquestioning loyalty.

Academically, the only subject that could raise even a twitch of interest from Henry was history, and this mainly by virtue of the imaginative skills of the staff; the experience of role-playing (very contemporary) rather served to bring out something of the actor in him and he discovered that he enjoyed the limelight rather a lot. Neither history nor the limelight is an interest which has ever really left him.

But school was merely an inconvenience compared to the risks of urban life during the blackout, which covered Britain like a giant wet blanket. During the day the neighbourhood was an extraordinary maelstrom of commercial opportunity and all three Cooper brothers worked, and very hard. Before school would be a paper round, after school would be errand-running and at weekends would be a busy round of collecting for the household commissary, whether liberating scraps of coal and coke from the local power station or joining the ever-longer queues at the various food shops, or collecting the randomly packaged relief parcels from the American Red Cross, or recycling horse manure, of which there was no shortage. Occasionally there was a chance to 'recycle' golf balls on the Beckenham course, too; they were free to the finder when picked up, but worth 2/- 6d at the back door of the clubhouse. Value added indeed. It would be a long time before Henry developed an interest in golf, but from that moment he had technically become a professional: he had made money out of it.

Coping on her own with three growing boys was a gigantic task for Lily; they simply shot up in height, as a natural result of her efforts in the kitchen. The challenge of feeding and clothing her sons was immense, but she proved well up to it. Many others in the same situation were to find themselves in debt by the end of the war, but not so Lily. It was part of her soul to spend only earned money, with the occasional unavoidable assistance of the local Co-op, without which many families would simply have starved, particularly later in the war, as food shortages started to bite.

The V1 flying bomb, the 'doodlebug', which nearly did for Henry, would have taken about 25 minutes from its launch site near Calais to arrive in southeast London. A prototypical cruise missile, powered by a simple pulse rocket motor, it would deliver a half-ton of high explosive warhead sufficient to destroy three or four terraced houses. The advent of these weapons was the early summer of 1944, the 'doodlebug summer'. Overall, 9,500 would be launched, and they would kill over 7,000 people and injure many more, but crucially, the fear of them would cause the hasty evacuation from London of over a million more.

The missile's approach was heralded by a characteristic farting drone, rather like an un-silenced motorcycle engine, which, once it stopped, meant potential trouble for those underneath its path. The V1 was guided only by travel time, it was not capable of manoeuvre: the more fuel, the greater the distance.

Once the V1 campaign started, a natural reaction was the disposition of more and more anti-aircraft guns, which were arrayed in order to shoot them down, which made for an even more random process as well as serious danger from falling shell splinters from the guns themselves. Despite the fact that Operation Overlord was under way as of 6 June 1944, the lives of the citizens of the southeast of England, particularly southeast London, were just as perilous as before and would indeed become more so when the V1's successor arrived.

Londoners became used to the doodlebugs very quickly. Lily had evolved her own strategy for coping with the impending arrival of these unwelcome guests. In many ways it made sense: run to the flimsy Anderson shelter with a chair cushion wrapped around the head. The cushion was never going to stop splinters, but it might reduce some blast effects.

For blast, as Henry was to find out at very close quarters, was the main danger of these weapons. On a clear Saturday in the summer of 1944, he and Bernard were selling football pool coupons quite close to home when the now-familiar sound of the V1 motor was heard. As it cut out, the pair dashed for the nearest Anderson shelter, and they very nearly made it. The explosion slammed Henry up against the structure and he was quite knocked out, while Bernard acquired a backside full of glass.

Such was the frequency of these events that Londoners, particularly children, became used to them very quickly. When the second phase of the V-weapon attack started, though, the difference was immediately clear. The V2, in effect the grandfather of the Saturn rocket, was a truly terrifying weapon, so powerful that it could destroy a city block, and not even hard-bitten and bloody-minded Londoners could think up a nickname for it. Even its inventor, Werner von Braun, was awed by it; he is alleged to have said: 'The only thing wrong with this is that it is being fired at the wrong planet.'

For children, providing they survived, the V-weapon raids were something of an adventure, and served very well to harden them up. Those who came through the bombing raids developed a carapace of callousness that was the simple and understandable result of being witness to total war. Henry's reaction was typical:

The day we heard Lewisham Woolworth's had caught it with a V2 rocket we ran all the way there, about three miles. It was one of the worst tragedies of the war. They were bringing out bits of bodies and, as one of the rescue workers came out with a carrier bag, we were told he had a head in it. We'd go back, and play afterwards. You knew it could happen to you, but it didn't keep you awake at nights, it didn't seem to penetrate. I suppose we were too young to have any deep feelings about it.

But by then the end of the war was in sight and the only evidence of enemy activity was the occasional earthquake thump of a V2. All that the Cooper household needed, particularly an exhausted Lily, was the safe return of Henry senior, which happened in late 1944.

So the family had survived intact, which was much more than could be said for some, including many neighbours and, as the Allies punched towards Germany, the thoughts of the twins developed about some more peaceful activities.

All three brothers had always been sporty. Bernard, of a lighter build, preferred athletics, whereas the twins both excelled at football and even cricket, but it was boxing that really interested them. They had never seen a match, except in the cinema, but there was definitely something about it that they liked.

Henry senior had no objection – one of the first things he did when he returned from the war, proudly wearing his XIV Army bush hat, was to spar with his sons on his knees in the family living room. Boxing was as deep-rooted in the culture then as football is now and, having boxed in the Army first time around, he was all for it.

CHAPTER THREE

Rumblings

'… Amateur sport, which is the best and soundest thing in England'
SIR ARTHUR CONAN DOYLE, *The Return of Sherlock Holmes.*

THE BELLINGHAM BOXING CLUB met weekly in the British Legion Hall and, drawing as it did entirely from the local community, had no shortage of talent spotters. One of these was a neighbour of the Cooper family, a fireman, Robert Hill. He had noticed the nine-year old twins sparring in the street, football socks wrapped around their fists, and saw something in them that rather interested him; he had himself boxed for the Fire Brigade and therefore knew of what he spoke. He approached Henry senior and asked him if he would be prepared to allow his twins to join the boxing club. He was so convinced that these two were serious prospects that he undertook to pay their subscriptions for the first year.

Unsurprisingly, the club was healthily oversubscribed; the generation of youths who had observed the war but who were too young to have taken part in it was to be an aggressive one, so there was a small delay before both the twins were able to attend, which caused some anxiety in the Cooper household. There were other clubs, of course – every neighbourhood had one – but the twins were inseparable and emotionally, if not physically, joined at the hip.

The purpose of the boxing club was primarily to teach the youngsters three things: training, the atmosphere of the gym and the rudiments of the ring. The object was not to make the boys aggressive (teenage boys are aggressive enough without that), rather it was to give them the discipline to carry on, as the attrition rate in amateur boxing is notoriously high.

The training rotation was relatively strict, even for young teenagers

– running, skipping, bag work and the speedball – and the methods of training had been handed down in the oral tradition, for there were few textbooks. The issue of diet was not a matter of particular scientific interest, particularly straight after the war and anyway, food rationing, in force until 1951, ensured that there were few unsuitably tempting items on offer to distract the ambitious athlete. Decent food could only really be discussed in the abstract.

Of course, at the most junior level, there was hardly any actual fighting done at all; Henry and George did not actually hit anyone seriously for some time, but they found the very fact of being fully fit satisfying enough to justify carrying on. They saw in boxing what Robert Hill had hoped they would and the Bellingham trainer, Matt Wells, had, in his time been British lightweight champion, so they were in good hands. It was not all harmony at Bellingham, though; early on in their time there, one of the junior trainers was asked to leave, for a reason which Henry blandly described to me as being 'the usual thing'.

At 15, as soon as they left school, the twins joined the Eltham and District Amateur Boxing Club and were thus now in the care of head trainer George Page, who would act as both their trainer and mentor for the remainder of their civilian amateur careers. If anything, according to Henry, the casualty rate at Eltham was even higher:

> In the early days I was about eight or nine stone, and I was in against this kid of seven and a half stone. He was no thicker than my little finger and I thought: 'He'll do, lovely.' I went in like a bull in a china shop, but this kid was a schoolboy champion and I had more left hands in my face than I ever thought possible... I never landed a glove on him. But George and me were keen and we went back the next week.

What the amateur ring really taught was an inner core of discipline, the ability to successfully manage anger, a thing that generations of adolescents, then as now, have usually found quite difficult to do. 'It's good to have a training routine which provides a discipline quite aside from the obvious physical improvements,' says Henry. 'But where boxing is chiefly character building is in the ring, where no kid can afford to lose his temper. If he does, nine times out of ten he'll be punished more. You go berserk and bonk! – your opponent is just picking you off.'

The difference between youthful anger and controlled aggression is very large indeed. The discipline needed to bang a left jab into another boy's face is not the same emotion as wishing to knock him over in the street. The narrow focus of the ring – that was a good punch, that was not – served to bring on a vast respect for the technical aspects of boxing itself, as opposed to a dislike or disrespect for the opponent, and success or failure would stem from there. Indeed, part of the 'psyching out' procedures of the professional ring really revolved about making the opponent angry as well as scared.

Henry enjoyed Eltham; both he and George were working hard at physically arduous jobs and the demands of regular training were even harder, so logically they were supremely fit, but Henry needed an indication of whether he was really temperamentally suited to boxing as a potential living; in 1951 he got it when he beat a PC Trevillion, then the national police champion at his weight (light heavy) in a four-round contest. He won the fight with his left jab, as he would so many, and the audience was appreciative.

These amateur fights carried prizes with them but, of course, no money. The prizes were typically things of some domestic utility: canteens of cutlery, toasters, coffee percolators and so forth. This was useful as Christmas approached, as the extended family was invited round to share the fruits of the twins' labours.

This was fine, but they had to work, too. They had left school in 1949 with a joint sigh of relief in order to earn a living and make a useful contribution to the household economy. Their choice of work was governed by a simple imperative: money. Neither had any particular ambition, save to earn as much as possible in order to make life easier for Lily as well as carry on their boxing – these two targets rather defined them. Initially they found that they could earn 9d (about 4p) an hour as labourers, stacking sheet metal for a firm called Burnham's in nearby Sydenham – not very good for the hands.

Research revealed that the wages at Sydenham Gasworks, from where they had carried sacks of coal to Bellingham during the war, the wages were a halfpenny an hour better, and so they promptly tried that. But even higher wages were available quite locally, on Bellingham Estate itself, where a builder was allegedly paying 10½d (just under 5p) an hour. It was dangerous roofing work, 60 feet up, with no harness. It was during this time at Bellingham that Henry had a nasty accident, which would revisit him in later life. While attempting to ride a bicycle with a chimney pot under his arm, he fell off and broke his left elbow. It was, of course, extraordinarily painful, but he needed to work. Unfortunately, there was a three-month waiting list at the local hospital, so the elbow was simply bandaged and he merely rested it a little, until the pain receded, but it later transpired that a chip of bone had been knocked off it and worked its way into the joint. It would stay there as well, slowly being ground down to a fine powder, both by the heavy manual labour he was doing as well as the increasingly arduous work in the gym.

When the twins discovered that the 10½d an hour was actually a fiction (it turned out to be 10d), they left in high dudgeon. Ultimately, their search for useful employment came as a direct result of their membership of the Eltham club; George Page had a good friend called Reg Reynolds, who ran a successful plastering contractor's business. It is a trade that George would never leave; better still, much later on, Reynolds would become his father-in-law. So, finally they had found a business that they could learn, and that would actually start to financially support them. Settled at last, they concentrated on their boxing to the exclusion of almost everything else.

The trade was quite good for them; Henry plastered with his left hand, George with his right and the effort required to mix a fair-sized load was considerable. Even the arm movements developed the right muscles so, coupled with the gym work, both boys quickly became extraordinarily fit.

But there was some debate as to whether he could go to Helsinki for the 1952 Olympics, to represent Britain at light heavyweight division; he was the Amateur Boxing Association (ABA) champion and had been since April, when he had outpointed Joe MacLean in the final, but the six weeks loss of earnings, perhaps £25, which would be the result, was economically important to the Cooper household at

Farmstead Road. If Henry didn't go, then there were plenty of boxers who could. In the end Lily simply increased her work rate and, by dint of even more charlady work, financed the gap.

The Helsinki Olympics had originally been scheduled to take place in the late summer of 1940, while Henry and George were still living in Lancing, and the Olympic village really dated from then. The British boxing team had high expectations, in fact, and had every reason to be optimistic, but the boxing was to be dominated by America.

The 1952 Olympics were extremely political, taking place as they did on the borders of the Soviet Union; not only was the Korean War in full swing, there was a particular local issue. Twelve years before, the Red Army had invaded Finland without declaring war, and the memories of that action were still fresh in the minds of the locals. As a result, security for the USSR contingent was strict, on the Soviet side to prevent defections and on the Finnish side to protect the athletes from being attacked, as the Finns had no reason to love its huge Eastern neighbour. It made for a rather tense Games. Henry's first bout was scratched, propelling him forward, but in the second round he came up against the Russian Anatoli Perov, who, of course, he had never met, for security reasons, and who beat him on a 2:1 split decision. Two out of the three judges were from Warsaw Pact countries, one from France.

Henry's defeat gave him plenty of time to watch the Games and even though he had no spending money to speak of he managed to enjoy himself and consider the prospect of his upcoming National Service as well as a rather bigger decision: the idea of turning professional.

He witnessed two future opponents, and the contrast between them was huge and certainly did not suggest to Henry that he would ever meet either of them, let alone that they would meet each other. The first was Floyd Patterson, at 17 one of the youngest competitors at the entire Games, fighting at middleweight. He won the gold medal and turned professional upon his return to New York. The second was a large and ungainly Swede, Ingemar Johansson, who put up such a lacklustre performance in the heavyweight division that he was thrown out of the competition for not trying. Given the large numbers of Swedes in the audience, this was embarrassing, to say the least, however much it may have amused the Finns. Patterson, fast and flashy, had impressed, but Johansson had definitely not

*

Before the Games Henry had had an interesting encounter with J.T. Hulls, the journalist who covered amateur boxing for the *Evening News*. It was Hulls's habit to visit the Cooper household for a general natter every Sunday and inevitably the subject of turning professional would arise. Hulls's advice was simple and sage: 'There is only one man to manage you – Jim Wicks.'

Hulls knew his business; he was one of the most knowledgeable of writers and, as Henry would find out, extremely well connected. Neither Henry nor George knew Wicks, who actually lived in Eltham – if he had ever been to the club they had not seen him. He hadn't, in fact, as it was Wicks's general expectation that people would come to him. He was right: they did.

The business of turning professional can be a tricky one. BBBC rules mandated that a fighter had to have a manager of record, but it was well known that these men varied widely in terms of their professionalism and honesty. A poor choice of manager can shorten a boxer's career just as surely as a detached retina, as many have discovered.

The twins and George Page accordingly made their way to Footscray Road, Eltham, where this apparent paragon of virtue lived. Hulls had arranged the meeting. They were initially rather surprised. '…we didn't know quite what to expect,' says Henry. ' I suppose we had visions of a boxing manager looking something like Noel Coward, with a cigarette holder and a silk dressing gown. But the Wickses seemed such a homely pair ...'

Of particular concern to the twins was timing, for both Henry and George were scheduled to join the Ordnance Corps for their spell in uniform in the late summer of 1952, straight after Helsinki. Should they turn pro before or after National Service? Wicks's counsel was straightforward, Henry remembers: '"If you go into the Army as professionals, you won't get any concessions," he told us. "If you box for them as amateurs, you'll go here, there and everywhere. As a pro you wouldn't be allowed to box for them."'

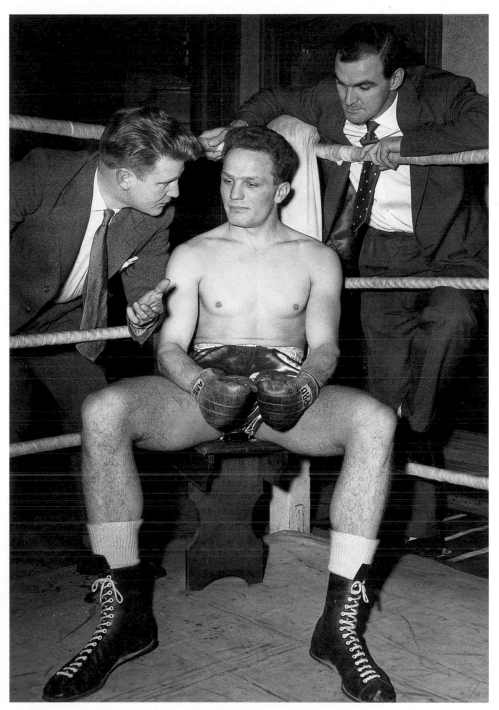

Donald Houston *(left)* and Stanley Baker *(right)* pick up a few hints from Henry at the *Thomas à Becket*. Both actors (along with their friend Richard Burton) were avid fight goers and fans of Henry.

Above: Disappointment for Henry at the Helsinki Olympics in 1952; his opponent Anatoli Perov of the USSR wins on points in the second round of the light heavyweight competition.

Left: 19 May 1957, Stockholm; Henry is dropped in the fifth round by Ingemar Johansson's 'Hammer of Thor'. You can beat Henry but you can never make a loser out of him.

Above: 12 January 1959; unlike his previous encounter with Brian London, when Henry fought London for the British and Empire titles, the fight went the full fifteen rounds and Henry won it on points 'I felt worse after this than after any other fight I ever had'.
Right: Henry, the new British and Empire heavyweight champion, looks down at his first Lonsdale Belt after his victory over London.

Left: 17 November 1959. Joe Erskine challenges Henry for his British and Empire titles. Erskine had beaten Henry twice professionally, so this was an important fight.
Below: Although it was one-sided and in Henry's favour the fight lasted twelve rounds.

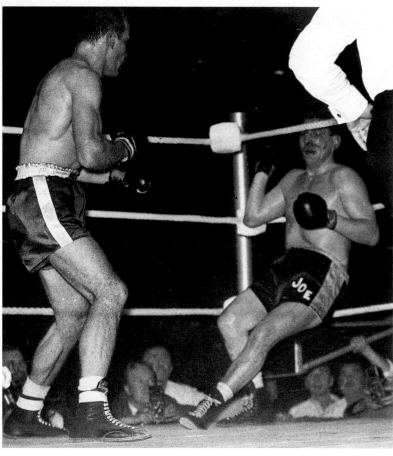

Above: Finally, Erskine ends up unconscious over the bottom rope 'we were really worried, we thought he'd broken his back'. He hadn't but Henry had broken his run of bad luck.

Below: 5 December 1961; When Henry fought Zora Folley for the second time he suffered the humiliation of a second round knock out. 'Chance only favours the prepared mind' LOUIS PASTEUR

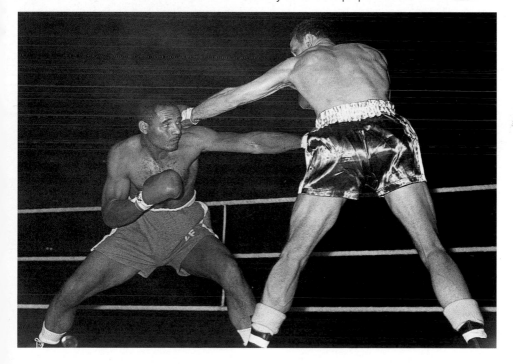

Above: 18 June 1963 the contrast could not be clearer as Henry goes for Cassius Clay from the bell in the first round. Clearly, Cassius is not expecting this.

Top right: The most famous moment in British boxing history as Henry puts Cassius on his pants with a mighty left hook in the fourth round.

Bottom right: Referee Tommy Little waves Henry to his corner after one of the worst cuts he'd ever received made it impossible for the fight to continue.

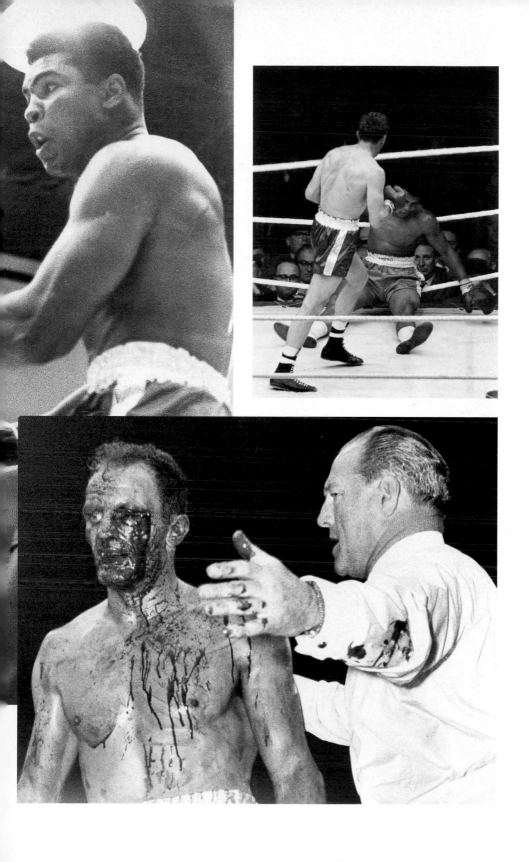

Above: The unique atmosphere of the upper room of the *Thomas à Becket* is apparent as Henry prepares for his second encounter with Clay (now Muhammad Ali) in May 1966. At the left corner stands Danny Holland with a bucket.

Below: Despite the fact that this was the first and last fight that Albina attended, she saw little of it. 'I just couldn't bear to watch' she said.

It was good advice, as things transpired. Accordingly, Henry and George both stayed amateur and reported for duty at Royal Army Ordnance Corps (RAOC) depot at Blackdown Barracks outside Aldershot within a few days of Henry's return from Helsinki.

Originally, when offered a choice of National Service destination, both brothers had opted for the Irish Guards; at 6ft 2in, they were well nigh perfect. And as Henry recalls: 'Well, we were both tall, and the Irish Guards had never won the Army boxing championship.'

But they were cunningly diverted from their original purpose. At a boxing tournament before the Olympics a Captain Eastlake had introduced himself. Eastlake was basically the talent scout for the 4th Battalion RAOC, a unit that was the main reason why the Irish Guards had done so badly. The 4th was known as the 'boxers' battalion' and with good reason. While it had a serious military function, which included the potential for dangerous overseas service in Korea, it had also established a rather proud tradition of the fistic art. Eastlake persuaded the twins to switch their allegiance – they did not regret it.

After six weeks' basic training – 'square bashing' – at Blackdown, they were dispatched to take a driving course, after which they were inducted into the battalion proper. 'I did very little soldiering, I must confess,' says Henry. 'Every morning after parade it was "boxers – fall out". Straight to the gym…'

The authorities rather turned a blind eye to the activities of the 4th Battalion. Company Sergeant Major Mick Cavanagh, in charge of the boxers, was a keen amateur himself; he had actually fought Henry just before the Olympic Games and bore him no ill will despite the fact that Henry had knocked him out. While CSM Cavanagh was in charge, he made sure that his boxers were not unnecessarily overburdened with military duties; good soldier though he was, he clearly had his own agenda.

Certain others were less considerate: one excitable officer was alleged to have grabbed the front of Henry's tunic when trying to make a point – the fact that under military law this was technically an assault had clearly escaped him. There was no need for the MPs, however. Henry simply growled with polite menace: 'Take your ruddy hands off me – sir.'

Quickly, under this generally benign but rather artificial regime, the twins established a routine. Given the discipline with which they ran their lives anyway, the routines of Army life were actually nothing new, but there was a high boredom factor, which, despite the diversion of boxing, set in quickly. Endless games of cards, particularly against the wily Joe Erskine, whom Henry had beaten in the ABA light heavyweight semi-finals in April 1952, were both tediously repetitive and extremely costly, as Erskine was a less than scrupulous card-player. Henry and Erskine would fight seven more times, in fact.

The twins managed to return to Bellingham for most weekends, and were permitted to fight in London at ABA events during the week, and it was in May 1953 that Henry beat the Australian Tony Madigan to clinch his second ABA light heavyweight championship. 'He was the best fighter I ever fought as an amateur…' Henry remembers. 'He came over here especially to win an ABA title. When I met him in the final, he'd stopped every boy in every round he'd had. He was a hell of a puncher, and tough, and I thought it the best fight I'd won – even if it was on points.'

Jim Wicks was in the audience and it was the first time he had seen Henry fight. 'He told me later that he thought I had a decent left hand and that I moved well against a two-handed fighter like Madigan,' says Henry. 'But I thought he'd forgotten us really.'

Despite the boost of the second ABA light heavyweight championship, Henry had trouble finding his form for the European amateur championships in Warsaw shortly afterwards. He was clobbered by another Russian, Yuri Jegorov, in the first round of the first eliminator. He was not knocked out, but very nearly so, sufficiently groggy that the referee stopped the fight. 'I never did any good at all in either the Olympics or the European championships,' he recalls. 'Looking back, I suppose the atmosphere was different – they were big occasions, and I hadn't yet learned to relax, to leave the worrying to others.'

Ultimately, he would do that, but it would cause him a crisis of confidence of a fairly high order before he realized that, while boxing is an individual sport, there are divisions of labour within it that serve to define both its evolution and thus its history. To mature enough to fully grasp this would take some time.

All in all, Henry would fight 84 senior amateur bouts and win 73 of them, which was an outstanding record, particularly allowing for the quality of the light heavyweight opposition in those far-off days. Henry senior, who attended as many bouts as he could, had discovered a magic tonic, which famously has worked for horse trainers for centuries: eggs beaten up in amontillado sherry. It is true that it can do wonders for horses and ponies, but its benefits to a prizefighter are dubious. Dutifully, though, Henry drank this unpromising mixture; he was trying to gain weight, an outcome which it would certainly accomplish, but it was about the only alcohol he would consume before turning professional.

Henry fought his last amateur bout in April 1954, four months before the end of National Service, an occasion to which he had looked forward, as the second year with the boxers' battalion had been rather more military and less fistic than the first. It was with a profound sense of relief that he and George resumed civilian life, although under the law they were bound to be registered for the reserve until 1957.

Unsurprisingly, they had been approached by a series of managers while still in the Army, inviting them to partake of their services as professionals but, having maintained contact with Hulls, they were determined that if they turned professional, they would do so with Wicks, and Wicks only. Sam Burns, who was an old acquaintance of Wicks's, going back to the days of the Blackfriars ring, had followed Henry and George's careers so far with interest and even dispatched his new prospect, Albert Finch, to see the twins to tell them what a marvellous manager he clearly was, but to no avail – their minds were made up.

A pleased J.T. Hulls re-established contact with Wicks, who happily agreed to see the hopeful pair. He willingly assented to be the twins' manager of record under BBBC rules, but he made no grand financial gestures, it was simply not his policy – he did, though, see the novelty value of managing a pair of identical twins who, he knew, under Board of Control rules, would never be allowed to fight each other. It would be very good for business. He arranged for the contract to be signed on live television, the BBC's *Sportsview* programme, followed by a little light sparring. It may have seemed to be an omen when the hastily built ring fell over, but if anyone thought it was, then no one said anything.

Wicks had every reason to be pleased; he currently had no rated heavyweights under his care (they had all been snapped up) but now no fewer than two of them had fallen into his lap, one immensely powerful right-handed puncher, George, the other, Henry, possessed of a rapidly burgeoning left, which rather suggested that he could expand his activities somewhat. As Henry ruefully comments:

> George was always a heavier puncher than me; he stopped more boys with his right than I ever did with my left … a lot of his fights never got beyond the first round. He also suffered from cut eyes more than me. His eyebrows were more prominent. But he lost a year's boxing through scarlet fever and in one of his last amateur fights he hit someone so hard that he broke his thumb in two places. It didn't heal properly, had to be reset and I don't think he never really punched so hard again.

Naturally, both twins were very familiar with the likely opposition. Joe Erskine, Brian London, Dick Richardson, Peter Bates and Joe Bygraves were the main British or Empire heavyweight prospects at the time; they were all reckoned to be fairly evenly matched and were all roughly the same age. The late 1950s would be rather defined by the six, together with Henry, as they fought time and again to establish the pecking order in the domestic division. By 1959 it would be sorted out for the next ten years. Being (unseasoned) professionals aside, little changed for the Cooper twins. They still shared a room at home, and carried on working for Reg Reynolds, learning their trade. Reynolds was quite content to allow them a certain flexibility as to their hours so that they could train; as a keen amateur himself, he was well aware of the demands and necessities of proper training and could see that they were extremely keen at both plastering and boxing and also very good at both. Further, with a potentially uncertain future, they calculated it was prudent to have a fallback, as it was now a very different world into which they contemplated stepping.

PART TWO

THE PROFESSIONAL
CAREER OF
HENRY COOPER

CHAPTER FOUR
'Tales of 'Offman'

'Something may come of this. I hope it mayn't be human gore.'
CHARLES DICKENS, *Barnaby Rudge*, (1841).

IT WAS SUDDENLY an extraordinarily interesting time for the Cooper brothers in a world that was clearly familiar to their new avuncular mentor. They also learned quickly that 'Mr. Wicks', as they were deferentially to call him for the first two years of their acquaintance, had a wide, varied and fascinating circle of friends. The centre of the London professional boxing world was Soho, just as it had been two centuries earlier, in the days of James Figg and Jack Broughton. Their establishments were long gone, of course, but some of their spirit clearly remained; indeed, much of the *milieu* of boxing, despite the rule changes and its current legality, was still fixed firmly in the past.

But Jim Wicks himself was headquartered to the south, at the *Thomas à Becket*, a tied public house on the Old Kent Road. He leased the first-floor function room from the brewery, Courage, whose pub it was, and converted it into a boxing gym, with a partitioned and rather ratty little office for himself. It served as a useful booster for the landlord's business, as the pub became a secondary focal point, a mecca for boxing south of the river.

The collective noun for boxers is 'a stable', and Wicks's stable of fighters was a formidable one. As well as the Cooper twins, he managed the fierce little Zulu fighter from Natal, Jake Tuli, who was the British and Empire bantamweight champion, as well as Alex Buxton, the British light heavyweight champion, and Joe Lucy, British lightweight champion. Also on the team was Brian Anders, who, while he may never have shone as a pro in the same way, was both wily and experienced. As a sparring partner and mentor, he was to prove invaluable. Wicks's senior trainer was Danny Holland, who was a master at dealing with cuts and would refine that art to new heights; sadly, he would need to.

At the time, the world heavyweight champion was the merciless and apparently unbeatable American, Rocco Marchegiano, who was a singularly hard act to follow. He would retire undefeated the next year. Rocky Marciano, as he was known, had the perfect statistical record of 49 fights with no defeats – *none*. He was no role model inside the ring, being both a crude and rather dirty fighter, but he had put the fear of God into a generation of others.

But the world title in 1954 was rather a remote thing. So, even, was a Lonsdale belt. The purpose of boxing for Henry was, in the early days, to learn the professional game and merely to 'earn a few bob' to help out at Bellingham. He knew he was good – nobody wins two ABA light heavyweight championships in succession against that quality of opposition without some merit, but he was uncertain, and his first fights were to be his professional education. Meanwhile, he watched bemusedly as his new manager went to work.

Wicks himself was a master of the telephone; he played it like a Stradivarius, which would offer some difficulties for the Cooper twins, as there was no phone at Farmstead road. Professionally, the twins did not really need one; it was always Jim Wicks who did most of the talking anyway and they met more or less every day at the gym above the *Becket*.

A particular crony of Wicks's was Albert Dimes, whose principal place of business (he had many and varied other interests, few of them legal) was a bookmaking office in central Soho. Dimes was an extraordinary character who was related to the Russian nobility. His sister's husband, known as 'Russian Bill', was a member of the Romanov family, whose collection of Fabergé Easter eggs Henry recalls admiring. Henry himself would, of course, become familiar with a very different Fabergé later on in his career...

But one of the best fights to take place in the 1950s was not in the ring at all; it was between Albert Dimes and the famous hoodlum Jack Comer, better known to his fascinated public as 'Jack Spot'. The issue was a simple turf war. One of Spot's protégés had been Billy Hill, a vicious loser whom Spot had employed, upon Hill's release from prison just after the war, as a strong-arm man and general factotum. Hill had prospered as a result. When Hill, who was a close associate of Dimes, had made his intentions clear, that he was going to take over Soho and manoeuvre Spot out of business (his core business was protection racketeering, spiced with the occasional robbery), it was Albert Dimes who sent the message out and an enraged Jack Spot came looking for him.

Spot found Dimes at around noon on 11 August 1955 and by three minutes past twelve, it was over. This incident, later dubbed 'the fight that never happened', rather caught the imagination of the general public, if only because Spot, who had also been the first employer of the Krays, was a celebrated gangster of the time who seemed to be fireproof by virtue of the fact that he was a major contributor to the private pension plans of many, many policemen – it was a habit the Krays had learned from him. But by 1955 the Krays had switched their allegiance to Billy Hill. Unfortunately for Spot, he did not know this.

Albert Dimes was taking his ease, chatting on the pavement in Frith Street when Spot approached him. According to one witness, Spot pulled a knife; according to another, he punched Dimes and knocked him down before setting about him with a razor. It was a blur of confusion. What all agreed on – perhaps a hundred people, including Henry, saw it – was that Dimes managed to make it as far as a grocery at the junction of Frith Street and Old Compton Street, The Continental Fruit Store, from where he obtained a paring knife and proceeded to mete out some poetic justice. Spot, like Hill, was well known as a 'striper'; he would use a taped razor – a chiv – to leave his calling card on his victims' faces, but what Dimes did to him was rather more comprehensive than that.

Aside from the punctured lung and perforated stomach, Dimes managed to sever the cheek muscles in Spot's face, which caused his jaw to hang open. He was unable to shut it again until a surgeon at the Charing Cross Hospital sewed him back together. Dimes himself was badly hurt with a stomach wound. He managed to stagger to a taxi, which removed him to the Middlesex hospital.

The collective amnesia suffered by those who witnessed the fight, coupled with some blatant witness tampering, ensured that while both men were charged with grievous bodily harm they were both acquitted. The episode marked the end of Jack Spot's ascendancy in Soho and from then on it was the territory of Billy Hill, who, happily for Dimes, was a close associate. Shortly after the acquittal, Spot was again assaulted on Hill's orders, one of the team involved being the now famous 'Mad Frankie' Fraser.

Albert Dimes was not new to violence in Frith Street. In 1941 he had been lucky to escape with a caution for unlawful wounding after the gruesome death of a criminal named Harry Distleman, who had been stabbed to death by a psychopath named 'Babe' Mancini, a particular chum (then) of Dimes, who was himself at the time on the run after deserting from the Royal Air Force.

Dimes has been written up by several boxing characters as a 'colourful character' of 1950s and '60s Soho. It is clear, though, that while he could be a truly dreadful enemy, he was also capable of a fair measure of loyalty.

Of course, boxers, as generally quiet men capable of extreme violence, were always quite near the top of this grisly but interesting food chain, simply by virtue of what they did for a living, which may have conditioned their attitudes to events such as befell Spot, but in terms of the sport itself, never mind the ancillary amusements, the big predators were the promoters. There were two senior ones: Jack Solomons and Harry Levene. Conveniently for a tactician like Wicks, they roundly detested each other.

By far the most powerful promoter was 'Jolly' Jack Solomons, as he rather liked people to call him. His base of operations was in Great Windmill Street, and his most often used venue was the Harringay Arena in north London. As well as promoting fights in his own name, he allowed others to front for him, particularly Freddie Mills; this allowed the illusion to persist that he did not exercise a monopoly. Having been a matchmaker before the war for the London promoter Sydney Hulls, from whom he had 'inherited' Harringay, he had had a good apprenticeship in the business aspects of boxing, as well as a controlling interest in the Devonshire Club, which was one of many similar institutions that served to both develop and exploit young fighters. His family business though, was originally wholesale wet fish.

The rise of Jack Solomons had been an extraordinary mixture of luck and opportunism. When Sydney Hulls had fallen out with the Board of Control in 1939, and effectively retired from promoting, Solomons was swift to fill the vacuum that he had left behind him. He promoted boxing all through the war years – it was inordinately popular – and at the end of hostilities he embarked on a whirlwind tour, by any means possible, of a war-ravaged Europe, which would create for him the loose associations necessary if he was going to play a dominant role in European boxing post-war. Solomons to that extent reminds us of no one so much as Robert Maxwell, who was, at about the same time playing a similar game with publishing.

Jack Solomons was committed to a vision of boxing that would recapture some (but only some) of the spirit of the National Sporting Club, which had – reluctantly – given way to the British Boxing Board of Control in 1935 as the regulator of boxing in Britain. As newsreel coverage, which was to give way to television, Solomons managed to achieve a certain classy intimacy to his promotions, insisting, for example, that the first six rows from the ringside should be dressed in dinner jackets, or should at least pretend to be, by wearing bow ties.

But boxing needs its promoters in the way that a car needs an engine. While they were not considered – quite – to be a necessary evil, all in the sport realized that in order to pursue a career then they had to be kept happy, for if they started to throw their weight about, a boxer would simply not work. And Solomons certainly did throw his weight about. He was intensely jealous of his turf, and while later on he would make the mistake of confusing the event itself with his own presence at it as being the prime attraction (he really did think he was wonderful box office), by the time the twins started their careers, he was merely nervous at the undercurrents he was detecting in the small world of professional boxing. He was suspicious about the motivations and actions of Harry Levene as early as 1953 and Jim Wicks did a fine job of fuelling his paranoia, while outwardly showing solidarity with him. Dark talk of sinister, organized syndicates moving in on the sport started to appear in the press, to which a chortling Wicks was quite happy to put his name.

In building his business base in the late 1940s Solomons had made some dreadful mismatches, particularly for Freddie Mills and Bruce Woodcock in 1946, both of whom were battered badly by American fighters hastily brought in to generate some fast cash flow. Joe Baksi, for example, beat the promising Woodcock so badly that he was nearly blinded by splinters of bone that were hammered north from his comprehensively broken jaw. Freddie Mills, also thrashed by Baksi, fared only slightly better against Gus Lesnevitch, but he freely confessed later that he could not remember anything after the second round, but sadly for Mills the fight had lasted for ten.

These ill-considered mismatches rather served to characterize the world of British boxing as controlled by Jack Solomons in those early post-war years, and it contrasted somewhat with the same period across the Atlantic. If one was searching for a golden age of boxing, it would be America in the late 1940s, whereas many a British hope was simply served up by Solomons to a series of American boxers who were not only simply better nourished but also clearly far better trained. There was, it seemed, a savage aggression about American boxing that was somehow lacking in Britain, and a succession of unwary British fighters, whose managers were in thrall to Solomons, paid the price.

That Jolly Jack did not particularly care about the controversy created by this policy was quite clear; to Solomons, a boxer was perhaps rather like a light bulb, to be replaced when broken, or even like a piece of fresh cod, to be simply re-ordered once it had been devoured. What was more important to Solomons was the rush for cash; a bewildering array of bouts, some arranged literally at the last minute, served, by the time Henry turned professional, to have propelled Solomons to the top of the heap and master of all he surveyed. In many ways, it was probably the closeness that Jim Wicks enjoyed, if that is the word, with Solomons that had led J.T. Hulls to recommend him to the twins as a manager in the first place. Certainly it was clear that any manager who did not have a useful working relationship with this uniquely dodgy character who single-handedly ran British boxing, then neither he nor his fighters would prosper. But Solomons, had he but known it, would be on the way out, and quite soon. The reason lay just around the corner.

Harry Levene, headquartered in nearby Wardour Street, had made a good business out of managing boxers who were generally considered to be over the hill. He had started out after the Great War as an adolescent and had made a consistently good living out of it, evidenced by the grand manner in which he lived – mohair suits, Park Lane apartment and all the trimmimgs. When Henry and George had visualized the boxing manager, as they had done, 'with a cigarette holder and a silk dressing gown', they could have been describing Levene perfectly, apart from the fact that he smoked cigars.

Levene also had, like most managers and promoters, several sidelines, but in 1956 he would declare his objectives by re-opening the Empire Pool, Wembley as a boxing venue; it had, unlike Harringay Arena, where Jolly Jack had prospered during the war, been closed down throughout the hostilities. Levene's reinvention of this venue, where Arthur Elvin had operated so many fights in the 1930s, rivalling Sydney Hulls, coupled with the advent of the widespread rise of television coverage with attendant intellectual rights, the potential of which he spotted immediately, would ultimately allow Levene to supplant Solomons as the UK's biggest promoter, a move that would do little for their already difficult relationship. As Henry recalls:

> Funnily enough, all that was originally nothing at all to do with boxing. Levene had a club with a restaurant, and Solomons' family business was wet fish; he used to supply Levene, and of course they were always breaking the rationing rules. One day, after a delivery, Levene got raided and fined and he always swore blind that Solomons had shopped him. He hadn't, actually, but he'd never believe that. After a while, they couldn't bear to be in the same room as one another – if one walked in, the other would walk out. They just never spoke.

For Wicks, and therefore for his fighters, this unarmed standoff would be handy, to say the least, particularly as Levene started to build his business with the aid of his later associate, Jarvis Astaire of *Viewsport*.

The pathological rivalry between the two promoters was to allow the Wicks stable to step neatly into the no-man's land that would open up between them. Not so other, less wily managers, who frequently joined either one camp or the other. Just as frequently, they often failed to read the small print, as Henry remembers:

> If a manager had bought a fighter – paid him money to turn pro, then obviously the first thing he's going to do is get his cash back, so if a promoter offers him, say £120, for his boy to fight so-and-so, as opposed to £100, then he'll just look at the big number – and this was quite a lot of money then.
> Jim Wicks wouldn't do that – he'd go through the whole thing – how much are you getting for radio, TV and so on – all that – and set a price that way.

To some less engaged observers, the feud between Levene and Solomons was merely a curiosity, just a spat between two outsiders, each of whom was probably quite as distasteful as the other, but in truth the conflict was to play a decisive role in the post-war development of British boxing later. The fact that Jim Wicks's own son Jackie worked for Levene (performing the tasks of at least four people) did not stop Wicks himself from dealing quite contentedly with Solomons; in fact Henry would not fight commercially in a Levene promotion until 1958, which was four years after he turned pro, and two years after Levene re-opened the Wembley Pool arena venue. Wicks's policy with the two promoters was that of a controlled, calmly orchestrated wind-up. There would be a price to pay for this strategy, and it would be a big one, but not for some time.

But, unlike many other managers, Wicks actually knew both men very well, although in fairness he knew Solomons rather better. Given that the two men refused to speak to each other except through intermediaries, Wicks could play a useful role in disseminating information (and disinformation) through the agents and bagmen whom both promoters used to gather intelligence on each other. Later, after Levene had announced openly that he intended to supplant Solomons, this would be important. The period of greatest rivalry would be between

1956 and 1966, after which Jolly Jack would go into a fairly rapid decline.

The two promoters also had rather different styles of business. Whereas Levene was a straightforward but very hard market trader, Solomons' style was more that of the wheedling rug merchant, always trying to renegotiate, pleading poverty, dwindling ticket sales, ailing relatives, a poor press, heart disease, or whatever else might work to drag the purse lower. Wicks, typically, would be flintily unmoved. ''E's spinnin' 'is tales of 'Ofmann again,' he'd beam grandly, while negotiating himself outside a giant bowl of *spaghetti alla vongole* at Peter Mario's bistro in Gerrard Street.

But both promoters invariably paid up, and promptly, however they had arrived at a contract, as Henry remembers: 'Levene might have been a hard man, but he'd never grumble. If he'd guaranteed £20,000 for a fight and only 12 people turned up, you'd still get paid.' With characters like Albert Dimes about, who indeed can be surprised?

James Wicks, aka 'Jim the Bishop', as he had been christened by the journalist George Whiting, had five passions in life: the turf, the ring, gambling, dog racing and food, in no particular order. He was, overall, probably the most senior figure in British boxing by the time the Cooper twins signed up with him, the grand old man of the business of the ring. He had even fought – only once – as a professional boxer himself. In 1915 he had participated in a prizefight at an unrecalled location, possibly the Blackfriars ring, and fought his bout, but discovered to his chagrin that the fly-by-night promoter responsible for the match had simply departed with the gate money before the fight had even started. Wicks was a quick learner. It was an experience that had rather guided his philosophy towards the fiscal aspects of the fistic sport since then. Although born in Bermondsey, he had Irish roots (which had led others to refer to him as 'Seamus') and after a period running a small string of pubs and co-managing the Blackfriars ring with another extraordinary character, Dan Sullivan, he had achieved something of a reputation as a tough independent.

A keystone to at least part of this reputation was a discovery he had made. Dan Sullivan (actually an Italian who changed his name by deed poll) managed Len Harvey, the well-known British heavyweight, and it was at a training camp near Windsor that Wicks had the bright idea of hiring four sparring partners for Harvey from the nearby barracks, which housed the Irish Guards. When one of the guardsmen – 'a nice-looking boy' – knocked Harvey down and, groggily, Harvey recommended that the boy be taken on, Wicks and Sullivan contributed £2 10/- each to buy Jack Doyle out of the Army. A fiver. They had grand plans for him, some of which came about after Doyle became a serious contender after only seven fights, but the pair were able to take a decent turn out of the transaction and put Doyle back in the care of the military by selling their management contract with him for £5,000 to a General Critchley, who was president of the Greyhound Association, in 1934, the year of Henry Cooper's birth. Clearly, global depression or not, there was no shortage of money in the fight game.

For Wicks, this financial triumph was followed by a period managing Wandsworth greyhound track, a connection that we need not belabour, where he also promoted fights, and earned the colossal sum of £500 a week in the teeth of the depression. However, he spent much of this on legal fees; the constant incursions of gangsters, notably three particularly irritating Maltese brothers, required him to make certain 'arrangements' to see them off, and quite often this muscle needed defending in court. Whatever his benign public face, the classic diamond geezer image, Jim Wicks came up the hard way and, crucially, everybody in boxing knew it. If there were bodies buried, Wicks knew exactly where they all were.

After a stint as a street (illegal) bookie, he found himself running a starting price office in Panton Street, quite near the *Union Arms* tavern that Tom Cribb had run after his retirement from boxing in 1822. Wicks was in partnership with a rather wet-behind-the-ears Jack Solomons. The pair prospered for a while, but Wicks's sense of independence led him to part company – more or less amicably – just before the war, as Solomons started to move other partners in. Wicks was a ferocious gambler and while he had the skill, luck and wit to generate truly vast amounts of money, he frequently saw it slip back through his fingers, but with no particular regret. 'The game, son, must be played,' he'd explain to Henry over a bottle or two of Krug and an extravagantly dressed Dover sole at Sheekey's restaurant. This was not merely a motto for Wicks, it was more of a mission statement. Jim Wicks was a sportsman in the same sense that Lord Palmerston had been a sportsman, but by the 1950s he was working hard to maintain traditions that had in reality been long dead before he himself had been born. He was something of a throwback, clearly in this for the fun of it as much as anything else, but the experience he had learned (and earned) was to stand Henry in good stead. For a start, Henry never gambled.

And Wicks never gambled with Henry's money, either. For a while he even charged his fighters zero commission on their earnings. It was his habit; it served to build up a mutual trust and, judging by the results, it worked. Given the time that his other interests already absorbed, he was quite relaxed about leaving his share of the twins' earnings on the table for them to pick up. He knew full well, because he knew boxers and he knew men, that their motivations for boxing were simple. Although primarily competitive, the Cooper brothers' agenda was also economic, and not immediately for their own benefit. All their lives they had witnessed at first hand how hard Henry senior and Lily had had to work. At the time of their professional boxing debut – pleasingly on the same card – Henry senior, with ten years' military service, a crushed hand, which still gave him trouble, and no particular thanks from the nation, was, at well past 50, still working hard, labouring at Deptford power station, where he scaled out hot furnaces for £11 a week. He was doing basically the same job that his grandfather William had done. It was a situation that the twins were anxious to change.

Wicks, having made no up-front 'investment' for his fighters, was quite relaxed about taking the long view. Further, he may have felt that to take 25 per cent of £25 – a typical entry-level purse, even for an ABA champion – was quite beneath his sense of dignity as a proper professional punter who regularly placed bets of an eye-wateringly high and sometimes plainly reckless value. 'Managers were entitled to 25 per cent of a purse after expenses,' says Henry. 'All through those early fights, until we were earning, say, four or five hundred quid or so for a fight, Jim Wicks, bless his heart, didn't take a penny off us; we kept it all.'

In fact, the twins were still working hard as plasterers, which was really their main source of income for some time. They were registered as professional boxers but had yet to spend all their time on it. The man they worked for, Reg Reynolds, was quite happy to accommodate their inevitable training schedules and because they were earning a modest living from this there was even less pressure to fight purely for the money, which suited Wicks perfectly. With no financial pressures upon him to recoup any investment, and his two heavyweights already gainfully employed, he could deal with matters of business with the bland confidence that made him such a canny negotiator.

The nature of the training for the professional ring was a process of total immersion; it was Wicks's habit to rent a riverside house near Windsor, not far from the site of his pre-war coup with Danny Sullivan over Jack Doyle, where the training camp would be established. Of course, Lily came, too, to offer her culinary support. She had proved during the war that she was a more than adequate cook, but the luxury of the ingredients now available, courtesy of Wicks, was a great freedom for her.

The first bouts the twins would fight were novice six-rounders, so it was understood that these intermediary bouts between amateur and full professional status were as much to get Henry and George used to the idea of professional fighting as anything else. The training was hard but not as hard as it would become.

The first fruit of that training, for Henry, came on 14 September 1954; it was a six-round Jack Solomons promoted supporting fight at the Harringay Arena, Solomons' favoured locale. His opponent was to be the bulky Harry Painter. There was no pressure, no pep talking for his tense fighters, as Henry remembers: 'Jim just said, "Take it easy and relax, don't try to over-impress."'

It obviously worked. Henry hit Painter with a left to the chin and dropped him, before knocking him out properly, all in the first round. George, who always fought professionally as 'Jim' Cooper, due to the presence on the circuit of another George Cooper, had a harder fight, going the full distance with Dick Richardson (never an easy task) to win on points. Henry recalls how they spent their prize money: 'I think we had about £100 between us, so off we went out and bought Mum and Dad a television set. I think we were the last people in Farmstead Road to have one.'

Quickly, the twins learned that the professional game bore only a superficial resemblance to the amateur one. A professional fighter, particularly a heavyweight, is training for a fight that, after the initial novice events of up to six rounds, will extend to ten rounds as a seasoned fighter and 15 for a championship. The training pattern would be in three-minute bursts of skipping, or speedball punching, or heavy bag work, punctuated by intervals that would start at a minute and shrink to 30 seconds. In this way, by compressing the intervals, a trainer could calculate the exact level of readiness of his fighter. Wicks had another trick as well: instead of eggs and sherry (the universal remedy for unmotivated horses), which had been the staple booster for Henry in his amateur days, he had invented a revolting cocktail, particularly confusing when taken on an empty stomach – a double port blended in with a pint of Guinness,* which, he calculated, would provide both energy and extended stamina. The training was thus proportionally much harder, not that either minded that, but the fighting itself was of a totally different order, and the refereeing of the fights reflected that. Actions that would automatically disqualify a fighter in a three-round boys' club event, or even an ABA championship bout, were tolerated, even encouraged in the professional ring. Harry Gibbs, of whom much more later, recorded in his memoirs the episode when Brian London complained of an opponent: 'He's butting me, Harry!' Gibbs's response was typical: 'Well, son, butt him back.'

The main purpose of 'careless use of the head', as it was somewhat primly defined, was to create a cut, any cut, but preferably above the eye on which the attacking boxer could then work, using jabs, to force the retirement of his opponent. It was purely a matter of vision, not pain. If a fighter loses the stereoscopic vision necessary to judge distance then he will eventually simply lose the fight, barring a lucky

---

* In the spirit of enthusiastic research, I have tried this brew – it is quite disgusting and cannot have helped Henry's gout, from which he sporadically suffered.

punch, but boxers learned very early on that luck was not something on which they could afford to depend. Damaging a nicked eyebrow with a series of twisting jabs, each of which land with an impact pressure of tons per square inch, is child's play, for even a boxer of modest talent, particularly because the opponent, operating at a heightened metabolic rate during a fight, his pulse running at 120 and with commensurately elevated blood pressure, will bleed copiously, and the Cooper twins, as many were quick to point out, had very prominent eyebrows.

Also, professionals, being more mature, were stronger and simply able to inflict more damage. They trained for body punching and the extra length of a professional fight allowed the boxer more time to wear down an opponent with blows to the heart and liver that would weaken him very fast. Henry knew this:

> I used to throw a nice little left hook to the liver. I've had guys literally scream out at that. They used to go down paralysed. I won a good many fights that way. I remember a Spanish boxer employed by Jim as a sparring partner. In the first round I noticed that every time we came away from a clinch he'd drop his hands. I told Bobby Diamond, the Spaniard's agent, to get him to keep his hands up or I'd catch him on the chin. So, next round he comes out with his hands up, exposing all his stomach. I gave him a hell of a left hook to the liver and he literally screamed and fell on the floor.

So, the boys' club mores of the amateur ring were clearly now a thing of the past. Obeying the spirit of the rules rather than the letter of them was the order of the day, as Henry recalls: 'A good trainer would massage the horsehair stuffing in the six-ounce gloves back and work it away from the knuckle, so you could land a hard punch more cleanly.'

Other dodges, it was suspected, included dusting the tapes around the boxer's hands with plaster of Paris or alabaster and, once the gloves were on, dribbling water down the fighter's wrist into the glove. Quite soon, the plaster set hard. It was allegedly this manœuvre that allowed Jack Dempsey to wreak such destruction on the bones of the hapless

Jess Willard's face in 1919, a beating that was to put Willard out of boxing.

The referee's job, then, was not simply to ensure that the fighters adhered to the letter of the law, rather it was to ensure a good fight within rules of safety and fair play that were outlined with a very broad brush indeed. He had in many ways to exercise a constant bilateral interpretation of an unwritten advantage rule and trainers and boxers were quick to exploit any weaknesses they identified in the referee as a man, or in his personal view of the rules, rather as a barrister might approach dealing with a judge. Refereeing, it must be said, was not an easy task.

Henry and George were not the only ones to take notice of the huge difference between the amateur and the professional game. George Page, who had worked so hard with them at Eltham and had initially accompanied them to work with Danny Holland at the *Thomas à Becket*, realized quite early on that the professional sport was really not for him. The Corinthian traditions of amateur sport, as praised by Sir Arthur Conan Doyle, via Sherlock Holmes, ran through Page as words run through a stick of Brighton rock and he discovered that the slickness and packaging that rather characterized professional boxing even in those far-off days was totally alien to him. He also rather disliked sharing the twins with Holland, having brought them skilfully to this level. Quite soon, he was to go back to purely training amateurs, which was where his heart truly lay.

Basically, Page disliked the fact that money was involved, any money. In his opinion it wrecked and degraded the game. Perhaps he had a point; after a novice professional fight, the ringside crowd would throw coins – 'nobbins' – into the ring in appreciation of a skilful or, more often, a bloody fight. To someone brought up in the rather Calvinist traditions of the amateur ring, such things were anathema, both patronizing and degrading, but all agreed that it was a lot worse when they threw bottles.

*

Not only did Henry and George buy their parents a television, but they also bought themselves a car, a perpendicular Ford Prefect, though Henry recalls that it was money earned from plastering that paid for it. Virtually all the cash the pair earned from fighting was spent either on the unavoidable costs of getting to and from the *Thomas à Becket* or helping the Cooper household financially. But from this modest beginning Henry was to acquire something of a grand passion for motor cars that has never left him.

In fact, once the twins had learned the basics of what was required to train, they worked together, which made Holland gradually almost redundant. He was officially their trainer of record, because Wicks was their manager of record, but in reality the discipline of rising at 4.a.m. for their road-work (carried out in Army ammunition boots) was all theirs. As they both remained working as plasterers for some time, it made for a rather long day, with little time available to chase girls. 'Oh, no, we didn't do any of that,' says Henry. 'Everyone else went off to a dance hall on a Saturday night, but George and me took boxing so seriously that we just trained and trained.'

But plastering was good training for Henry's left hand and George's right, and both brothers started to become observably asymmetric. Because both were completely monodextrous they started to resemble not so much identical twins but more mirror images of each other and naturally enough, any athlete whose sport demands some sort of polarity will start to favour the strong side in preference to the less strong, but Henry took this to unusual levels – he used his left for everything .

So, gradually, the standard of living at Farmstead Road was raised, to the clear and predictable envy of certain of the neighbours, as the Cooper twins started to achieve some modest fame. Their local celebrity was not long in coming, indeed, they had featured as an interesting curiosity, as twins often do, as far back as the days of the Bellingham club, but if they had thought that that had been fame – and they had – then that was quite inadequate preparation for what Wicks had in mind for them.

He insisted that they behave in certain ways, and his list of do's and don'ts was short but absolute. When Henry was invited by a friend to accompany him to one of the perfectly innocent but private drinking clubs with which Soho was liberally dotted, for example, Henry's response was perhaps curious. 'No,' he said, 'Jim wouldn't like it… it just wouldn't look right.'

In essence, Wicks was teaching his boys to behave like champions, to be not as other men. Henry quite saw the sense of this, as the little anecdote suggests, but it also hints that Wicks was man possessed of a formidable personal authority. In truth it was never in Henry's nature to while away afternoons propping up a bar, a fact that made his later friendship with Oliver Reed such a dangerous one, for there is perhaps a slight streak of the puritan in Henry.

Wicks really didn't miss a trick. The more exposure, he reasoned, the more celebrity, and the more celebrity, the more money, both for boxing and for other activities. His fighters were not the first to perform a string of public relations exercises, and they were certainly not to be the last, but for Wicks all was one; he had a full agenda, and it was not totally concerned with boxing.

But the Coopers, of course, were not the only twins in boxing: there were the Krays, too. The Kray family hailed from Hackney, so they had no social acquaintances in common with the Coopers in their early years, but Jim Wicks knew of them through boxing, as both Krays had tried their hand at the professional game a year before the Coopers, albeit at a lighter weight. They were good, too, if hard to train properly, but had given the fight game up for more obviously lucrative activities in 1954, just as the Cooper brothers turned professional.

Interestingly, the Krays never really went back to it. Had they put their minds to it as a business activity, history might have been very different. Henry remembers them from the early days:

We got to know them quite well, in fact. I remember once – this was much later, of course, they called Jim to ask us if we could all go to a bash they were having. They had taken over Hackney town hall and when we arrived half the local CID were in there, all drinking in the mayor's parlour. They had organized a trip for some pensioners somewhere and wanted to publicize it. They were always doing something like that, or presenting an old people's home with a TV set. What they never said, of course, was that they had threatened to take some poor bloke's ears off unless he gave them the set in the first place. They were OK, though – until they went mad.

So, even the Krays didn't dare upset Jim Wicks, they always asked politely. But they also clearly had no particular interest in muscling in on boxing. They were frequently present at gyms as well as fights but really their primary motivation was publicity. If celebrities went boxing, so would the Krays.

'I remember when the biggest thing on television was *Sunday Night at the London Palladium*, says Henry. 'Almost every single American star who went there – and there were hundreds – wound up in some Kray night club or other having their picture taken with them. They just couldn't get enough of that. They were basically publicity seekers.'

Under Wicks's firm hand, Henry's career started to build. There was no particular pressure but by 26 April 1957 Henry had an almost perfect record of nine victories out of nine fights, all but two inside the distance. His first defeat came that evening at the hand, or rather the head, of the Italian Uber Bacilieri at Harringay Arena. Henry sustained a badly cut eye – his first serious cut – in round two. The speed with which Wicks threw in the towel was startling but he knew full well that the identical twins had this potential weakness, if only because poor George was suffering badly from the same problem and had been stopped quite frequently.

Henry would get his own back on Bacilieri when he knocked him out in round seven of their rematch in September, after stopping Ron Harman in June. On 15 November 1957, though, he encountered Joe Erskine for the first time in the professional ring. The pair had fought as amateurs in the Army, as Henry recalls:

I first met Joe in the light heavyweight semi-finals of the ABA championships in April 1952. Already he was a good boxer technically, a good left jabber, a good mover and a hard boy to box. Whenever you thought you were out of distance, sure he wouldn't sling a left hand, he did, the crafty so-and-so. And he had a poker face. You could hit him, and you could hurt him, and he would never show it. You'd wonder – have I hurt him? – and while you were thinking, he'd have recovered. He never showed any emotion in the ring.

Erskine as a professional was even stronger, despite his lack of a big punch, and he outpointed Henry at Harringay Arena in an eliminator for the British heavyweight title. It was a disappointing loss, but going the full ten rounds, even if he did lose the fight, marked the end of Henry's apprenticeship.

All in all, in his professional career, Henry would fight Erskine five times, and if there was ever an opponent who had a psychological edge over him in their early encounters it was this one, but it is also fair to say that at each full-blown championship encounter the two men had, Henry was always able to reach deep and beat him.

From the start of 1956 Henry's work rate logically started to ease off. Having built his résumé over a fairly intensive two years, and established that he was a formidable boxer, Wicks could now commence phase two of this great adventure, which was to gradually position his fighter for a serious crack at a national title: a Lonsdale belt. Henry had already popped his head into the higher reaches of the division with the match with Erskine and Jim Wicks's job was now to ensure that he stayed there.

Pacing a fighter's development is utterly critical to his future. History is scattered with examples of badly managed fighters of great talent (Erskine was one of them, Zora Folley another) who are brought to a peak too early. There is only a certain number of top level fights that a boxer is capable of delivering, as a sturgeon has eggs, and an unscrupulous manager, while he is constantly on the lookout for new talent, will exploit his seasoned fighters for his shareof their purses. It happened to so many in the earliest days of the ring, and was still happening when Henry commenced this vital part of his career, but more particularly in the USA.

Boxing may have been inordinately popular, but planning a fighter's finances was a business fraught with practical problems. For a start, it was difficult for a boxer to live anything but a hand-to-mouth existence. It was inordinately hard for a fighter to get credit, for example, if only because there was a higher than normal risk that he would be incapacitated at any time, so the pattern of a fighter's life tended to be fairly well circumscribed. Boxers simply did not live as other men and were in many ways totally dependent upon their managers as a contact point with reality and day-to-day business. Some were particularly unlucky or ill-advised in this respect. Henry was not.

Wicks was a patient man; not only was he fiercely protective of his fighters – he really cared about them – but he managed to disguise this behind a pink, scrubbed exterior mask of world-weary wit, which journalists in particular found extraordinarily attractive. The private face of Jim Wicks lived amid a frenzy of telephones in his ratty little office off the gym in the Old Kent Road, with its curling linoleum, cheap furniture and unmistakable 'atmosphere', whereas the public face of Jim Wicks was to be seen regularly in his favoured booth at Simpson's restaurant (or one of a host of other venues) from where he handled the increasingly vital element of his portfolio of responsibilities – public relations. He was, happily for the twins, in the autumn of his life, so as the rest of his stable slowed down and retired, he did not replace them now. Soon he would be left with just the twins and, quite shortly after that, just Henry.

*

Harry Levene finally managed to promote a Cooper fight on 28 February 1956 but it was a charity event, at the Albert Hall, just prior to the re-opening of Wembley. The opponent was Maurice Mols, the French heavyweight champion. Henry totally outclassed him, putting the clearly overweight Frenchman down no fewer than four times in the fourth round. He accomplished this by a succession of sickeningly solid left hooks to the body, which caused referee, Tommy Little, to stop the fight and deliver Henry's tenth win inside the distance.

Mols may not have been the classiest fighter Henry had faced (Erskine clearly was, up to then) but he was the first title-holder Henry had ever fought. The ease of the victory did not create an air of over-confidence, as Mols was clearly overrated, but it was an important win, as it allowed Wicks to select and negotiate more selectively, as he understood that in boxing, like so many other areas of activity, a fighter will be commercially judged almost totally by his last effort, which is a phenomenon that naturally works both ways.

Next up was Brian London, who was unbeaten in 12 professional fights. In a sense, London, whose father, Jack, had been British heavyweight champion himself, was becoming the Henry Cooper of the North. He came from Blackpool and his family name was actually Harper, his father having changed it to reflect his admiration for the writer of that name, the author of *Call of the Wild*. London had fought as an amateur under the name of Harper, as had his brother, Jack junior. Henry had beaten Jack London as an amateur, whereas Brian had beaten George as a professional, so there was no lack of potential rivalry. Henry even went so far as to make a prediction. He was asked before the fight if he planned to knock his opponent out. He nodded. When? Eighth or ninth? He shook his head, holding up one finger. 'Just one,' he said, quietly.

Henry remembers Brian London in the early years as '... a surly so-and-so, never smiling in his pictures, and a difficult man to get along with. From his attitude at the weigh-ins there was no love lost between us. He could be quick-tempered in the ring, too...'

The two men were very different. Henry, whose sunny disposition was already making him inordinately popular, was up against a man whose dour disposition made him exactly the opposite, at least in the South. The match took place at the Empress Hall on 1 May. It did not take long. Henry whacked London onto the ropes in round one with a rare right hook to the body. As London dropped his guard, Henry moved in with the rapidly developing left and delivered it serially to London's jaw. The referee, Tommy Little, leaped in and stopped the fight after 2 minutes 35 seconds of the first.

This had been a startling and accurate performance, as important for Henry it was a heartbreaker for London. The aggression Henry had shown, not to mention his ability to fight two-handed, was appreciated. Suddenly, after that fight, he was a name to conjure with, particularly for Jim Wicks. Winning fights at this senior level with such apparent ease as well as such versatility was vital for him. He was not yet at the level where Wicks could charge whatever he wanted for Henry's professional services, but he was already getting close to it.

He would fight Brian London twice more, in fact, and always beat him, but not necessarily with the same ease.

After such a brief fight, which had caused no damage whatever to Henry's eyebrows – London had barely landed a single blow – there was no need for a sustained layoff, and less than two months later, on 26 June, he fought the ungainly Giannino Luise, of whom he had never heard (and would never hear again). It was a relatively pedestrian fight until Henry landed a hard, hacking left to his opponent's liver, which stopped the fight in the seventh round.

With three such authoritative victories in a row – Mols, London, Luise – and a career now fully launched, Henry had every reason to believe that those vague ambitions of childhood, those images of Joe Louis, were leading to something. Everything seemed to be cruising along, going exactly to plan, without any clouds on the horizon. Life was good.

CHAPTER FIVE

Into the Abyss

'Cheer up! The worst is yet to come!'
PHILANDER CHASE JOHNSON, (1920).

IF HENRY THOUGHT that his straightforward stopping of Giannino
Luise was a portent for the future, he was to be sadly mistaken.
Statistics are seldom the measure of a man but a glance at the record
book suggests that there is an exception to every rule. In Henry's case
the signs of trouble ahead were certainly not clear at Belle Vue,
Manchester on 7 September 1956 when he put Yorkshireman Peter
Bates down with a massive left hook to the mouth for what might well
have been added to his résumé as a first-round knockout. Bates stayed
down for a nine count (not tactically – he was severely dazed) but
then, amazingly enough, got to his feet. The next four rounds were all
Henry's, despite a small smear of fresh blood on his left eyebrow.

In the fifth, though, a concerned Wicks saw from the corner that
'coming out of a clinch' (as one report had it) there was a very serious
cut over Henry's right eye as well, probably the worst cut that he had
received so far. In a situation like this a boxer needs a fast knockout
but Henry simply could not land a repeat blow to the one he had produced in round one. Without further ado, Wicks threw in the towel
at the end of the fifth. It was not a particularly important fight but,
while Henry was well ahead by five rounds to none, the damage was
severe; he was cut to the bone, but there was clearly nothing wrong
with his boxing.

A disappointment, to be sure, but not a catastrophe; boxers get cut
all the time. After a five- month layoff, Henry faced Joe Bygraves, the
muscular hard man from Jamaica, all 15 stone of him. This Earls
Court fight, on 19 February 1957, was an important one, for the

British Empire heavyweight title no less, which Bygraves had seized in June of the previous year.

Henry had beaten Bygraves before, of course, but at the weigh-in he found that he was now only a pound short of 14 stone, which for Henry was an unheard-of bulk. He had discovered that his ideal fighting weight was exactly 13 stone 7lbs; the difference may not sound much, but over a prizefight, the extra baggage always shows. In fact, under modern divisions, Henry Cooper would be a cruiserweight.

The extra poundage certainly showed as this fight got under way. Henry was the slowest he had ever been and looked it, even against Bygraves, who was not the fastest mover in the division. Bygraves took the fight to him and Henry seemed unable to make any impression at all. Of more concern was a cut to the left eye (round three) and a haematoma under the right, which burst messily.

The end, when it came, was humiliating. In round nine Bygraves landed a crushing punch to the solar plexus. Winded, Henry just managed to beat the count but as soon as he arose Bygraves simply did it again. This time Henry simply could not get up and was counted out. Henry's friend Danny Cornell, who went to the dressing room, accompanied by Derek 'Del' John, the lightweight boxer from Catford, describes the scene:

> The place looked like a morgue. Cooper, bruised and bitter, sat on the edge of the rubbing table, while Danny Holland worked on his face. Then, looking up, Henry spotted Del: 'How's the nose, Del?' Del had broken his nose a week earlier in a bout at the National Sporting Club. It impressed me that he could be that considerate about a friend at such a moment.

In the audience was Ingemar Johansson, who, since September 1956, the month of Henry's misfortune with Bates, had been the holder of the European heavyweight title after taking it from Franco Cavicchi. Three months after that, Johansson had dispatched Peter Bates in two rounds, breaking his jaw in the process. He had actually thought that Henry had boxed well, in fact, but he needed to find out what he might be up against, for Jim Wicks had, as soon as Johansson had taken the title, put Henry's name forward with the European Boxing Union (EBU) as a contender. Ambitious, perhaps, but he had faith in the emerging Cooper left hook, which was developing into a punch of awesome stopping-power, even if it was not yet fully formed. It was merely fearsome, if not the devastating blow it would become. Certainly, it had been noticeably absent against Bygraves. But Wicks was philosophical. 'Have a couple of months out,' he wheezed. Which Henry did, before challenging Johansson for the European heavy-weight title in Stockholm on 19 May 1957.

Johansson was not actually best pleased at the prospect, as he recalled in 1961:

> The EBU instructed me to defend my title against Henry Cooper. We were not especially happy. Cooper had been knocked out by Bygraves in London. It was one of those things which can happen. Cooper ... jumped on a punch. From the public's point of view it didn't look good, but Edwin [Edwin Ahlqvist, his manager] chose Johanneshov [the stadium in Stockholm] and figured that Cooper would draw a full house in Stockholm in spite of everything.

Ahlqvist was right – 10,000 baying Swedes turned out, along with a few cautiously optimistic British scribblers. Lainson Wood of the *Daily Telegraph* wrote: 'Cooper is certainly keyed up for the fight of his life and I do not think he will let Britain down. He is a better boxer than Johansson. Let's hope he pulls it off.' And the view of the *Boxing News* was not dissimilar: '...on paper, this is the most open fight imaginable...'

But there was more to this than pure boxing. Johansson was not technically an inspiring boxer but he was possessed of a truly terrifying right – 'The Hammer of Thor' as he later called it. Anyone who got in its way was almost certainly going to go down, and hard, as poor Cavicchi had recently discovered when it had connected with his midriff, 'dropping him like a log', as one rather uninspired report had it.

Henry, though, had not actually lost very much weight; he was still 13 stone 12lbs, and, in an attempt to shed some avoirdupois, he went running, accompanied by an extremely fit and cooperative waiter from the hotel where he was staying.

The fight was staged in the open air, on a fine early summer afternoon. 'It was really bright,' says Henry, 'and there was muggins, sitting in the corner with the sun right in my eyes.'

It was in truth a fairly plodding and uninspiring contest, and Peter Wilson of the *Daily Mirror* scored the first round even, with Henry perhaps marginally ahead in each of the following three, but by the tiniest margin. In the interval, after round four, Wicks advised Henry to take the fight to his opponent. Both men were nervous about the attitude of the crowd and, ever mindful of the fact that Johansson had been thrown out of the 1952 Olympic Games for 'not trying', it seemed logical to introduce a little ginger. This was a mistake, as Johansson recalls:

> Nothing much happened in the first rounds. I punched a couple of intentional misses with the right to limber up and make sure that the right hand was in order. He had probably thought that I would be beginning the fight by pouring on everything I had. But I rapped him with the left. I wanted to make him cocky and lure him out. He had thought, of course, that I would be a violent smasher as I had knocked out so many opponents.

His knockout record was 10 out of 16, in fact. After 2 minutes 47 seconds of the fifth round, the punch that Henry never saw coming landed on his chin. It was a classic left, left, followed by a blinding right cross and Henry became Johansson's seventeenth victim. Peter Wilson wrote sadly:

> The Englishman's eyes were staring blindly at the blue sky above, his limbs twitching helplessly. He was lolling finally against the ropes as he fumbled with them, trying – oh, so desperately – to pull himself upright before the count of ten had been reached … He was slogging his numbed muscles, but he was like a man who had touched the live terminal of a high voltage wire and had been shocked out of his senses.

Yes, quite a punch. 'It was so quick, I didn't see it coming,' said Henry. 'Dat's de whole idea,' artlessly responded a justifiably smug Johansson. But as Henry would discover again, you never do.

Actually, Ingemar Johansson rather liked Henry, as he recalls in his memoirs:

> Henry Cooper is one of the most pleasant people I have met, and in many ways an unusual boxer. He really seems too kind for boxing. He is so like his twin brother that I can't tell the difference between them when they are together. They must be together before I'm sure of not calling them by their wrong names.

All in all it was a rough day for the brothers Cooper. George, Henry's main sparring partner, was disqualified against Albert Finch, Johansson's sparring partner, for an alleged low punch, although Sydney Hulls of the *Daily Express*, perhaps trying to salvage something constructive from such a dismal day, rather plaintively disagreed: 'I did not think Cooper's two-fisted spasm of body punches had landed below the belt. The blows appeared strictly and energetically on the target area.'

But that opinion was little consolation as the lowered little team flew back to Blighty. Two title fight losses for Henry – Empire and European – in depressingly quick succession. Wicks, however, had kept the faith, for he had already made his plans clear in Stockholm. 'First Henry needs a couple of fights at home to get back his confidence,' he'd gurgled to a depressed and more than slightly sceptical press corps.

What Wicks actually had in mind for his slightly reduced fighter was another crack at Joe Erskine for yet another championship, the British one. If this seems a rash policy with the gift of hindsight, then it should be borne in mind that Erskine, although a supreme tactician, was not a particularly strong puncher. Conversely, whatever he lacked in brake horsepower he made up for in guile. Joe Erskine really was a very fine boxer indeed and any deficit he suffered in the ability to create a punch was further offset by his ability to take one, as he himself was to find out.

In truth, the action outside the ring was almost as interesting, and serves as an exemplar of the seamier side of the sport. Joe Erskine had discovered that his manager, Benny Jacobs, had, not to put too fine a point on it, been stealing money from him. The two men were by now communicating only through the medium of Erskine's trainer, Archie Rule. It seems that Jacobs had a severe gambling problem and was not above being economical with the truth concerning – ahem – the exact amount of Erskine's purses. Erskine fired him on the eve of this fight. He would re-engage with him later but on the night of his fight with Henry, he was, to say the least, understaffed. But it didn't show.

*

The attention span (and collective memory) of a fight crowd is astonishingly short; the bout went down in history as being supremely dull but the first seven rounds were, in fact, swift and rather full of action, including a warning to Henry in round four for 'steadying' the back of Erskine's head before punching him. Henry, in fact, landed at least three crushing lefts, one of which nearly dropped his opponent, but Erskine responded with strong (but not debilitating) body punches and from round eight the chubby Welsh fighter simply plodded back to win narrowly on points. Harry Carpenter calculated the margin to be a quarter of a point, the smallest possible.

For Henry, this marked his fourth defeat in a row: Bates, Bygraves, Johansson, Erskine. If this continued, it was going to become hard to make a living. There was always plastering, of course, but plasterers did not as a rule eat lunch at Simpson's in the Strand or, indeed, wear hand-made suits. The nagging self-doubt that invariably accompanies such a string of defeats was growing to such an extent that he seriously considered quitting.

One of his main difficulties, which first arose with the Bates fight, was the vulnerability of his eyes to damage, which, while it was relatively painless, invariably laid him open to defeat. He had started to become defensive, a tactic which, while it certainly served to make him a technically far better boxer later on, was not what was required now if he was to take full advantage of his rapidly developing left hook, which, when all was said and done was, apart from his agility, the main weapon in his armoury.

Wicks's counsel on using the hook was quite subtle. He held that there was actually no need to connect with it all the time; for some opponents its mere existence would be enough to threaten and compromise their mental composure. 'Just let them feel the wind of its passing, son,' he told Henry, ' just the wind of its passing. Just let them know it's there.'

Meanwhile, Wicks took the view, as he always did, that Henry should get on with his business and his corner men should be allowed to get on with theirs. It was something of a pet theme of his, this tidy division of labour. Danny Holland had developed a novel approach to dealing with cuts: an adrenalin compound, mixed with Vaseline, ensured that the astringent chemical, which served to neatly close off broken blood vessels, could be applied using his own hand-made swabs, and be expected to last most of a three-minute round. It worked well as a tactic, for with less than a minute to repair such debilitating damage, speed was of the essence. The British rules did not permit some of the more exotic substances commonly used in America, which were little more than crude hard-setting fillers for cuts, and which had contributed to the ruination of many a fighter's eyebrows, and therefore their careers.

But now, after this little string of defeats, Henry's commercial value was suddenly very little, at least domestically; his stock was at a very low ebb. Other fighters who found themselves in a similar position always ran the risk of being 'overboxed' in ludicrous mismatches by cynical managers, so that at least they would earn something out of them before moving on to other hopefuls. Wicks, it must be said, was not cut from that cloth; he was fully convinced of Henry's long-term value and while he was concerned at his boy's plummeting morale, the pair maintained their agreeable routine. At a time when self-doubt was nagging Henry, Wicks was a rock of stability.

*

Given the iron grip exerted by Jack Solomons and Harry Levene on the promotion of the sport in Britain, there was a small gap in the market: Germany. The clear reluctance of the two main Jewish pro-moters to accommodate German fighters meant that boxing in Germany was developing on a separate but parallel path from that in Britain, cut off from it by both culture and recent history. To be sure, the purses were smaller, as neither Marshall Aid nor the ludicrous exchange rate seemed to have had the same effect on boxing as it had on BMW, but at that stage Henry was still faced with the simple imperative of rebuilding his résumé and the money was really quite secondary. There was also the possibility of exacting some sweet revenge for the near miss from that doodlebug in 1944.

Swiftly, Wicks organized a fight with the German heavyweight champion, Hans Kalbfell. The German boxer was 2 inches taller and more than a stone heavier than Henry who entered the ring at 13 stone 6lbs, more or less his perfect fighting weight. Clearly, something had happened, as Henry gave the German champion a comprehensive boxing lesson and scored a runaway points victory; it is unlikely that the hapless Kalbfell won a single round out of the ten.

The crowd was remarkably unpartisan (possibly buoyed by a large contingent from British Army over the Rhine, who cheered their ex-comrade very hard indeed) and appeared delighted as they chaired Henry round the Westfalenhalle, celebrating what was probably his finest technical career performance to date. What this must have done for poor Hans Kalbfell's morale can only be guessed at but it had all certainly served to motivate Henry.

That single (but vital) victory over a national champion went a long way toward rehabilitating Henry in the eyes of the sport and, more particularly, in the eyes of the promoters, but Wicks felt that there were other German boxers who probably made obvious matches, particularly those who had faced top Americans in the ring. Kalbfell had actually boxed Archie Moore, for example, and a further logical choice was the ex-European champion Heinz Neuhaus, who, while possibly over the hill ('past his best', as the boxing euphemism went), was still apparently formidable. Back to Dortmund the cheered little team went.

There was another reason to return to Germany, as Henry's rather spartan training regime had clearly not ruined him for the manliest game of all; her name was Hilda. With typical media savvy and promotional deftness, Wicks announced grandly, in the wake of the well-reported defeat of Kalbfell, that Henry had profited hugely from a motivational encounter with an eccentric and reclusive German shrink, 'Doctor Whassisname', as Wicks christened him. The gullible British press, who had a huge respect for Henry, and shared his low morale concerning the future, rather latched on to this. Had they known the truth, that Henry's German girlfriend was helping to relax him more than any fictitious mad professor ever could, there might even have been a xenophobic backlash, particularly from a disapproving Levene or Solomons, but just as probably from the tabloid press, which was as ethnocentric then as it is now, however gullible they were where Wicks was concerned. The Bishop certainly knew his business; he was able to conjure up a huge amount of attention on the flimsiest of pretexts. As well as being a good manager, Jim Wicks was himself absolutely wonderful copy, particularly during the silly season.

But on returning to Germany for the Neuhaus fight, Henry learned that the rules of the ring as they had evolved in Germany were not necessarily consistent with complete fairness. The convention had emerged that a fighter had to win a bout by a margin of five clear points in order to be awarded the referee's decision if there was no knockout. Henry had certainly accomplished that against Kalbfell and in his opinion he did so again against Neuhaus but the decision was to be disappointing: a draw. Although Henry was dropped in round four, he fought back strongly, but not, alas, strongly enough. But a draw was better than a defeat.

Both boxers and crowds hate draws. A boxing match, like any other duel, is supposed to resolve something and the better referees took the job of judging a close fight very seriously indeed, and occasionally took the odd risk in coming to their decisions, which is why a draw is a relatively rare occurrence in professional boxing.

There was one more encounter to come in Germany, but this time in Frankfurt, on 19 April 1958. The opponent was the German light heavyweight champion, Eric Schoeppner, and the fight was to lead to the only disqualification of Henry's career. Wicks was of the opinion, having seen Schoeppner already, that Henry would knock him out easily but the German's management was convinced it was a fair match.

Henry recalls Schoeppner as 'useful, but a bit flashy'. Naturally, as a light heavyweight, he was fast, and possibly even ahead on points for the first five rounds, but in the sixth, Henry managed to put him on the ropes with a left and followed through with a mighty left hook just as the German turned away. As the punch connected, Schoeppner dropped to the canvas, quite senseless. In fact, he had to be stretchered out of the ring and was to be hospitalized for five weeks. It was to prove the end of Schoeppner's ambition to fight for the world title against Archie Moore. But the celebrations in the Cooper corner proved to be both precipitate as well as short-lived, as the announcement came over the tannoy that Henry had been disqualified.

The disqualification was both unexpected and unwelcome. The reason – rabbit-punching – was, given the speed of a fighter's reactions, hard to justify. It had been said of Joe Louis that an opponent would be on the canvas before Louis realized that he had even hit him; it is a trait shared by many top class professionals and Henry was no different.

As well as a disqualification, Henry was fined the equivalent of £700 – half the already meagre purse – which, it later emerged, the German Boxing Federation sorely needed; the German economic miracle had clearly not trickled down into its coffers, as it was forced into some difficult financial gymnastics from time to time. Of course, the disqualification did not in any way invalidate the efficacy of the punch itself; it was, after four years in professional use, clearly developing into an awesome weapon.

Heavyweight fighters can take more time to mature than those men in the lower divisions, it is often said; one reason for this must be the sheer variety of their opponents. Any man from any weight can technically fight at heavyweight, there is no minimum or maximum, so over his career a heavyweight fighter might be called upon to fight men of a huge range of skill and weight, from less than 12 stone to more than 16, which makes the top division both unpredictable as well as arduous. Henry was, by that late spring of 1958, starting to mature nicely. He had learned to live with the risk of cuts, as Wicks had known he would, and his burgeoning faith in Holland's skills allowed him a degree of relaxation that had been rather obviously absent before.

He had grown up to trust only family, particularly George. There was a closeness about the Cooper household, and a particular closeness between the twins; they could even at times finish each others' sentences, which could make for a slightly fractured conversation if others were present – most confusing. Henry's willingness, initially wary, after that short string of defeats, to accept the input and judgement of others, marked a sea-change in him and the pleasing succession of fights in Germany (plus the fringe benefits) allowed him a reserve of energy that he had previously wasted on fretting and worrying, clearly a trait he had inherited from Lily.

So, it was clearly time for a UK comeback now. The chosen opponent, on 6 September 1958, would be the very rough Welshman, Dick Richardson, whom George had defeated on his own professional debut in 1954. The arena would be home turf to Richardson: the dreadful, seedy Coney Beach Arena at Porthcawl on the South Wales coast. The Welsh fighter enjoyed a 17lb weight advantage over Henry, as well as the extra edge of enjoying his own very liberal interpretation of the rules. Henry had known Richardson as something of a thug and a bully in the Army and had wisely given him a fairly wide berth.

This was a now a critical fight for Henry. The three encounters in Germany had not paid particularly well – £1,500 or so each – and, although they had served to restore both his credibility and his self-confidence, he needed to shine against Richardson if the level of his purses was going to rise. In the event he would receive £6,000, which, although it was the equivalent of four fights on the Continent, was still not a vast amount, given the level of expenses he was incurring. Henry was confident, if wary.

Richardson attacked immediately, a thing that Henry had thought he might do, for he knew his man: 'Dick realized that very few referees were strong enough to disqualify a man in the first round.' That is presumably why Richardson overtly head-butted Henry and opened a huge vertical cut on his eyebrow, which bled profusely. Henry managed to hold the charging, swinging Richardson off, protecting the eyebrow so that Danny Holland could effect some useful running repairs between the rounds, but this was not looking promising. It looked even worse in round five, after a fairly well-balanced second, third and fourth rounds, when Henry was floored by a painful right to the body. Richardson, assuming that he had his opponent exactly where he wanted him, went dashing in and promptly impaled himself on what was probably the best left look that Henry had yet delivered in his career. As he launched it, it was already near textbook perfect, and Richardson's own momentum made it even better. His feet actually left the canvas and he was quite out cold before collapsing. It was such a fine punch that even the usually partisan Welsh crowd cheered.

It had been two years since the loss to Peter Bates and the forced reassessment of his career. To a professional fighter, that is a very long time indeed, but Henry had proved, in this win over Richardson, that it had been well spent. He showed, in succession, that he could take a punch, recover from a knockdown, deal with cuts and also deliver a classic left hook of truly terrifying power. Some fighters, even the most highly rated ones, can perhaps do one or even two of these things. To be able to do all four was remarkable. He had also showed enormous courage, as well as an enormous left.

Obviously this splendid punch needed a name, and naturally it was Jim Wicks who thought one up. Ingemar Johansson had 'The Hammer', so now ''Enery's 'Ammer' had arrived. It would dominate the upper reaches of the heavyweight division of British boxing for more than a decade and almost change the course of sporting history.

CHAPTER SIX

The Comeback Kid

'I loved the garish day, and spite of fears,
Pride ruled my will; remember not past years.'
JOHN HENRY NEWMAN, (1834).

CHARLES 'SONNY' LISTON was not, it must be said, considered by many to be a perfect role model for American youth – particularly black American youth, given that the administration of the sport was entirely white. He was boxing's perfect bad boy, illiterate, violent (when drunk), an ex-convict (coached to box in prison by that almost inevitable Catholic priest) and managed by the mob. He was also possessed of what was probably the hardest punch in the history of the ring. The Cooper left was, some maintained, but a friendly caress by comparison. Unfortunately, Liston also enjoyed using his huge ham-hock hands (15-inch circumference) on policemen, which made him to say the least unpopular with the forces of law and order.

In the office, however, his behaviour was different. Harry Gibbs described Liston as being 'fearsome to look at, but a gentleman in the ring'. Jim Wicks had actually never heard of him; this was not of itself unsurprising, as Liston had, since 1955, been dividing his time between prizefighting and breaking legs for low-level gangsters in St Louis. He had not fought at all in 1957 (he had pressing business else-where, mainly in the Federal Penitentiary) and thus only appeared on the radar screen of *Ring* magazine, in early 1958 after having comprehensively demolished a hapless boxer called Billy Hunter in January. In August of that year he knocked out a hopeful Wayne Bethea in round one. After that brief encounter, Bethea's distressed seconds removed no fewer than seven of their boy's own teeth from his gum-shield. Liston was, in the parlance of the day, bad news, the sort of fighter every sane man dreads. And Jim Wicks was a very sane man indeed.

It was Wicks's friend Jim Norris who tipped him off; the two men, both extreme gamblers, were engaged in a little gentle betting in Jack Solomons' office in Great Windmill Street: 'If you're offered a fighter called Liston, don't take him,' came the clear message.

And Jim Norris had every reason to know. Despite a vast inherited fortune, which came from family interests in the grain business, based in Chicago (much of which was redistributed among the bookmaking fraternity around the world) Norris took an all-consuming interest in the fight game. As head of the International Boxing Commission (IBC), which had, since its formation in 1949, acquired controlling interests in the fortunes of a large number of fighters as well as a managing interest in Madison Square Gardens, Norris was a close (some say the closest) associate of Frank Carbo, the gangster and alleged assassin of Bugsy Siegel, who had recently acquired a controlling interest in Sonny Liston's career and who would shortly be invited to spend 25 years in prison. Carbo owned Liston just as surely as if the emancipation of slaves had never happened. 'Jim Norris got a bigger kick out of making $5,000 crookedly by stealing from a boxer than he did from making $10 million legally; he just made a lifestyle choice," Henry recalls, with no particular fondness.

Harry Levene, who was extremely keen to promote a Henry Cooper fight rather than see Jack Solomons put on yet another one, had other ideas about Sonny Liston; he had already opened negotiations with Miami-based Chris Dundee (brother of Angelo), who was at that time a promoter of Liston. As a result of the upcoming fixture between Henry and Alex Miteff being called off due to Miteff's injuries from a fight with Willie Besmanoff, Levene needed a replacement, and urgently. A black American fighter would be a good idea, he thought, for Henry's first bout under his promotion. In the event he got one, but it would not be Liston. It would never be Liston, in fact, certainly not a matter of particular regret to Henry, and one of profound relief to Wicks, whose view was eloquently summed up: 'I'm not going to let my boy fight that mahogany wardrobe; we don't want to meet this geezer walking down the street, let alone in the ring. He's too ugly, we only take on good-looking boys.'

As Jim Wicks and Harry Levene settled into negotiations concerning the upcoming fight, Wicks casually but firmly ruled out both Liston and Nino Valdes, the hewn-from-solid Cuban who had recently been defeated by Zora Folley. Valdes had also been ruled out by Norris, not on the basis that he was necessarily dangerous for Wicks's boxer, but simply because Norris made a hobby out of denying fights to Valdes's manager, Bobby Gleason, whom he hated.*

Levene was naturally piqued because he had virtually made the Liston match with Dundee but had done so without consulting Wicks or, it must be said, particularly researching Liston. But then Levene was a businessman, first and foremost. The prospect of ancient Archie Moore was an enticing one, but 'The Old Mongoose' was almost dormant by then, at least as a heavyweight, deservedly picky and extremely expensive.

However, the man who had beaten Valdes, Zora Folley, was, rather to Wicks's surprise, prepared to travel to London to take on Henry, even for the modest amount of money the famously tight-fisted Levene was prepared to guarantee. Presumably, Folley was at something of a loose end due to d'Amato's reluctance to match Patterson with anyone if he could avoid it. On the face of it, Folley/Cooper was a fair match in terms of weight and reach, and Folley had no reputation as a savage. On the contrary: a blameless private life, a sunny disposition (in fact rather like Henry himself) and everything that Liston was considered not to be. The match was set for 14 October 1958.

The difference in approaches between Wicks and certain other managers is chillingly well illustrated by a conversation between the columnist Joe Liebling and the aforementioned Bobby Gleason, who comes down to us as an interesting study, if you happen to be a herpetologist. Having railed at the IBC concerning the difficulties he was having with Norris, Gleason remarked casually, 'So, what of it? I can make as much with ten fights a year for ten thousand as I can for one big shot for a hundred grand.'

---

* The character of 'Mountain Rivera' played by Anthony Quinn in 'Requiem for a Heavyweight' (1962) was loosely based on Nino Valdes. Aptly, his crooked manager was played by Jackie Gleason, who was, so far as I am aware, no relation of Bobby's.

Liebling was coolly scathing: 'Ten fights at ten thousand dollars apiece entails ten times as much fighting as one at one hundred thousand, but Gleason wasn't going to do the physical fighting, which is after all a mechanical detail. It is why I think of him as an economist.'

There were many other critics of the sport at this time. By far the most vociferous was Edith Summerskill. Her ranting tract *The Ignoble Art* was first published in 1956, at the end of Henry's professional apprenticeship and, to coin a phrase, the book pulled no punches. As an MP, a Privy Councillor and not least a qualified doctor, Edith Summerskill's opposition to boxing was quite merciless and, as Henry was to find out later, she offered little room for compromise. In her opinion the sport should be banned at all levels, amateur and professional. There was no talk of improving safety, head guards, body armour or whatever – she was against it. She viewed it, essentially, as a nothing short of a criminal activity.

As a classic Whig, Summerskill felt almost as incensed that people enjoyed watching boxing as she was that the boxers might actually enjoy fighting. The fact that it was bad for the fighters was one thing; a critical element of her crusade, though, was that it was bad for the spectators. In 1953 she had engaged in a debate with Jack Solomons, which, in almost exclusively male company, she had narrowly won. Freddie Mills was there, too; when asked to defend himself, Mills reportedly responded by standing up and proudly displaying his gent's natty: 'Do you know how much this suit cost, Missus?' Or words to that effect. Summerskill was unimpressed.

Jolly Jack professed his intention of wreaking his revenge for his defeat upon her by standing for her Fulham parliamentary seat as an independent but only, he announced, after paying for some public speaking lessons. He did neither, in the event.

*

Zora Folley, who hailed from Chandler, Arizona, did not pass through the annals of boxing history with the credit that was due to him, possibly as a result of his tragically early death at only 41 in a stupid swimming pool accident in the summer of 1972. He was a prodigious athlete and potentially an extremely difficult opponent; he was, rather like Henry, a skilled boxer with the added edge of a powerful punch. He was also, by all accounts, a most considerate and charming man. In the early autumn of 1958 he was 28, near to the top of his form and (by a clear margin) the man most likely to succeed Patterson if only he could manage to manoeuvre himself into a ring with him.

It was this fight, more than any other, that lifted Henry out of his two years of relative obscurity and put him firmly back in the public eye. The pre-fight comments from the sporting press were, to say the least, cautious. While all agreed that his demolition of Brian London in 1956 had been impressive, he had fought nine times since then and lost five times, drawing once. His victory over Dick Richardson only six weeks previously might, it was contended, have taken a lot out of him. Further, Folley himself had already fought 45 bouts and lost only two. Despite the physical statistics of the two men being close, Fleet Street did not view it as an even match. The assessment of *The Times* was depressingly straightforward: 'I believe that he will find the American too strong and too experienced to be hurt seriously and then he will have to avoid being discouraged (a failing he has shown before) and concentrate on boxing his way. Folley must be the favourite but Cooper has a chance to make his name, even by surviving the 10 rounds.'

Oh dear. It was further ominously pointed out that 'Folley ... has defeated Nino Valdes, the conqueror of both Erskine (Henry's nemesis) and Richardson. He has won eight of his last fifteen bouts inside the distance and is reputed to be a clever boxer with an accurate left jab.'

Well, he was certainly a clever boxer, Folley, but he had a mighty right hand as well. Clearly, despite his world ranking status, he had not been well researched.

Donald Saunders, for the *Daily Telegraph*, was only marginally more optimistic, and pointed out a further source of personal pressure for Henry:

During the past few weeks those isolationist Americans who take it upon themselves to name each month the 10 best heavyweight boxers in the world have been forced for the first time since the war to glance over their shoulders towards Europe.

On September 14 they were obliged to note with some dismay that their compatriot Eddie Machen, whom they called the No. 1 contender for the world title, had lasted only 2 min. 16 sec. against the powerful right hand of Ingemar Johansson, the European champion.

Sixteen days later the unexpected news reached Broadway that Willie Pastrano, of New Orleans, rated the fourth best heavyweight in the world had been beaten by Britain's unconsidered champion, Brian London.

They are hoping that Folley will restore American prestige. But they are worrying, lest Cooper completes a unique hat-trick for Europe.

The splendidly jingoistic piece went on to reflect exactly the uncertainty that was descending over the heavyweight division:

…The record book helps us little. It merely causes confusion by showing that Cooper stopped London, who in turn stopped Pastrano, but that Cooper was knocked out in five rounds by Johansson, who knocked out Machen, who drew with Folley.

But I think that Folley will prove to be more skilful than Cooper, even if the young Londoner is at his best. And should Cooper slip back into his old irritating ways, Folley may well win inside the ten rounds.

In fact, if Cooper is to earn the world title contest promised tonight's winner, he must quickly relax, must avoid the eye injuries that in the past have often upset him and must use that left hook with the speed, power and determination shown against Richardson.

Saunders finished the piece with a touch of classic hedging: 'All this, I think, is too much to expect. But Johansson and London have recently hinted that now is the time for optimism.'

Plenty of local pressure here, then. The upsets in the heavyweight division caused by Johansson and London that had propelled Folley to the status of number one contender were the cause of considerable confusion. Henry had beaten Brian London (and quickly) but had also been well and truly pole-axed by Johansson's 'Hammer of Thor' and so, it was supposed, he sat somewhere in the middle. London, despite the fact that he had very effectively taken out Willie Pastrano, was never rated as highly as he probably deserved to be. Johansson, 'Thor's Hammer' aside, was considered to be a very nice man but perhaps somewhat idle; he even took his girlfriend, who later became his wife, to his training camp. Because Folley was known only vaguely in Britain, there would, all recognized, be a very partisan crowd, which could only help Henry. Even so, Folley entered the ring as favourite at 2–1, odds probably encouraged by the generally pessimistic forecasts by the pundits as well as the clear realization that, quite simply, black men might make better boxers.

Initially, the pundits seemed to have been absolutely right, or perhaps Folley too was aware that he was under the invisible burden created by the recent defeats inflicted upon his fellow compatriots. The first three rounds were a blur of savage and accurate combinations that firstly opened cuts above and below Henry's left eye and secondly, after a huge right, dropped him to the canvas. Henry took a count of seven, which was wise if not necessary. As he put it years later: 'When he put me down in the third, I didn't have a price ...'

All who were present assumed that the fight was basically over. But then Folley changed his tactics; he stopped boxing and started punching, to finish a fight that he now assumed he had won. But as he slung long, looping rights, he metaphorically opened the door and Henry did not need prompting. For the next three rounds he managed to insert himself inside the American's punches and responded with a series of wicked lefts, which rapidly started to even up the scorecard. A telling left hook to the face drew blood. By round nine Harry Carpenter, who was at the ringside, reckoned the fighters to be almost level, with Folley, having little left, perhaps a quarter point in front, but, of course, it was the referee, Tommy Little, whose opinion counted.

The last round was a simple, intimate toe-to-toe slugfest: Henry's left versus Folley's right. Both fighters were a mess. Henry's left eye was now cut in three places; the manic corner work of Danny Holland, with his faithful adrenalin and Vaseline swabs, had plugged the leaks, but by the time the final three minutes started, the blood was flowing freely from both men.

An astonished Jack Wilson of *Boxing News* reported:

> Folley started proceedings in the last with an over arm right to the chin which shook Cooper into quick retaliation. There was a vicious exchange of body punching and Cooper held his own. Out shot those superb lefts, Folley ducked and countered, tossing rights in desperation but Henry stayed with him and matched him punch for punch.
>
> Now it seemed that the whole place was in uproar. The crowd was mad with excitement and the central characters played out their last desperate parts to a tumultuous roar of approval.

Such was the noise that neither fighter heard the bell. Only when Danny Holland and George Page climbed through the ropes did Folley drop his guard, followed by a cautious and clearly exhausted Henry. Tommy Little did not hesitate; he raised Henry's arm in victory as the ring was invaded, the crowd led by a delighted Stanley Baker. Folley's corner men, who come down through history as being quite as unpleasant as their fighter was charming, half-heartedly disputed the decision, but to no avail. The British referee's view is holy writ, as Henry himself would come to regret many years later. With that decision, Folley's ambitions to seize the title from Patterson lay in ruins; having lost to Henry, who had not, it must be said, registered much on anyone's radar screens until that morning of Wednesday 15 October, d'Amato had no valid reason to dodge the match. But dodge it he would.

The *New York Times*, despite its fastidiously lofty and seigneurally dismissive editorial attitude to the noble art, (rather a litmus test of the liberal left) was predictably indignant:

> Henry Cooper, an unheralded Cockney plasterer, tonight won an upset ten round decision from Zora Folley, America's top-ranking heavyweight contender. It was another crushing blow to American boxing prestige. Folley became the third leading

American Heavyweight to go down to defeat on this side of the Atlantic in a month.

More cheerfully, humble pie was wolfed down along the length of Fleet Street. *The Times*, so dubious about Henry's prospects before the fight, reported graciously of the final moments: 'Then came one more great gust of sound as Cooper's hand was raised in triumph, and we were all left to marvel at what we had seen.'

Despite the fact that Folley had not lived up to his reputation as a 'classic' fighter, this was a huge victory for Henry and, only six weeks after stopping Dick Richardson, gave notice that he was well and truly back. But in three separate fights, the fourth, third and now second contenders for Floyd Patterson's heavyweight crown had been beaten by outsiders – what on earth was going on?

Henry's target was clearly now the world title – he was aware that making such an authoritative comeback would involve a vast amount of work, but first things first; the third leg of this remarkable recovery would now be to challenge for the British and Empire heavyweight titles. The fight was scheduled for 12 January 1959, the night when Henry Cooper went after Brian London.

*

The lantern-jawed London was not the swiftest of movers, and could even manage to make himself look flat-footed at times, but he made up much of any deficit of elegance by virtue of his immense strength and courage. This fight was to prove one of the bloodiest spectacles anyne had ever witnessed (or indeed would ever witness) in the UK heavyweight division. So savage was it that even some seasoned veterans turned away. The fight (perhaps unfairly, with hindsight) was to last the full distance and Henry was later to describe it as the hardest one he ever endured, and with good reason. Even at the distance of over 40 years it is a sobering, even distressing, encounter to watch.

There was still some serious needle here; despite the fact that that Henry had dispatched the Blackpool fighter almost without breaking sweat in 1956, London had given George a severe mauling, which Henry, ever the loyal twin, was determined to avenge, and with interest. The rivalry between the two was an open secret and it made wonderful copy for the scribblers.

Mindful of his first-round humiliation by Henry of two years before, London made a tentative start and, despite accurate and effective jabbing and some well-aimed hooks from Henry, London was able to respond in the second round with a colossal right that connected between Henry's eyes at that vulnerable junction of capillaries at the very top of the nasal septum. For the rest of the fight the challenger had to put up with a steady stream of blood pouring straight down his throat. This was not just some nosebleed, this was the kind of haemorrhage which had killed grandfather George all those years before.

By round four Henry was also cut below the right eye and London relaunched his attack to score his first (and, as the record reveals, only) winning round. The champion concentrated on the eye and by round seven the referee, Ike Powell, was showing proper concern about the resultant damage. Happily for Henry the cut was below the eye so that restricted vision was not a particular problem, and he simply swallowed the blood from the damage between his eyes. Shades of Eurydamus the Argonaut. The outcome of the fight and the championship now depended on Henry's ability to defend the eye as well as inflict meaningful damage on his energized opponent. The middle rounds of the bout were the fulcrum upon which Henry's championship hopes depended. He had to reach deep, as it transpired ...

Round eight was the point of no return. Despite the ferocious assault he had endured, during which London was warned for 'careless use of the head', Henry finally managed to unleash the mighty left hook, which simply shook the champion rigid and nearly took him down, but London was a very, very strong man. More of the same followed, with Henry scoring heavily on aggression and accuracy, and London inflicting even more damage on the badly cut eye (but little else) before Henry took final control with complete authority. The last four rounds were a savage blur of jabs and hooks that confused London so badly that he actually raised Henry's arm at the end of the fourteenth round, effectively conceding victory, although he had to endure another three minutes of the most brutal punishment that an exhausted Henry could mete out. It was for fights like this one that a boxer trains.

As an awed Donald Saunders described to his readers in the *Daily Telegraph*, the fight was '…15 of the most bitterly contested rounds I have ever watched … both warriors looked as if they had been fighting with meat axes.'

'It took more out of me than any other fight in my career,' says Henry. 'I felt worse after this, more exhausted and in more pain, than with any other. It took me weeks to recover.'

The loss of blood alone would have dropped most men on the spot; it dropped Henry only shortly afterwards: 'We got back home (Farmstead Road) and I remember asking George to run me a hot bath, just to help ease some of the pain away. Well, as soon as I got into it, I just fainted clean away, totally out. George had to drain out the bathwater and lift me out.'

So the new British heavyweight champion was not in any condition to enjoy his laurels; the 3lbs of congealed blood that he had ingested, a giant *blutwurst* really, also took some time to remove itself: 'I was so swollen up and sore, I couldn't even wear trousers for over a week.'

But more pleasingly, this second defeat of Brian London, and indeed the terrible nature of it, served to mend the fences between the two men. Donald Saunders was clearly grasping for something nice to say about the truly ghastly spectacle he had witnessed: '…These one-time enemies clasped each others' shoulders and let everyone know that as far as they were concerned, honour had been well and truly satisfied.' On Henry's terms, of course.

No one was in any doubt that he had earned this rather Pyrrhic victory, as well as casting the pecking order in stone. He was back, and it had been a remarkable turnaround from the previous disappointments of only a year before. Apart from the pleasures of being champion with a seat at the top table of British sport, the boost of confidence that came with it allowed him to relax a little. In quick succession he had beaten three worthy opponents, won the British and Empire title and suddenly entered the world rankings. 'To think,' a bemused Henry had said to Saunders after the Folley fight, 'I am the number one contender for the world title!'

He had every reason to think that the fight with Patterson for that world title was now a given, but if he did, he reckoned without d'Amato; astonishingly (or perhaps not) Floyd Patterson's manager accepted a fight with Brian London, only so recently beaten by Henry, but would not countenance a bout with Henry himself. While that may have been something of a compliment, it was also hugely frustrating. D'Amato was in the process of attempting to create a counter-monopoly, in order to defend himself and his champion against the forces of evil as he saw them: the IBC.

D'Amato was in danger of devaluing Patterson, in fact, by taking the path previously trodden by Joe Louis in 1940–41, the well-honoured tradition of the 'bum of the month', whereby Louis defended his world heavyweight title no fewer than 14 times without breaking serious sweat in any of them. Brian London was no bum, of course, far from it, but the implication from the d'Amato headquarters was clear – he would be his own matchmaker, thank you, and he was justifiably nervous of exposing his boy's weak jaw to Henry's left hook. Behind all the obfuscation and delay, though, was something even bigger: a genuine fear of Charles Liston.

Patterson knocked out a surprisingly durable Brian London in the eleventh round on 1 May 1959. But even then, if Henry thought he could now step forward, he was still mistaken. D'Amato selected Ingemar Johansson as the next fighter to be served up to Patterson, and Johansson knocked him down seven times in three rounds before the astonished referee stopped the fight. Naturally, a rematch was part of the contract, which put Henry to the back of the queue. Despite this frustration his equilibrium was back. It had taken two years and a vast amount of hard work, leavened with equal dollops of dangerous self-doubt. To be sure, there were still opponents of whom he was right to be nervous (particularly his nemesis Joe Erskine), but seven months after the bloody encounter with Brian London he demonstrated that South African Gawie de Klerk was not necessarily one of them. This was to be another cruel fight.

The plucky policeman from Pretoria challenged Henry for the Empire title at the dire and dismal Coney Beach Arena, Porthcawl (the site of Henry's previous defeat of Dick Richardson) on 26 August 1959. Ten thousand people turned up to watch. Initially, Henry appeared 'ring rusty' as one commentator had it, which he rather showed by allowing himself to be clobbered early on by a wild, unorthodox over-arm right, and for two rounds he was less than impressive, behind on points and with a bad cut under his left eye. One of the dangers of fighting inexperienced opponents (the SP on de Klerk was a pessimistic 5–1) is that because they are unpredictable, they can be occasionally lucky, particularly if they deliver the unortho-dox, which de Klerk certainly did.

It was a fight somewhat characterized by clinches, during which some fairly rough 'inside work' was done by both men but, as Henry started to unlimber the left hook, the balance started to shift in his favour. He had much catching up to do, and finally scored his first round, the fourth. There was little hint of what was to come, and Ingemar Johansson (who was in the audience again) may not have been particularly impressed (not that he would need to worry over-much, in fact) but after a minute of the fifth round de Klerk was unwise enough to drop his guard as the pair disengaged from a clinch, and Henry let rip with the hammer.

The blinding, perfectly timed left hook that he released detonated under the challenger's jaw and the rib-bending right hook to the liver that followed it dropped an agonised de Klerk for a count of nine. But the South African was brave: he rose, and Henry went in to finish the job, assaulting his opponent as before and dropping him again before referee Eugene Henderson finally stepped in and stopped the fight. De Klerk, rugged and extraordinarily courageous, had nothing left. After the fight, it was discovered that his jaw had been broken in two places. Most observers felt that the fight should have been stopped earlier or even that there was a technical knockout the first time; the count had perhaps been a little slow.

The *Boxing News* was appreciative: 'Cooper needed no advice from manager Wicks as to what to do. He stalked across and belted the open mouthed and glassy-eyed Springbok with all he had …' The non-specialist press, however, was rather more mixed. A red-blooded reviewer of the fight in the *Western Mail,* Alan Wood, was deeply impressed:

Cooper is a vicious opportunist … in he went to pound de Klerk to the canvas for a further count of nine. As he staggered back to his feet Cooper went in again to beat the South African around the head and body and the referee had to call a halt. It was a perfect performance from Cooper and I would not now like to forecast the result of his next meeting with Erskine. He could well prove the best heavyweight fighter we have seen in twenty years.

The reporter on *The Times* was less enthusiastic, if somewhat toadyish in another direction: 'I turned to Ingemar Johansson, the world heavyweight champion, who was sitting in the third row of the press seats, and he remarked "Impressive." True enough, but Johansson could have finished the job four rounds earlier.' There really is no pleasing some people.

Mischievously, or perhaps in response to this rather softball questioning, Johansson remarked enigmatically to the *Daily Mail*, 'I'd rather meet Cooper than Erskine.'

For Joe Erskine was on the card that night, too. He was fighting Bruno Scarabellin, a 30-year-old (and extremely game) pork butcher from Venice and, while Erskine outpointed the hugely tough Italian fairly comprehensively, he did not dispatch him with the finesse that the Welsh audience quite expected. Erskine therefore also witnessed the quite pitiless attack that Henry had unleashed on the hapless Gawie de Klerk. Perhaps that was unwise of him; Erskine was challenging Henry for the British and Empire titles on 17 November. While he may well have dominated Henry in the two professional bouts they had fought before, he could surely see that while this was clearly the same man he was also by now a radically different opponent. Something had changed.

*

Henry's third encounter with Joe Erskine would provide one of the British sport's most enduring images, that of a completely unconscious Erskine spread across the bottom rope, dead to the world. The fight, at Earl's Court, was to be controversial, in fact, but not immediately for that reason.

Despite the aggression and maturity that Henry had shown four times in a row, there was still a measure of uncertainty on the part of the pundits as to whether this was merely a 'good run' or something more than that. Was this a re-invented and remotivated Cooper who could now be taken seriously as a world-class fighter? Ever pessimistic, Donald Saunders of the *Daily Telegraph* had his doubts. In an unusually convoluted piece on the morning of the fight he wrote:

> Erskine, as he proved when out-speeding and out-smarting Pastrano, on his night is the best boxing heavyweight in the world. Cooper, by stopping Richardson, indicated that his left hook is as powerful as that of any current heavyweight and his brilliant points win over London also shows that he knows plenty about the Noble Art. In effect, the artist who cannot punch opposes the craftsman who hits hard. With some temerity I chose the artist to triumph.

Saunders would see for himself later that evening the degree to which Henry's aggression, quite counter to his nature, had asserted itself.

Henry started as he meant to go on. In round one, when Erskine slipped, Henry caught him with a mighty left, which dropped him to the canvas. When he got up, Henry simply hit him again. Erskine was able to respond with a few overarm rights, one of which opened a cut at the side of Henry's left eye. It was an eventful first round, and Danny Holland produced the Vaseline/adrenalin rather earlier than he would have liked.

Erskine, technically one of the best boxers the British ring had ever produced, closed in for round two, negating Henry's slightly longer reach, but some of the best punches travel mere inches, and a hard hook to the body had the Welshman in trouble again at the end of round two. One spectator commented: 'Henry Cooper won this fight in the first round.'

And he may well have done, but there were, in fact, many more to go. At the end of round five Henry clobbered Erskine a 'split second' after the bell after the challenger dropped his guard. It was a perfect but quite undefended right. It was indeed a blatant foul and there were predictable and justified howls of protest from Erskine's corner. Benny Jacobs, by now reinstated – reluctantly – by Erskine as his manager, leaped into the ring and berated first Wicks and then referee Eugene Henderson. Henderson calmly ordered Jacobs out while Erskine's corner men worked frantically to revive their dazed prospect. At the start of the sixth Henderson cautioned both fighters, but particularly Henry. He may well have been too surprised to issue a formal warning. Henderson had witnessed (very close up indeed) the damage that Henry had inflicted on de Klerk, but sneak punches had played no role in that.

Erskine continued gamely but it was clear that he was fighting by 'courage and instinct only', as one report had it. The end came in the twelfth round. Henry dropped his hapless foe for two counts of seven before lashing out with a blinding combination left/right to the jaw that propelled poor Erskine clean off his feet and left him draped inelegantly over the bottom rope, totally out cold. There were only five seconds to go and Henderson, who, as we have already seen, was not a referee to stop a fight unless he absolutely had to, declared the contest over, which it certainly was. It had been a brutal experience for Erskine, a real heartbreaker; truly, this was not the same Henry Cooper to whom he had given those boxing lessons before. 'We were really worried,' says Henry. 'We were convinced that Joe had broken his back.'

Even with this totally authoritative (if perhaps slightly grubby) display, which involved Henry giving perhaps the finest technician in the sport the worst thrashing he ever received, the praise was faint. '… I cannot see Cooper ever taking that crown off Ingemar Johansson, who has already beaten him in five rounds,' said Harry Carpenter. 'Cooper can be hit too easily ever to stand a chance with a really heavy puncher.'

Which rather begs the question: what on earth does a man have to do in order to be taken seriously? In fact, Henry would be denied again a chance at the world title, a match to which he had every right since his win over Folley, for in June 1960 Floyd Patterson, driven by the humiliation of losing his title to Johansson a year before, knocked the giant Swede out. In five rounds.

With the recovery of Patterson's crown (a unique event at the time) the US heavyweight division promptly deteriorated into an unseemly farce; Cus d'Amato, Patterson's manager, knew full well that the only challenger who had, by right of conquest, an entitlement to fight for the title was Sonny Liston, who had shot up the rankings to undisputed number one contender with dizzying speed by stopping Nino Valdes, Zora Folley and Eddie Machen, who were all themselves fighters whom d'Amato had refused. D'Amato was no less protective of his boy than Jim Wicks was of Henry. Clearly, Sonny Liston was not going to go away unless somebody shot him (a thing which more than one policeman would have been happy to do had anyone asked them nicely) and so a ridiculous logjam built up – everybody wanted a crack at Patterson, nobody wanted a crack at Liston, but Liston's brooding presence, coupled with Patterson's (or d'Amato's) clear reluctance to engage with any of the top five (apart from Johansson, whom he was to beat again in 1961) meant that the world title as defined by the World Boxing Council (WBC) was quite literally inaccessible. It was to stay in virtual cold storage until Liston finally got his chance in September 1962, proving that Patterson and d'Amato had been entirely right to avoid him – he totally flattened Patterson in a terrifying display of barely controlled aggression – in just 126 seconds. The bad boy, who had announced before this fight that he would like to 'run Patterson over with a truck', had arrived on the world stage.

For Henry Cooper, though, these dramas were all in the future as he reflected upon his remarkable transformation. He had won five bouts in succession, including the one against the US number one contender (as Folley had been then) and he had even beaten his nemesis Erskine, but he was still not, as we have seen, quite yet the darling of the press. The pundits were not yet believers, indeed many never would be. However, he had other objectives to fulfil as the 1950s gave way to a new decade – for Henry Cooper, British and Empire heavyweight champion, was engaged to be married.

CHAPTER SEVEN

A Married Man

'Chance only favours the prepared mind...'
LOUIS PASTEUR, (1854).

IN THEIR STATELY PEREGRINATIONS around London's better restaurants, Henry and Jim Wicks had settled into a comfortable routine. Monday usually saw them at Simpson's in the Strand and Friday usually saw them at Sheekey's, the famous fish restaurant off the Charing Cross Road quite near Jack Solomons' Soho office. In between, there were rich pickings to be had in a bewildering variety of places; lunch with Solomons, a decreasingly frequent event as he surrendered his turf to Levene, would invariably be at Jack Isow's, the kosher restaurant in Brewer Street. Then, of course, there were the Italian bistros.

*

Henry had been casting an appreciative eye over the new waitress at Peter Mario's, a restaurant in Gerrard Street, for some time before he finally summoned up the courage to ask her out. She was the niece of Maria, the wife of the owner, Peter Rizzi, and her name was Albina Genepri. She had in fact been in living London since 1948. Forty-five years on, she recalled to me their disastrous first date:

> He asked me what I was doing one Saturday night, and I said 'nothing'. So he asked me if I'd like to go to the cinema and I said 'yes', but I really didn't think he was serious. I thought he was taking the mickey! He was so tall and I was so tiny, and I simply couldn't imagine what he saw in me. So, I didn't think that he meant it, but he turned up on the Saturday evening, and I gave him a cup of coffee and just carried on working.

After about 40 minutes he asked me when I was going to be ready and I said I was busy. Oh dear! He didn't come back for three weeks, I was really worried.

After this rather unpromising start, Henry tried again and this time managed to be taken seriously. Gradually an understanding simply emerged that they would marry and they drifted towards an engagement. There was the matter or Henry's religion to be considered, as he was technically Church of England, but he had no issues with Catholic doctrine, in which he was instructed prior to the wedding, and nor did his parents.

The pair married in January 1960, honeymooning on the Italian Riviera. On their return they stayed with Albina's family and went looking for a house, which they found through the classifieds of the *Evening Standard*. It was in Ledway Drive, Wembley, far removed from the tribal lands south of the river.

Despite marriage, Henry and his twin brother were still quite inseparable, and so George came too. Henry and George both worked hard on the house, and Albina, schooled as she was in the traditions of the rural Italian family, saw nothing out of the ordinary in sharing her new house with a brother-in-law. The idea of George staying in Farmstead Road on his own seemed absurd.

With the departure of the twins, Farmstead Road was depressingly empty for Lily and her husband. As soon as his earnings from boxing had permitted it, Henry had insisted that his father retire. 'Well, he was only making £11 a week,' says Henry, 'so I told him to give it up, that I would pay him £10 a week to stop working.'

He also bought his parents a small tobacconist and dry goods business; it was in Hounslow, unfortunately near the Heathrow airport flight path and very noisy. Already under pressure from the burgeoning supermarkets nearby, it did not particularly prosper. In fact, Henry's parents were to find it quite difficult to settle; although there was never any ill feeling about the role that Jim Wicks was playing in their son's life, it is hard to avoid the impression that they felt rather rudderless.

*

Albina was to discover in August 1960 that despite the deceptively routine nature of Henry's daily commute down to the *Thomas à Becket*, the five-week isolation required to prepare for a fight meant that her only communication with him would be on the telephone. In one sense it was no different from a husband being on a business trip (although she was all too aware what the business was to be) but it was made harder by the fact that more often than not he was in some London suburb other than Wembley, merely a few miles away, but on a different planet. With the arrival of children, this would become even more difficult.

Meanwhile, Henry was engaged to fight Roy Harris in September 1960. Harris, from the quaintly named town of Cut & Shoot, Texas, was the state champion and appeared to be a good yardstick; he had actually knocked down Floyd Patterson in an August 1958 title fight, although the bout had been stopped in the twelfth in Patterson's favour. The encounter should prove interesting.

It wasn't, particularly. The message, that Henry's left hook was a thing best avoided ('just let them feel the wind of its passing, son') had clearly come through and Harris was wisely reluctant to put himself in harm's way. After a clash of heads, an event in which Henry invariably came second with a cut eyebrow, he took the fight to Harris, but only put him down for the first time in round eight, for a count of six, after which it became something of a slugging match. Harris proved to be durable, in fact, but referee Jack Hart gave Henry the clear decision after the ten rounds were over.

The fight that had been called off in October 1958, between Henry and Argentinean Alex Miteff, the cancellation of which event had produced the Folley encounter, was now back on for 6 December 1960 at Wembley. Originally, Henry had been scheduled to fight Joe Erskine but that fight was now delayed until March of 1961.

Henry knew full well, having researched him in preparation for the postponed fight, that Miteff, having been schooled in the American ring, was likely to be something of a handful, and so he was wary. He spent nine rounds simply picking up points with his left jab and seemed comfortably ahead when in the tenth and final he made the mistake of trying to mix it with his aggressive opponent, as he recalls:

...he slung a big right-hand punch, which put me down. It shook me and I was in a bit of trouble, but my head cleared. I got up, and signalled to Jim that everything was OK. Then I got back on my bike again, started pumping left hands and took the decision. But it gave Jim and the Wembley crowd a bit of a shock.

The prospect now loomed of keeping forever the Lonsdale belt that he had won by beating Brian London in 1959. The belt was a rather special one; it had originally been made for Tommy Farr and, while most Lonsdale belts were silver, this one was of gold. To keep it he had to beat the game Joe Erskine, who was challenging for the British and Empire titles at Wembley on 21 March. It would be the fourth time the two men had met in the professional ring and, although Henry's previous dramatic defeat of him had rather served to break the psychological hold that Erskine had exercised, he was always to be a tricky opponent. Jim Wicks had been so bold as to predict: 'Erskine would be lucky to last five rounds with Henry.'

In the event, Henry started as he meant to go on, by stamping his total authority on the fight. It was obvious that Erskine's eyes were now a weakness and Henry concentrated on them, alternating with hooks to the body. It was clear that Wicks was right; the fight was really very one-sided indeed and after Erskine came out for round five with one eye almost closed and a large cut on his forehead, never mind what looked like a broken nose, Henry barely had the heart to carry on. He switched his attention to body blows, and it was inevitable that this was really a fight that should be stopped. At the end of the fifth, it was, as Erskine's manager retired him.

While that first Lonsdale belt was a pleasing thing to own and a significant rite of passage for Henry, there was frustration at the Games being played in America. Two weeks before that Erskine fight, Floyd Patterson had knocked out Johansson for the second time in a year and showed no sign of accepting a fight with anyone who stood the vaguest chance of beating him. The serious risk now was that Henry might miss out if Patterson's pride compelled him to accept Liston, for Henry knew that Wicks would not sanction a fight, whatever the prize, with the 'mahogany wardrobe', as there was little doubt that Liston would win.

Wicks, as frustrated as Henry at the sheer inaccessibility of Patterson, suggested a rematch with the ever-ready Zora Folley, which, with the advantage of hindsight, was not to be one of his better ideas, and one that many observers found frankly perverse.

Since Henry had comprehensively wrecked Zora Folley's chances at the world title in October 1958, the Arizonan had fought 16 times against Henry's six. One of Folley's bouts had been against the strong heavyweight contender Eddie Machen; Folley had beaten him. Another had been against Liston and he had been KO'd in three. The rate of work put in by Folley since October 1958 had been prodigious and had led some observers, Jim Wicks included, to conclude that he was 'boxed out'.

Henry's preparation for his second fight with Zora Folley was, as he readily admits now, less than perfect. Folley had slumped in the rankings to seventh, as a result of his defeat by Henry three years before but he had held onto his recognition by dint of simple hard work. He was now ranked number six but there was still turmoil in the upper reaches of the heavyweight division, caused by Floyd Patterson's clear reluctance to fight Liston; in fact, on the same day as the Cooper/Folley rematch, he was busying himself with a little light exercise 'burying a body', Tom McNeeley. A straw in the wind for Patterson was that McNeeley, a relative novice, dropped Patterson twice. Henry was himself ranked three, his best ever rating. If he beat Folley there was a good chance of leapfrogging over Liston for a serious crack at Patterson.

The situation was neatly and elegantly summed up by Robert Daley of the *New York Times*, ever perceptive in matters fistic:

> Cooper will have the crowd going for him, plus a splendid left fist, plus the knowledge that he beat Folley here three years ago on points. He won narrowly after having been down for a count of eight in the third round with both eyes already slashed open by Folley's punches. Cooper also has a greater need to win than Folley. Cooper thinks he will get a shot at the heavyweight

title once Folley has been knocked over. Folley, who was the number one challenger in 1958 before losing to Cooper, no longer appears to have any designs on the world championship. But he does have six children, so his incentive to fight is there. This may or may not be the right incentive for a winning prize-fighter.

Experienced British Cooper observers were fussed about the match, several wondering why Henry was fighting Folley again at all. *The Times* declared:

> Logical matches are rare in boxing and rarest of all in the heavyweight division. Coming only a few hours after the bout between Floyd Patterson and Tom McNeeley as it does, the ten-round contest between the British and Empire champion Henry Cooper and the American Zora Folley at the Empire Pool, Wembley this evening seems almost reasonable.
>
> Yet it is to be regretted that Cooper's manager saw fit to put his charge against a man Cooper outpointed as far back as 1958 rather than meet a more highly ranked contender like Eddie Machen. It will be ironic if Folley, as is quite possible, upsets the applecart by defeating Cooper and removing him from contention for the world title.

So it was clearly perceived as a very high-risk strategy indeed. Henry had little to gain and much to lose and, despite the fact that he was 5:2 at the bookies, Donald Saunders, although generally optimistic, shared the overall concern:

> In my opinion, the man who should be in the other corner tonight is Eddie Machen, of California. Apart from Sonny Liston, who has just resumed his career following a brush with authority, and the currently inactive Ingemar Johansson, Machen is the only heavyweight available to prove whether Cooper is good enough to fight for the world title.
>
> Cooper's manager Jim Wicks points out of course that Folley

beat Machen last year. My answer is that the verdict was disputed and that Machen has regained his form and Folley has
lost his.

That last remark proved to be very premature indeed, as matters
unfolded.

There was a further issue, unremarked on at the time, which
would count heavily against Henry, that of training. As Johansson had
remarked that very year when his memoirs were published, 'Henry
Cooper is too nice to be a boxer.' The surest way of overcoming this
aggression deficit is the monkish routine of the training camp, and this
was not a ritual to which Henry looked forward at all, particularly as
a newly married man and proud father of a one-year old. The farmers'
hours required – rise at 4 a.m., bed at 9 p.m. – had never particularly
suited him at the best of times, and certainly not in November, so he
made the error of training 'at home'. For a man with a nature like
Henry's, this was to prove a virtually impossible task.

So on 5 December 1961 Henry was cheered into the ring at
Wembley Pool by his apparently loyal fans. Due to the nervousness in
the informed press (the tabloids were predictably jingoistic), his odds
had narrowed slightly to 7:4. Five minutes and eights seconds later, all
the misgivings expressed by the more informed commentators proved
to be sadly correct.

Initially, after a fairly uninspiring first round, there had been a
murmur of unease at the sight of Henry's cut forehead and grazed eyebrow after a clash of heads, but the damage was contained swiftly by
Danny Holland during the break. Henry seemed tense to some
observers, whereas Folley moved with a smooth assurance; he was
obviously immensely fit, as a man who had fought 16 times since the
pair had previously met should be, but there was no hint of what was
to come as the two fighters squared up for the second round. A minute
into it, after exchanging a series of inconclusive left jabs with Henry,
Folley let rip with an unorthodox, sweeping right that was almost a
hook. It connected between Henry's jaw and ear and simply dropped
him like an empty suit. One report read:

Cooper was sitting upright before the count even started. He was staring into Folley's corner, a half-smile on his face. At first glance, he was trying to get up.

But the count went on and on and Cooper didn't move and his smile didn't change. Only then did ringsiders note that his eyes were unfocused.

As the count reached ten, referee Bill Jones moved to help Cooper up. Standing, Cooper lurched toward Folley's corner, holding his guard high and looking for someone to hit. There was no one there.

The crowd who had cheered him in five minutes before now booed him out, as an anxious George escorted his brother from the ring. 'I didn't see the punch at all,' said Henry later. 'All I remember was Folley coming close to me and I found myself on the floor. I suppose I shall have to start all over again.'

As for Folley himself, perhaps to balance the truly appalling behaviour of his seconds, who had openly sneered at the dazed loser, he said gracefully, almost in implicit apology:

> I didn't think it would end so quickly, but I came into this fight much fitter than last time. When I fought Cooper last time, I made the mistake of not using my right. During training I concentrated with that hand … I've waited six years [to fight Patterson]. Henry Cooper is a gentleman and if I win the title then I will come back and give Cooper a shot at it.

Well, history shows that he never got the chance to fight Patterson, as the champion finally had no option but to give Liston a shot at the title, with famously embarrassing results. In fact, Folley would have to wait six years for a title fight, and it would be against Muhammad Ali, not Liston, by which time he too, partly as a result of over-fighting to feed his large family, was past his best. Ironically, after all Zora Folley's hard work, Henry would get his own crack at the title ahead of him.

Generous though Folley's offer of a rematch was (and the cause of much appreciative comment), Henry's fans, the more informed of

Two peas in a pod – Henry and George sharing a chair circa 1936.

Above: Training with the army – the habit of wearing ammunition boots when training never left him.
Right: 7 December 1960. The proud father. Henry, fresh from his victory over Alex Miteff, holds his son, Henry Marco, for the first time.
Far right: Henry *(left)*, George *(right)* at an art gallery.

Left: Henry receiving the Knighthood of St Gregory from a delighted Basil Hume, Archbishop of Westminister and a long-time boxing fan. 8 June 1978.

Above left: Albina , Henry Marco and Henry Cooper OBE outside Buckingham Palace on 18 February 1969.

Above right: Sir Henry Cooper OBE with grandson Henry after receiving his knighthood on 22 February 2000.

Below: Which one of them hit me? George *(left)*, Muhammed Ali and Henry at Henry's 50th birthday celebration in May 1984.

Right: 1975 sees Henry playing Jack Gully in his cinematic debut. The film is *Royal Flash*; here we see Gully sparring with Otto Bismarck played by Oliver Reed.

Bottom right: Henry sizing up Billy Walker in January 1965 in his first ring-side commentary job. He would fight Walker within two years but meanwhile Billy knocks out Charley Powell in this fight.

Below: Two against one. Henry, Paul McCartney and Ringo Starr, 1964.

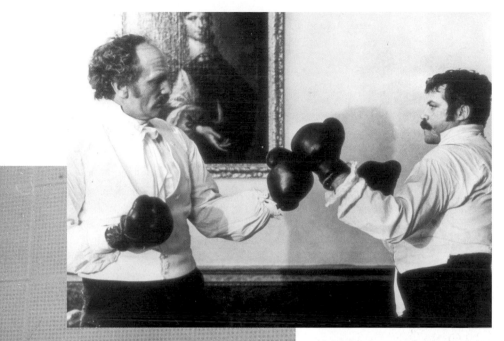

A reflective Henry before his attempt to recapture his European title from José Urtain. October 1970.

whom had been nervous about this fight in the first place, were appalled for him at the disaster. *Boxing News* wrote:

> According to our ratings, Cooper was Number two challenger to World Champion Floyd Patterson. That was before Tuesday night. Now, we are afraid, it is a rather different story. Poor Henry has tumbled down to number six. When the excitement dies down, when the gun smoke clears we must look around and see where we [meaning Cooper and British boxing] stand. We understand that Cooper ... was earning something like £10,000 from the fight alone. Victory must have meant at least another £100,000.

Others, including Donald Saunders, estimated that a fight with Patterson for the title would have netted him even more but, of course, neither man would get the opportunity. *Boxing News*, however, offered some sensible advice as well as a good and relevant parallel:

> It has happened before: it will happen again. On June 26, 1959, in New York, a so-called Swede-basher [Ingemar Johansson] smashed American Floyd Patterson to defeat in three rounds. They said it was the end of America's grip on World Heavyweight boxing. They said it was the end of Patterson; but Floyd hid himself in the backwoods for exactly a year, and trained and trained and trained. Now he's back at the top.

But whatever the level of the opportunity cost involved, this unnecessary defeat was a huge setback for Henry, both personally and professionally. He had made the classic and clear mistake of under-training for the fight, thus effectively committing the cardinal error of underestimating his opponent. Quickly, another bout was arranged, for 23 January 1962. The opponent was to be Tony Hughes, who was something of an unknown quantity, save that he was the protégé of Rocky Marciano, who had retired as undefeated heavyweight champion in 1955. Marciano, with some justification, had been just as feared as

Liston, so there was a buzz of anticipation, firstly at the prospect of actually seeing this great but terrifying man in the flesh, as well as evaluating his presumably promising prospect. A man like Marciano, it was reasoned, would surely only sponsor someone cast completely in his own image, if that was possible.

After the disaster of that second Folley fight, Henry and Wicks had sat down to have a serious talk about the issue of training; Henry had ruefully agreed that to attempt to work at home was a mistake that had cost him dear, so this time round he threw himself into it with great intensity.

Henry was fascinated to meet Marciano, whom he had long admired, but never particularly wished to fight. In 1952 Marciano had knocked out champion Jersey Joe Walcott with a terrifying punch that had famously been caught on camera and it had appeared that poor Walcott's jaw had almost become detached by it. Marciano had christened this punch the 'Suzy Q' and Henry was quite interested to meet its owner. 'He was the quietest, most softly spoken guy you could ever wish to meet,' he remembers.

The fight with Hughes itself was a straightforward and inelegant brawl, which took place at the Olympia Circus Arena, complete with caged animals nearby. 'God, they stank the place out,' recalls Henry but, in the parlance of the game, so, alas for him, did Hughes. Happily, he possessed neither a 'Suzy Q' nor great abundance of either discipline or ability. Straight from the bell he windmilled away at Henry for four rounds before being caught by a left that put him down at the end of the fourth. In the fifth, spectators witnessed a rare sight: Henry attacking with both fists in equal measure. It certainly worked, and a dazed and bleeding Hughes was forced to retire.

The use of the right hand was, however, significant. Henry had started to suffer from that dreaded puncher's ailment, bursitis, an inflammation of the knuckles caused by calcium deposits and exacerbated by judicious 'management of the glove'. Given that he used the left approximately 30 times more often than the right, and didn't even brush his teeth with his right outside the ring, it was the left hand that was starting to deteriorate into a truly dreadful condition. His left elbow was not much better, and it was was now starting to hurt in the days that followed these fights.

The knuckle damage went back to his Army days, when Henry had banged the top of Joe Erskine's very hard head. The knuckle had been split and swollen but little had been done about it. Now, ten years later, the (already big to begin with) joint was severely calcified and enlarged to the size of a golf ball and, despite treatment in 1955–56, it was still giving trouble, and always would. Hot wax and massage treatment helped to disperse some of the deposits but it remains to this day an interesting sight.

The second fight in this rather flurried and hasty comeback was arranged barely a month later, on 26 February, against the dentally challenged Wayne Bethea, whose features had been so comprehensively rearranged by Sonny Liston in August 1958. Bethea was by now well past his best and this fight was only possible because he was on a general European trip fighting purely for the money. History records that Henry scored a points win but oddly it is not a fight he remembers well now.

On 2 April Henry fought Joe Erskine for the last time, defending his British and Empire titles. It was a bloody encounter, with Erskine's puffy eyes offering an obvious target, and the referee, Frank Wilson, stopped the fight in round nine. It was to be Erskine's last title challenge, in fact. Although he was (like Dick Richardson) the same age as Henry, he was tired. Despite unrivalled ability as a technical boxer, he had always lacked a seriously heavy punch, and the extra work he had been forced to do as a result had probably weakened him enough, never mind the machinations of his crooked manager, Jacobs. 'I really think that if Joe Erskine had developed a really heavy punch and had had a decent manager, he would have been world heavyweight champion without a doubt,' says Henry. ' He was just a superb boxer. He gave me more trouble than Richardson, London and Billy Walker put together.'

So, after another successful rehabilitation of almost unseemly haste, Henry had earned himself a decent layoff. He had hardly laid eyes on Albina and his son, Henry Marco, in four months, and now he would go back into regular training – just a day at the office, really – for almost a year, before another encounter with Dick Richardson. But there was plenty for him to do. Wicks, never idle and usually scheming something up, had had a rather good idea.

Using the full breadth of his contacts, he was even able to secure a walk-on part in a *Daily Mail* cartoon strip, *Carol Day*, penned by David Wright, which had been run from 1956 and would carry on until Wright's sadly early death in 1967. Actually, it was a baddie; Henry would model for the character of 'Gene Miller', an apparently 'brutal' boxer, who was one of the many and varied male friends of the eponymous heroine. The Miller character was actually rather well drawn, and was also very obviously Henry Cooper (or possibly even George, of course). It was this kind of trick, very contemporary now, that served to keep either the name or the face of 'Our 'Enery, as the tabloids would impertinently christen him later, in the centre of the limelight.

For a man who is naturally fit and enjoys being so, there are many worse existences than being a boxer in daily training, particularly if your manager is both a good friend and counsellor and a trencherman of London-wide repute. Wicks was approaching 70 years of age but was never to lose his appetite for the good things of life. He also eschewed any nonsense about 'my body is a temple', so the combination of hard training and workouts, coupled with a fairly sybaritic lifestyle in terms of food, made for a rather idyllic existence for both Henry and George. The lunchtime round, alternating between the Strand and Soho, continued, with the combination of the highest protein diet imaginable, washed down with some of the best wine these establishments could offer, was not by modern standards the height of dietary excellence but it seemed to work. Wicks's main aim was to keep his senior fighter in a fit but relaxed state, just near enough to a peak of fitness that a gruelling five-week training camp could then bring to an acme of both condition and aggression. The problem with Henry was always going to be the second rather than the first. He had, since the early fights, quickly calculated that his optimum weight was exactly 13 stone 7∆lbs, which, although there never has been a minimum weight for a heavyweight (anyone can have a go) would today put him in the lists as a cruiserweight, and a light one at that. This inability when fit to gain useful weight was always to handicap him.

But, as the Wicks *équipe* maintained its stately progress around the West End of London, with 'The Bishop' holding court at a succession of favourite and pre-ordained tables, it was becoming clear that, serene though the outlook seemed to be, with the only thing concerning Wicks being perhaps his age, then the conflicts within the prize ring were as nothing compared to the conflicts outside it.

If it was not clear to Jack Solomons that he was on the way out as Britain's senior promoter, then it should have been. The writing had probably been put on the wall since the sale of Harringay Arena at the end of 1958, which had been London's favourite venue, but Solomons did not see it. At the opening of the new decade Solomons was consistently attempting to underbid for fights, believing that his position was still that of a monopolist. A good example was the way he attempted to secure the services of Terry Downes, the British middleweight champion, for a relative pittance. In July 1960 Downes effectively jumped ship, accepting a fight in a Harry Levene promotion. Solomons' response was to threaten, via his creature Sam Burns, 'that Downes would never work again'.

But the rise of Harry Levene, in concert with Jarvis Astaire's newly established *Viewsport* operation, now served to put Solomons under great pressure to bid , and bid high, for fights. This period marked the peak of the competition between the two men and Wicks was now beautifully positioned to take advantage of it. His willingness, on the part of his fighters to be quite ruthless about matters of money on behalf of his fighters did not endear him to the promoters nor, in particular, to the matchmakers employed by them.

It was Wicks's practice to 'make the matches' himself. Despite the fact that the name of Mickey Duff would always appear on the fight programme as being the matchmaker of record when Harry Levene promoted a fight with Astaire's cooperation, this was not actually so. If Henry was top of the bill, then the promoter's matchmaker (whoever it was) would be responsible only for the supporting bouts – the under card, as it is dismissively referred to, and this was a matter of great frustration. But Wicks did not care. At his age he was a man with few ambitions left and even fewer illusions. He was thick-skinned enough not to bother.

Jim Wicks had moved with the times. Even though he had originally had a far better relationship with Solomons than with Levene he had neatly managed to step between the intense commercial (and personal) rivalry with them and play a pivotal role in his fighters' careers, over which, when all was said and done, he held an iron grip, operating almost *in loco parentis* for a much younger person. His uncompromising attitude was total. 'I often wondered why Henry senior didn't resent Mr Wicks,' Albina told me. 'I know that a lot of other fathers would have done.'

For Albina, who had yet to witness a fight, the strain and worry, despite Wicks's confidence, were vast. She was buoyed by the knowledge that Henry's career would not last forever and that she would have him back one day but she was also imaginative enough to realize that he could be hurt or, God forbid, even killed at any moment. The long break after that final Erskine fight was a godsend to her and, although Henry trained, she was more or less able to put boxing out of her mind. Pleasing to her was the sound of the Alfa Romeo arriving back after another hard day's work at the *Thomas à Becket*. 'Once the front door was closed, there was no talk of boxing,' she says. 'I didn't like it and Henry knew that I didn't like it, but I also knew that it was his living.'

But after a fight she would pitch in professionally. Although Henry's metabolism meant that he was generally struggling to put weight on rather than take it off, he had little trouble with that awful risk that has damaged so many boxers: pre-fight dehydration. It is the curse of the lower weight divisions and one of the main reasons why the casualty figures are so high. A boxer under pressure to meet a lower weight will, like a jockey, run the risk of dehydration, which can affect the brain's ability to absorb punishment. If anything, Henry had the opposite problem: 'I could lose five to six pounds easily during a full-distance fight, and feel terrible afterwards, so Albina always had two huge jugs of orange juice ready in the fridge when I came home. The first thing I'd do would be to sink them both as fast as I could.'

Disapprove as she might, Albina was very good at coping with the results of her husband's uniquely dangerous career. She was pleased, though, that he healed so quickly.

CHAPTER EIGHT

That Fight

'Yon Cassius has a lean and hungry look;
He thinks too much: such men are dangerous.'
WILLIAM SHAKESPEARE *Julius Caesar*, (1599).

THE EMBARRASSING CHAOS at the top of the US (and therefore the world) heavyweight division was gradually resolving itself. The remorseless Liston had finally achieved a match with Patterson, held on 25 September 1962. Patterson's acceptance of the bout had led to an emotional split with the nervous Cus d'Amato but the philosopher/manager was still loyally present in the champion's corner to witness the total humiliation of his protégé. As is traditional before a fight, champions past and present, as well as current contenders, were introduced to the crowd. All the hopefuls were cheered heartily. All, that is, bar one.

Cassius Marcellus Clay, 20, light heavyweight gold medal winner at the 1960 Rome Olympics, was dutifully booed by the press corps as he climbed through the ropes to take a bow. Many of the hacks were literally on the payroll of Norris's IBC and Clay's independence from that organization was awkward, to say the least. He was managed by Angelo Dundee, the brother of Liston's one-time promoter Chris but, more importantly, he was financially supported by an 11-strong group of local worthies from his birthplace, Louisville, Kentucky, each of whom had lobbed in a tax-deductible $3,000 a year to have a stake in their local boy and keep him from the clutches of the Mob's regiment of obedient shadow managers. Cassius Clay was guaranteed a living, and a good one, until 1966. Each of the Louisville Sponsoring Group, as they called themselves, was probably as wealthy as Norris, so Clay was in good hands. However, his reputation as a loudmouth sat ill with the world of boxing writers; that, they reasoned collectively, was rightfully their job. White to a man (and some of them more redneck than many) they took the view that if Floyd Patterson represented the 'good' (cooperative) Negro then Liston was therefore the 'bad' (downright dangerous) Negro. Clay, at that stage in his career, was merely the 'noisy' (uppity) Negro, quite outside the script of this cynical morality play and reckoned to be a thoroughgoing nuisance of dubious (professionally, at least) fistic quality.

Famously, Liston demolished Patterson in 2 minutes 6 seconds, and if this spectacle gave Clay pause for thought it didn't show much. This handsome young man (already known as 'gaseous Cassius') was, at the time of Liston's first destruction of Patterson, the victor of 15 professional fights out of 15. His opponents had not been in perhaps the top ranks (with the possible exception of Alonzo Johnson), which is why he was scheduled to fight Archie Moore in November. This was to be a rite of passage, a normal and even faintly honourable transaction of boxing, that moment when the newcomer beats the established master, to which he looked forward. Moore had also helped to train him before Angelo Dundee had taken over in early 1961 and, despite his persistent disobedience, Moore had a great affection for him. The pair amused themselves by 'doing the dozens' in public – demonstrating by verbal sparring that they both had adequate supplies of 'mother wit'. Clay would knock 'the old Mongoose' over in the fourth round. It did not go unnoticed that Moore was approaching 50 but then by some calculations so was Liston.*

*

Henry, meanwhile, had recovered well from the defeat by Folley with his pleasing succession of four wins. He had secured his first Lonsdale belt as a result of the Erskine fight and had, it seemed, thoroughly reconciled himself to the burdens of training as against the responsibilities of fatherhood and marriage.

---

* There had been a fighter called Charles 'Sailor' Liston who had fought before the war – it has been assumed from time to time that they were one and the same. Birth records in certain parts of the Deep South were approximate at best.

The Clay fight was arranged for Waterloo Day, 18 June 1963. It would go down in history as a most important encounter because the winner would almost certainly face the winner of the Liston/Patterson rematch, a contest scheduled to take place barely a month later, which may have given Jim Wicks some mixed feelings. It was generally held, correctly as it transpired, that Liston would steamroller Patterson once again.

As a sparring partner, Wicks had hired the gifted Alonzo Johnson, who had gone the distance but been narrowly beaten by Clay two years before. Johnson therefore had an agenda of his own, valuable experience and a great talent for aping Clay's style, which was blindingly quick if somewhat unorthodox. Clay actually moved like a middleweight. For his input, Alonzo Johnson was paid his fare, board, lodging and food, and $500.

As for Clay, who arrived in Britain three weeks before the fight, he worked out at White City, at the Territorial Army gym. For publicity purposes he was chauffeured every morning at 5.a.m. to do his roadwork up and down Pall Mall. It made for a good picture – a bowler-hatted Cassius metaphorically knocking on the door of that 'swell pad', Buckingham Palace. He would take this regal imagery even further later on.

Cassius Clay had a lot of ground to make up, in fact. His previous encounter, with Doug Jones, had not been an impressive affair, at least from Clay's point of view. He had both outreached and outweighed Jones but the more experienced man, actually a light heavyweight, was consistently able to sneak inside Clay's huge reach and counterpunch him very effectively. For his part, Clay certainly didn't hurt Jones and the crowd were unappreciative of the points verdict in Clay's favour, so much so that they bombarded the ring with any piece of rubbish that came to hand. They were not happy.

For a fighter with an agenda like Clay's, this was disconcerting, to say the least, but any shortcomings he was exhibiting in the ring (and he was) were in large measure offset by his pre-fight antics. In Las Vegas Clay had encountered a professional wrestler, George Wagner. Wagner was 46 and had carved out an interesting niche for himself as 'Gorgeous George'. He was the first wrestler to address himself entirely to the opportunities offered by the media. His long blond hair and narcissistic manner – he has been memorably described as 'a Liberace in tights' – were balanced out by a bloodcurdling litany of pre-match threats. A fairly typical offering would be something like: 'I'll tear his arms off! If this bum beats me I'll crawl across the ring and cut all my hair off! But that ain't gonna happen, because I'm the greatest wrestler in the world!'

Cassius loved it as much as the little blue-rinsed old ladies who made up the bulk of George's fan club did. He had first come across Wagner when the pair shared a radio show and, given that he had been coming up with this nonsense for years, and had clearly prospered from it, Cassius listened to him.

'A lot of people will pay to see someone shut your mouth,' he is alleged to have counselled told Cassius, 'so keep on bragging, keep on sassing, and always be outrageous.'

That the stadium was full, that the capacity crowd could witness the destruction of this middle-aged mediocrity, was lost on no one, least of all the impressionable Cassius.

*

Sledging the opponent is as old as boxing, of course; as far back as 1748 a fighter called Ned Hunt had advised his prospective opponent, William Cutts. to 'bring his coffin with him', when he turned up to fight in some unremembered field, but Cassius Clay brought the art to new heights, in boxing terms at least. His training sessions were actually rather popular and as he would spar up to five rounds he would turn to the audience and say: 'This is the magic round. This is the round of the annihilation of Henry Cooper.' Obediently, the spectators lapped it up. It was observed that Clay's sparring was somewhat one-sided. He had three sparring partners, one of whom, Don Warner, he slugged quite happily and the other two, his brother Rudolph and their friend Jimmy Ellis, he simply dodged. This was, to say the least a little hard on Warner, who was scheduled to fight George Cooper on the same billing at Wembley.

In conversations with journalists, Clay showed himself to be a *faux* angry clown. On paper his remarks about his latest opponent were astonishingly rude. In reality they were delivered with an impish charm (or as impish as someone who weighed in at 14 stone 12lbs could be), which quite captivated some and left others, who did not necessarily appreciate the verbal legacy of George Wagner, totally cold. 'Henry Cooper is a bum and a tramp,' he announced with a twinkle in his eye on the eve of the fight. 'He has no right to be in the same ring with me.'

For British observers this was something rather new, although the tabloids lapped it up; 40 years on we are quite used to such prattle from boxers but in Clay's case it was as light-hearted as it was rude. Partly, perhaps, such clowning served to bleed off inevitable tensions as well as carrying on the contest at a different, if experimental, cod-psychological level. For on the day before the fight he changed his prediction of victory from five rounds to three or even to one. It rather depended on whom he was talking to, as well as whether he could manage to find a rhyme, for he had taken to extending Wagner's repertoire somewhat, to versifying – of a kind. He also affected to be offended by the fact that the British media had not wholly embraced him and his truly dreadful doggerel, complete with dodgy scansion:

> This will be an annihilation.
> If the bum don't fall in five,
> I won't come back to this nation.

Pure 'Gorgeous George'. Well, he was only 21, but this was possibly the most excruciating verse in English since the days of William McGonagall. Holding court over dinner in a Soho restaurant, Clay, surrounded by his entourage, announced: 'I'm real mad, the way I've been received. I stick to all I've said about Cooper.'

Henry, on the other hand, was calm, philosophical. He opined said to Jack Wood of the *Daily Mail*, also on the eve of the fight: 'I appreciate what Clay's done for the box office, but tomorrow night at 9.30 we'll be equals. Before the night is much older I expect to prove that the Lip is a better talker than a fighter.'

He meant it, too. Because, even at this distance, the fight that put

Henry Cooper on the path towards the state of grace he would achieve so far as Britain was concerned was characterized by an astonishing and quite untypical display of early aggression from him. If Clay had been seeking to rattle Henry's cage, then he may very well have succeeded, but he would wince at the outcome of this strategy, which came very close to changing boxing history. Donald Saunders pointed out, cautioning Clay:

> But his somewhat unsophisticated tactics of ridiculing the opposition could act like a boomerang. The insults which have poured out of the American's camp might have changed Cooper from a comparatively mild Englishman into an angry fighter. And, unlike many boxers, who are most effective when they keep cool, the British champion is far more dangerous when his temper flares.
>
> In his last contest, for example, an exchange of punches with Dick Richardson after the bell so upset him that he stormed out in the next round and quickly knocked out the Welshman. If Cooper could reproduce that sort of mood tonight then perhaps Clay would be rather quieter than he has been so far for the remainder of his visit to Britain.

Saunders was entirely correct; he, like many others in the sport, had spotted the same deficit of aggression, the lack of overweening ego that seemed to power so many sportsmen (and particularly fighters) but that seemed so entirely absent in Henry. When he became cross he was formidable, but, as Wicks had experienced, and Ingemar Johansson and Max Baer had already both observed (long before this fight), Henry was clearly slow to rile. As Piero Tomasoni would discover later, when its owner became angry, the Cooper punch assumed a life of its own. Getting Henry to a proper level of focused aggression was a long and frustrating process and it often actually took a fight to do it. This aspect of his character could make him a slow starter in a fight but it would also ensure him a reputation outside the sport which would endear him to millions.

The psychological banter extended to the weigh-in at the London

Palladium, where Clay's weight advantage, 207lbs versus Henry's 183½, was clear. Cassius had managed to excavate a theatrical crown from the back reaches of the props department when he went exploring and, needless to say, he would wear it into the ring. As well as serving to maintain the royal *leitmotif,* which had rather characterized his PR campaign, it also made him look even taller – and he was quite big enough already. The legend on his gown read modestly: CASSIUS THE GREATEST. The most famous fight in British boxing history – up to this point – began at 9.30 p.m.

Wicks had realized that the exceptional training that Henry had done for this fight had fined his weight down to, observably, well below 180lbs. He reasoned that two can play at this game and he cleverly inserted two 2½lb lead plates into Henry's boxing boots, and also slipped him a lump of lead to conceal in each hand. Only in this way did Henry even manage to register the weight that he did. It was a harmless ruse but, Wicks and Henry felt, probably a necessary one.

But the tenacity and aggression that Henry would show in this fight had its roots in more than Clay's banter. Henry was facing an opponent who enjoyed a 2 inch reach advantage, an inch in height and, if the real truth were known, over a stone in weight. Clay was not noted as a big puncher but his hard twisting jab was formidable. Above all, his speed was extraordinary. Not even his sparring partner Alonzo Johnson's imitation of the Clay style had served to prepare him for the sheer pace of his opponent. Henry knew that he needed every ounce of his resources to make up the difference, so, he rather uncharacteristically 'went for it'.

Straight out of the corner, Henry attacked as he had seldom done before, catching Clay with two powerful lefts to the head, which clearly shook him. Close work by Henry in the clinches was very near the knuckle and elicited howls of protests from Cassius, if not his corner. Clay was simply not used to this style of fighting – also, a few seconds of protest buys valuable time if you have just received two massive blows to the head. The referee, Tommy Little, airily gave a general warning to both fighters but, as Henry confessed later: 'When I caught him off the ropes and we went into a clinch he just held me, waiting until the referee said break. I tried to be as rough as I could inside. I really roughed him up. I belted him to the body, tried to uppercut him on the inside, pushed him, anything almost, except using the elbows.'

Round one was definitely Henry's. The BBC radio commentary, from W. Barrington Dalby, ex-referee and boxing veteran, was appreciative:

> This is unbelievable. Cooper, always a slow starter, decided tonight he'd start fast and he started with a beautiful left hook that shook Clay and from then on that was exactly the stimulus that Cooper needed to make him wicked. Cooper, once he gets a man on the hook, very rarely lets him off and after that he chased Clay round the ring. Cooper's certainly done a grand job on him so far. If only he can keep this up, well, we don't have a thing to say.

The second round started well, as Henry banged three assertive lefts into Clay's face in quick succession, but Cassius showed remarkable powers of recovery and delivered a short right-hand counterpunch, which nicked Henry under the left eye, offering Cassius a clear and obvious target. He went to work and, by the end of the second, the eye was bleeding. At the interval, Danny Holland, well prepared as usual, went to work. The BBC continued: 'Well, Clay managed to wriggle off the hook. He was boxing better in that round but it was Cooper's round very clearly. Now Cooper has a slight cut under his left eye but nothing very serious.

Dalby spoke a little too soon, for in the third, although Clay's punch rate dropped and Henry's increased, the eye started to look worse and worse. The impression given by the commentary, however, is that Henry was comfortably ahead on points on the basis of the number of blows he was managing to land on target, despite rapidly occluding vision. So bad was it that he even led off with his seldom-used right and caught Clay twice.

At one point in this round Clay dropped all pretence at fighting, to the extent that William Faversham, head of the Louisville group, bawled at Dundee: 'Angelo! Make him stop the funny business!'

In fact, as Clay said later, he was merely trying to keep out of the way and conceal the damage he had sustained. He was not, contrary to appearances, enjoying this fight; he had never been hit more often, and harder, than on this June evening. It was a sobering experience, but he was as good an actor as he was a boxer. He certainly fooled Jim Wicks who, Henry recalled, was tempted to throw in the towel during the third round.

Now the whole stadium had also started to realize that, despite Holland's marvellous work with the adrenalin and Vaseline, not to mention the damage Henry was doing, there had to be some doubt about whether he could now go the distance. Dalby commented: 'That was Clay's best round, but he still didn't win it. Now I think Cooper's judgement of distance is faulty because of the certain amount of blood running into his eye and he's probably worried about that. Clay was able to be rather cheeky about that.'

Round four was the one that nearly changed the course of boxing history. While Cassius carried on working on the eye, using his trade-mark long, twisting, flicking jab, Henry tried to keep out of trouble. He was three rounds up despite the cut but he desperately needed to survive.

His eye was now pouring blood and the situation was becoming quite critical. Five seconds from the end of the round, Henry finally found his distance and delivered an absolutely perfect left hook, which simply pole-axed Clay: Henry recalls:

> ... it was now or never... At times, I left myself exposed, but that was the chance I had to take. I went after Clay, throwing as many left hooks as I could, hoping that one would land. Suddenly, I had him. I jabbed once, twice, three times. Every time, he went back, back, back. But now he was right back on the ropes – he couldn't go any further. The fourth punch hit him, a genuine left hook, a more curved punch than the jab, which went from out to in, with all my power behind it.

An appreciative Robert Daley described the moment:

The punch came from a long way back, with Cooper lunging forward as hard as he could. Cooper put everything into the punch. It caught Clay on the side of the jaw and Cassius went over backwards through the ropes.

He rolled back into the ring then got dazedly to his feet. He was gazing off into the distance again, this time starry-eyed. He wobbled forward, gloves low. He started to fall, but his handlers caught him.

Henry takes up the story:

> ...there was a count of five, Clay started to get up and then the bell went. For Clay to get up like that was really a classic boxing error which he was lucky to get away with. It's a mistake a guy can make who's never been on the floor before.
>
> When you are down, you should stay down for as long as possible. Your head may clear, but you have to consider your legs, as well, and the longer you rest, the more the strength will come back into them. It's what the old-timers mean by taking the long count. Clay wanted to prove that he hadn't been hurt, but he walked back to his corner like a drunk.

Correctly, Little carried on the count until the bell went, which nobody heard, such was the uproar, at which point all hell broke loose in Clay's corner, where Dundee had some serious work to do. The use of smelling salts – carbonate of ammonia – was and is expressly forbidden under the rules of the BBBC but Dundee did not hesitate to use them to bring Cassius round, while slapping him hard around the face. He certainly needed to; he further drew attention to the small tear in Clay's left glove, near the thumb. He was later to admit quite cheerfully that he made it worse by jabbing it with his finger in order to buy time. The glove was not changed, for the simple reason that there were no spares. The manoeuvre with the glove was the mere gamesmanship of a trainer with few options open to him – furthermore, the use of smelling salts was blatantly illegal but probably saved the day.

Dundee recalled to Thomas Hauser in 1991:

> He'd split his glove on the seam near the thumb. Actually it happened in the first round. I spotted the tear then and told him, 'Keep your hand closed.' I didn't want anyone to see it, because everything was going our way, if you know what I mean. Then, at the end of the fourth round, he got nailed. And Cooper could do one thing; he could whack with that left hand. Cassius was hurt, no doubt about it. He got hit with that hook right on the button. So when he came to the corner I gave him smelling salts. Then I helped the split a little, pulled it to the side, and made the referee aware there was a torn glove. I don't know how much time that got us – maybe a minute – but it was enough. If we hadn't got the extra time, I don't know what would have happened.

Actually, subsequent analysis of the film of the fight, and indeed the radio commentary, put the extended interval at 66 seconds. To normal men, six seconds is nothing; to a fit heavyweight boxer, particularly one made groggy by one of the hardest punches in the sport, it is a vast amount of time.

So, revived and fortified by the smelling salts and the vital extra few seconds of rest, Clay went out into the fifth round in an instinctive flurry of savage jabs, most of which were aimed at the eye. The stuffing now coming out of the glove served to increase the abrading quality of his flicking jabs.

The *New York Times's* Robert Daley, ringside, was sympathetic to Henry's plight: 'In two minutes 15 seconds, he nearly tore Cooper's head off his shoulders. Few men have absorbed such a beating in so short a time. Blood was everywhere; it was now gushing out of Cooper's wounds.'

But, as the appreciative crowd and commentators pointed out afterwards, despite the apparent punishment Henry received in that shortened fifth round, he stayed on his feet.

Suddenly, Clay was not clowning any more. It did not take long to reopen the wound and two minutes into the fifth, Henry was quite a dreadful sight, with blood pouring down the left side of his body. The crowd, clearly distressed at Henry's plight, collectively moved by his courage and upset at his lost opportunity, roared at Little to stop the contest, throwing their newspapers and programmes into the ring. Fifteen seconds later, Little finally obliged. Clearly, the damage was so bad that it was beyond even Holland's skill to repair it. Quite unable to see clearly, Henry had absorbed more than enough punishment.

Clay may have done massive damage to Henry's eye but in the process he had learned that while he himself clearly didn't have a glass jaw (he received several such lefts in the earlier rounds) he had discovered a few things about punching and in-fighting that he clearly hadn't known before. In his career to date he had simply never experienced a punch like this one. The bragging stopped as he realized how lucky he had been not to lose this fight; only the intervention of Dundee with his chemistry set had saved him.

Curiously, Little did not disqualify Clay for Dundee's tactics though he would have been quite entitled to do so. This fight has always been controversial from the point of view of the attempt by Dundee to exaggerate the tear in the glove rather than for anything else and, while Dundee makes mention of the smelling salts cheat in his recollection of the fight, time has served well to obscure it. But watch the fight and it is clear that technically, by the letter of the regulations, Henry should have won it, for that infringement alone, as Clay was clearly quite out of it as he reached his corner.

So it was a relieved and subdued Cassius Clay whose hand was raised in victory; there was no clowning, bar a wordless gesture of five fingers once the gloves were off, and the crown stayed firmly in the corner. Afterwards, he said of the fight: 'Cooper was great, the toughest I have met by a long, long way. I wasn't clowning; I was trying to conceal how much damage his punches were doing. The punch which put me down at the end of the fourth was the hardest one I have ever taken. He shook me up – he hit me harder than I've ever been hit.'

He appeared cross with Tommy Little, though: 'He's a dirty referee and I'm telling the world. Henry Cooper hit me on the break and the referee wasn't doing anything about it.'

Little hadn't done anything about the smelling salts either, but naturally no one mentioned that, not even the supine Board of Control.

Clay's split boxing glove, liberated from the ring by some enter-
prising agent of his, appeared the very next day in the window of
Albert Dimes's betting emporium in Soho, from where it soon disappeared. No doubt it (or something resembling it) will turn up one day.
It is more likely, realistically, that at least four of them will.

*

Aside from the eye damage, which was hideous to behold, Henry was
not, despite Robert Daley's concern, particularly hurt, as he explains:
'When I fought Clay, even the second time, after he'd changed his
name, he was never really going to hurt anyone. He had this long,
flicking punch which was very fast, and it could damage an eye, but it
wouldn't actually hurt.' That statement, of course, is entirely relative:
'But oh, he was fast, you've got to give him that. He was the fastest
heavyweight I've ever been in a ring with, there's no doubt of that.'

Certainly he had impressed. He had even used his right fist to good
effect and, although Wicks was probably relieved that his fighter was
not going to be obliged to take on Sonny Liston, Henry himself, who
had little say in the matter at the time, recalls: 'The press, particularly
the American papers, had really built up Liston to the point where he
might has well have had four arms and two heads. He was a good
boxer, Liston, but a bit crude. I'd have fought him if I'd had the
chance; better him than Marciano.'

Of course he never would; Clay's next fight was against Sonny
Liston for the world title. It took place on 25 February 1964, and
famously Clay, having taunted and mocked the champion for weeks
beforehand, totally outwitted him. At the opening bell of round seven
Liston quit while still on his stool, a thing that had not happened since
Jess Willard had done it against Dempsey in 1919. But as we have seen,
Willard had a rather better excuse.

But with that victory over Liston, the legend was born. To the
infuriation of many, black and white alike, Clay promptly confirmed
the open secret: that he was already a member of the Nation of Islam
and would be henceforth known as Cassius X. Shortly afterwards he
would accept the name Muhammad Ali.

CHAPTER NINE

'Our 'Enery'

'Unhappy the land that has no heroes!'
BERTOLT BRECHT, (1939).

ALTHOUGH HENRY HAD BEEN STOPPED by Clay, that encounter, still the most famous in the history of the post-war British ring, did more than perhaps any other to boost his career, particularly after the humiliation of that second Zora Folley fight. ''Enery's 'ammer' had now passed into the lexicon of sport, indeed of the nation, as having a personality of its own, at least among those who had not been clobbered by it. The Clay fight created a huge interest in him among a wider circle. He had long enjoyed a huge popularity among boxing aficionados but now his appeal was apparently countrywide. He would appreciate this soon.

The defeat had not been a personal disaster; neither had there been any particular shame in losing the fight on the basis of a bad cut, and everyone knew it. As Robert Daley had been quick to point out in the *New York Times*, the 'Badly cut Briton was never floored'. The post-match endorsement of Henry supplied by Clay, a complete *volte-face* from his pre-fight histrionics (and not a policy he would adopt often again), had actually served rather well to boost Henry's stock.

However near he had come to glory, though, there was still the small matter of earning a living. His near knockout of Clay (and the American's victory by dint of the clear cheating in his corner) had ensured that his value as a boxer was as high as it ever had been and would go higher still. His fight against Zora Folley in 1958 had (at the time) seemed just as important a match, with Folley as senior contender for the world championship. Now that Henry had shown that he could, up to a point, handle cuts – unless they were as bad as the one he had suffered here – his value was assured. No British fighter would, during Henry's career, earn more from the ring than he did, even though the income tax situation was crippling, and would get even worse.

The damage by Cassius to the left eyebrow had been horrendous and took several months to heal properly. The difficulty was simple: surgical stitching repaired the outer surface, whereas the inner damage merely knitted together to form hard subcutaneous scar tissue. If another punch landed on the healed outer wound, the encysted scar tissue underneath acted as an anvil. Something would have to be done (and would be, later on) but meanwhile Henry went about his usual routine, training in the gym above the *Thomas à Becket*, downing his unique cocktail and lunching in the West End, as Wicks proudly paraded his boy about.

On 24 February 1964 he had his third and final encounter with Brian London. Defending his British title was one thing, but there was a second outright Lonsdale belt at stake, too, as well as the European title, which had fallen vacant on the retirement of Ingemar Johansson. The fight was hard but nowhere near as remorseless as their previous effort. The two men were actually on much better terms than they had been before Henry had both firmly satisfied Cooper family honour in 1959 and seized the title for the first time. Henry won on points after a tiring but not particularly punishing 15 rounds. At one stage the crowd even slow hand-clapped; they were looking for the sort of fire-works that had lit up the Wembley football arena against Clay but it was simply not to be. Happily, the left eyebrow repair remained more or less intact this time.

An example of the high-handedness of the Board of Control had popped up literally minutes before the fight with London. Quite arbi-trarily it had been decided, but not announced, that the amount of protective tape a boxer wears under the glove would be more than halved. This was dangerous for two reasons. Firstly, when heavy-weights hit each other – and you have to be there to grasp the sheer power behind the punches – the impact of the blow will serve to spread the knuckle laterally and invariably damage the joint. Bursitis is often the result. Secondly, the risk to the opponent is correspond-ingly increased. When Holland saw the amount of tape provided he protested and Wicks backed him up, as did Harry Levene, for whom the cancellation of the fight meant financial disaster. Quite calmly, the Board of Control officials, Onslow Fane and Teddy Waltham, reversed the decision and issued Holland with more tape. It wasn't enough, as it transpired, as Henry damaged his left hand on London's head during the fight.

But, despite the disappointment of the Clay fight and the irritating behaviour of the Board of Control, Henry was now as close to the top of the tree in Europe as he could be. There was trouble in store, however, but it came not from the British regulators this time but the European Boxing Union (EBU). Henry had been challenged for the European title by the hefty Karl Mildenberger and the fight was arranged for 9 September 1964.

The fight was actually scheduled to take place in Germany because neither Levene nor Solomons was prepared to promote a fight with a German boxer at that time and the simple truth was that, as a result of the British promoters' reluctance, their German counterparts invariably bid less, despite the fact that the challenger was a countryman of theirs. Even though it was a mandatory defence, Henry would still have to pay Wicks his 25 per cent but now out of a much smaller pie. He was now commanding at least £20,000 a fight at home, whereas his share of any European championship purse would be less than half that.

But a few weeks before the fight Henry's left elbow started to give him trouble and the two specialists he consulted advised a fortnight's complete rest. Obviously a boxer in training for a fight simply cannot rest and, therefore, Wicks requested that the fight be postponed. Unsurprisingly, the EBU refused and Henry was unceremoniously stripped of the title he had won from London. He used the time to do as the specialists had ordered.

Unwisely, Henry accepted a fight as a late substitute in a match against Roger Rischer at the Albert Hall in November. It was a match hastily arranged by Mike Barrett. The main event had been originally intended to be a lightweight fight but Dave Charnley, who was a very big draw indeed, was unwell. Henry, still smarting from the EBU's decision, only had a fortnight's notice for the match. Winter training was never his particularly strong point and he paid the price for his hasty preparation. 'If anyone asks me which fight of my career I want to remember least,' he recalls, 'then this was it.'

Roger 'The Dodger' Rischer, a black Californian, was experienced, crafty and crude. He even managed to put Henry on the canvas twice in the eighth round. It was a complete mismatch of styles and was not only a particularly tedious fight but did no good to Henry's reputation. He lost (and clearly) on points; the referee was Harry Gibbs. Henry's behaviour after the fight was revealing. Interviewed on television he was asked if he agreed with the verdict, and the public waited for the embarrassment of boxing's traditional 'we-wuz-robbed' argument. Of course, they didn't get it. 'Oh yes,' said Henry, apparently relaxed, 'he was well on top.'

Henry, despite his frankness with the press, was rather lowered by the outcome of the Rischer fight as well as the behaviour of the EBU, and Albina saw her opportunity to suggest that he might consider retiring. This was, as she told me, less than wise: 'I did ask him to quit … I remember when Henry was very disillusioned. He told Jim Wicks that I wanted him to stop. Mr. Wicks rang: "Listen, you just look after your house and leave the business to us." I was quite clear about that message – you mind your Ps and Qs and get on with your work.'

'Woman, mind your house, woman, mind your place,' were the clear and perhaps even slightly sinister messages. She refers to Wicks in that rather formal way not, I must point out, because he exercises any particular influence over her even from beyond the grave, but rather more because she has innate Italian courtesy. She never asked Henry to retire again. When he finally did, she felt quite reborn.

Albina was never part of boxing, had never yet even seen a fight, and the Coopers as a couple did not, as a rule, socialize with other fighters. 'I could never really became close or friendly with another boxer's wife,' she says. 'I've never mixed with them. It's such a cold sport. I don't feel there was ever any warmth it. You can't get close to someone whose husband is going to fight yours.'

Likewise, Henry found it quite difficult to spend leisure time with anyone he might have to hit. Retired fighters were different, of course, because they had a wisdom about them that a working boxer always finds valuable, and the ex-boxer is usually keen to impart, but dinner with Brian London, even after their reconciliation? No.

So, although the Rischer fight was an embarrassing error, both before and during, that winter brought an interesting approach from the Nation of Islam. The subject was a potential rematch between Henry and Muhammad Ali, as the world champion now styled himself. The caller was Malcolm X, displaying that same naivety that would ensure that he was dead by the end of February 1965. He was, despite the avowed hostility of the Nation of Islam to boxing, actually attempting to negotiate a fight.

Wicks was unmoved. He agreed to a meeting, which took place in Marylebone, but nothing came of it. It was clear to Wicks that Malcolm X knew little of boxing or its commercial imperatives so blandly, but with no particular sense of irony, he referred him to Harry Levene.

Malcolm X had, until the previous year, been a close friend and associate of Muhammad Ali, but was so no longer, as a power struggle for the soul of the American Black Muslim movement had forced Ali into making choices between Malcolm and the spiritual leader of the movement, Elijah Muhammad. The two men were at loggerheads; Malcolm X had realized that some of the tenets of the movement were frankly absurd and attractive to only the most gullible. Stating this would cost him his life. He was assassinated on 21 February 1965 on the orders of Elijah Muhammad.

Interestingly, when the Cooper/Ali rematch did take place in 1966, Wicks received a request for a commission from the Nation; again, he referred them to Levene and that, predictably enough, was that.

Of course, Henry was extremely interested in a rematch with the world champion. He had proved, the vulnerability of his eyebrows apart, that given the right circumstances he had Ali's measure but meanwhile there were titles to defend and a living to make; clearly the two activities did not necessarily coincide. Wicks, sticking to his principle of rejecting 'ugly' fighters, turned down a request for Henry to defend his Empire title against that rough handful, George Chuvalo, in Toronto. The reason was actually money for the purse offered by the

Canadian promoter was a paltry £8,000. 'Jim would never let me take my coat off for less than £20,000,' says Henry. 'After all, I could fight anywhere for nothing.'

There was a persistent buzz of interest in a return fight with Ali that died down rather rapidly in the backwash created by the new champion's second defeat of Liston, the implication being clear that Liston had taken a dive, or 'swallowed it'. Rumours grew about a deal between the Nation of Islam and the Mafia, for example, and it was this fight, which took place at the obscure location of Lewiston, Maine, on 25 May 1965, that put paid to the established convention of an automatic rematch between any fighter and the man who had deposed him. In future, such rematches were to be a matter of pure negotiation.

Of the six fights Henry fought after losing to Rischer only one was of any importance: the defence of the British and Empire title against Johnny Prescott. Previously he had put away two Americans, Dick Wipperman in round five at the Royal Albert Hall, followed by Chip Johnson at a match at the Civic Hall in Wolverhampton. The Johnson fight offered some needle for Henry, as it was this fighter who had effectively ended George's career in the ring by inflicting a huge cut on his eyebrow. After losing to Johnson, George had, in fact, announced his retirement and chose to fall back on the experience he had gained with Reg Reynolds and build up his own plastering business, which was to prosper.

Rather as his first fight with Brian London had shown, the way to rouse Henry to heights of aggression normally unseen was for his opponent to have beaten his brother. Johnson was unwise enough to announce to the press that he would take care of Henry as he had taken care of George and seize his rightful place in the world rankings. Henry, of course, was informed of this:

> The revenge angle was being played up pretty big, and as far as I was concerned quite legitimately. It was one I wanted to win above most. As it turned out, I didn't have to wait long. Suddenly he gave me an opening in the first round – Wallop! It was a good left hook, his legs started to quiver and he went down.

As George returned to the plastering trade, Henry was diversifying and, with hindsight, this was probably an error. He had met, while on holiday in Las Palmas, a businessman, coincidentally named Harry Cooper, who owned a greengrocer's stall in Holloway market. It obviously paid but he was attempting to expand his enterprise to include a shop. He had thought that Wembley might be a good location and asked Henry's advice as a resident. Henry gave it, that it was a good location, and thought little more of the matter.

However, once back home in Wembley, the phone rang. It was Harry Cooper, with something of a hard-luck story; his business partner had, apparently backed out of the proposed transaction, leaving him dangling somewhat. Henry obliged with some funding and his name, and the business, 'Henry Cooper of Wembley' at 4 Ealing Road, Wembley, was duly established. It was to go well for a while, even though it seems fairly clear that it was something of an ambush.

*

Henry had encountered Johnny Prescott before, as a sparring partner at the *Thomas à Becket*. The young Midlander was very much the rising star. Danny Cornell's report of their curious encounter read:

> A largish crowd gathered to see them spar. They saw instead a one-sided war with Cooper in the role of destroyer. I have never seen him look meaner, and in the end, they had to stop it. I have often wondered about that day... it was one of the rare occasions when I didn't much admire Cooper. And judging by the look of him as he left the ring that day, I don't think he much admired himself.

It was an interesting aberration, this meanness, which seemed so untypical of Henry but so routine in other fighters and which surfaced at such inappropriate moments. A professional sparring partner is paid, and paid well, to be knocked over, but the Prescott episode was as much an exhibition as anything else, whereas Henry seemed to be determined to turn it into a full-blown fight, which was unusual behaviour by his standards. It all rather served to make him, unconsciously, a slightly enigmatic figure, despite his popularity.

The Prescott championship fight, promoted by Jack Solomons in partnership with Alex Griffiths, was a rather one-sided affair, the more so after Henry sustained a cut eye. Prescott was warned for 'dangerous use of the head' but the incident served to make Henry change up a gear, as he had learned to do in response to a bad cut. Basically he did to Prescott in the ring what he had already done to him above the *Thomas à Becket*: he hammered the challenger to the canvas with a left hook in round eight, and twice more in round ten, at which point Prescott's manager, George Biddles, who also managed another hopeful Midlander, Jack Bodell, threw in the towel. One more defence of the British title and Henry would break the national record of winning and holding no fewer than three Lonsdale belts.

Ex-marine Amos Johnson had fought Cassius Clay as an amateur and, indeed, had defeated him. Henry was scheduled to fight Johnson (no relation to Chip) on 19 October 1965 at Harry Levene's favoured venue, the Wembley Pool. Johnson had started his career as a southpaw and rather unusually 'converted' to the orthodox style of boxing. It showed a bit, too, as he had clearly not dropped all the habits of his previous approach, nor, indeed, some of the habits of the battlefield or bar-room. He hit Henry low in the first round, which dropped him, and his kidney punches, coupled with another low punch in the sixth, were probably illegal enough to disqualify him, had the referee not been Harry Gibbs, who controversially gave the decision to Johnson after the ten rounds were over.

Almost as if in compensation for that bruising encounter and its highly questionable outcome, emotional rescue was at hand – a classic *deus ex machina*. The Queen issued an invitation to Henry to lunch with her at Buckingham Palace. Jim Wicks, who had received an enquiring call from an equerry some days before, was initially nonplussed until the pasteboard flopped onto Henry's doormat in December; he had assumed that it was a practical joke.

But, of course, it wasn't. The esteem in which Henry was now held was bone-deep in the nation and cut across all levels of society like little else ever had since the days of the nineteenth-century heroes of the ring. But, for Henry, the knot of tension that emerged in his bowels on that December morning was quite as bad as that before any prizefight, for there was no institution, not even Jim Wicks, for which he had (or has) a more well-developed respect than the monarchy and in particular the Queen. In fact, in 1957 Henry had – semi-seriously – challenged John Grigg, the Tory polemicist, to a boxing bout in response to certain criticisms Grigg had made about the royal family. He meant it, too, and would have knocked him out in order to simply punish him. Wisely, Grigg declined Henry's offer.*

A month later, on 25 January , clearly energized by the encounter at Buckingham Palace, which had quite charmed him, as well as confirming to him that he was indeed fighting for his country, he took on Hubert Hilton, a truck driver from Long Island, NY. Hilton was at the time ranked well up in the top ten contenders for a crack at Ali and had also achieved something of a reputation as a basketball star. He had also stopped both of George Biddles's great hopes, Bodell and Prescott. He had never even been knocked down, let alone knocked out. Until now.

Henry was quite merciless. The speed with which he dispatched his opponent, by introducing him to the left hook in round two, was quite outside Hilton's experience. As he retreated to his corner, clearly stunned and in the middle of the round, the referee, Bill Williams, simply took one look at him and stopped the fight.

But stopping Hilton was not Henry's fastest career victory; that was actually coming next, and he savoured the prospect of it. The victim was Jefferson Davis, from Mobile, Alabama. Like Hilton, he also had never actually been knocked out in 35 professional fights and had gone the distance with both Karl Mildenberger and Ernie Terrell. He had, more significantly, also beaten George Cooper in seven rounds (another cut) on a previous visit to the UK in October 1963 and Henry was rather tired of his pre-fight pronouncements that he, too, was going for 'the double.' The word had clearly not gone out that

---

* Although this episode is cited in Grigg's obituary – he died in 2001 – Henry does not recall it. It is quite likely that he may have said something privately and Wicks, seeing an opportunity, spun the tale out of all proportion.

defeating George 'Jim' Cooper would not necessarily put luck in a boxer's corner if he ever met his brother. Henry went after Davis on a simple search and destroy mission, just as he had with London and Johnson. He found him quickly and dispatched him even faster.

The fight lasted exactly 100 seconds and was very similar in nature to the Johnson fight. After a minute and a half the Alabama fighter was unwise enough to leave a gap in his defence and Henry as ever did not need prompting; he lashed out with the left and Davis slumped to the canvas for a full count.

While these minor but pleasing defeats of a succession of American fighters had been going on, Wicks had been in negotiation with Arthur Grafton, the attorney in Louisville who took care of contracts for the syndicate who still supported Ali. The management and pro-motional contracts they had with their fighter actually expired at the end of the year and they knew that he would fall into the clutches of the Nation of Islam, which was something they were keen to avoid. They had all enjoyed a huge return on their tax-deductible $3,000 per annum and, it must be said, they had enjoyed the experience, however much they were suspicious about the motivations of Elijah Muhammad. They were also fond of their boy, despite his frequently odd behaviour, which was often the result of Elijah's son Herbert whispering in Ali's ear.

Wicks had already put out some feelers to the non-boxing com-munity, which rather suggests that he had ambitions to stage this one himself, independent from either Levene or Solomons. He certainly approached Leslie Grade, who quite saw the commercial value in a Brit fighting for the world title on his home territory, but Grade was clearly a man who knew his limitations, and he passed.

As he often did, Wicks handled the purse negotiations himself. He had always preferred to act as his own matchmaker rather than use Harry Levene's own man, Mickey Duff. The two men had developed a profound dislike of each other, on Duff's part because there was no aspect of the business of boxing where his knowledge outstripped that of Wicks, and on Wicks's part because Duff did not necessarily always seem to understand that fact. To Wicks, Duff may have merely appeared to be just another flashy bagman for the promotion industry.

Very few men ever managed to put one over on Jim Wicks and he was not about to let Mickey Duff even try.

But the negotiations, when they took place, brought the full weight of Harry Levene's extended organization into play and it became clear that for Henry this would be a very big payday indeed. The fight was scheduled for 21 May 1966 and would take place not at Levene's favoured locale at Wembley but at Highbury Stadium, home of Arsenal football ground. It was the biggest event Levene had ever handled. He was, for events of this type, in partnership with *Viewsport*, the company created by Jarvis Astaire in order to exploit both satellite and closed circuit coverage. The arrangement enabled Levene to offer realistic guarantees to both the fighters and the hosts, Arsenal, who had cheerfully undercut the price of £25,000 offered by Wembley. Henry's guarantee was £50,000, Ali's £100,000, reflecting the fact that the last world heavyweight championship bout held in Britain had been in 1908. The last Brit to actually win it had been Bob Fitzsimmons, in 1897, so the significance of this event was lost on no one.

Naturally, this was something of a media frenzy, assisted by every ounce of spin the promoters and Wicks could muster. There was, it was felt, a serious chance that Henry might pull it off; he was clearly at the top of his form, as he had demonstrated against the four Americans he had beaten in the previous calendar year. The hook that had dropped Ali in 1963 was clearly as strong, or even stronger, three years on.

The popularity of this fight was such that the cash value of the ticket sales actually outstripped those for the Wembley World Cup Final of 30 July of that year. Arsenal's stadium would be filled to its 55,000 capacity and even Albina consented, somewhat reluctantly, to attend. It would be the first and last fight she ever saw. But even she conceded that her husband deserved her support – this was, after all, the world heavyweight championship.

The distance Henry had travelled since those days spent sparring with rolled football socks on the Bellingham Estate was vast, almost immeasurable; after two serious career dips, which had triggered such serious self-doubts, here he was, about to fight for what was, despite the widespread moral opposition to it, the greatest prize in individual sport. Even boxing's most ardent opponents, apart from Summerskill, found themselves well able to put aside their moral scruples as they settled down to hear it on the radio, for it would only be screened in certain selected cinemas. This single fact caused a small but fairly public debate: was it fair that such an important fight should be only available to those who could afford it? The government was keen to be seen to promote the interests of 'the ordinary viewer' and a token round-table conference was held, hosted by Anthony Wedgwood Benn, to which all interested commercial parties were invited. Levene and Astaire pointed out that without factoring in the cash value of all the various ancillary rights, the title fight could simply not take place in Britain at all. After a protest for the record, the government turned its attention to other things, notably the World Cup Final.

Since the retirement of Stirling Moss in 1962 Henry had probably become the country's most well-respected sporting figure (although Jim Clark, of course, had come up fast) and it was a status all agreed he had earned. He was probably as important to sports fans in Britain as the entire England football team and as such a popular hero he had his political uses; the issue over his fans' access to the fight was a clear opportunity to generate some useful brownie points with the electorate.

*

Training for his promising encounter with Muhammad Ali was no different from any other preparation Henry had made before. The team stayed at the *Duchess of Edinburgh* in Welling, in Kent, where Henry, accompanied by George, did his early morning roadwork, whereupon, after a shower and a rest, they drove up the Old Kent Road, through Grandfather George's old stamping ground, to the *Thomas à Becket* for midday sparring.

Henry had always eaten a high protein diet, albeit in rather more agreeable circumstances than many. The culinary rituals established by Wicks did not change particularly, partly for reasons of familiarity, partly for reasons of publicity. It was important to maintain a high public profile, which in turn demonstrated a higher level of confidence.

So a regular intake of medium-rare grilled steaks, potatoes and green salad (no onions, they can cause burping) washed down with half a bottle of Fleurie were the order of the day at Simpson's, *osso bucco* or veal escalope at Peter Mario's, or some predictably exotic piscine confection at Sheekey's, with the traditional Krug to go with it. Only in the last week did the diet become spartan; any sensible boxer, like any sensible racing driver, does his stuff on an empty stomach, for obvious physiological reasons. 'It was important to be totally cleaned out,' recalls Henry now.

He had learned this painful lesson very early in his amateur career, when he had innocently downed a huge portion of Lily's bread pudding before a fight, with predictably disastrous results. 'You can't fight on an empty stomach,' she'd advised. Since that early fiasco he had learned that you have to do exactly that, and not just for speed, either. A full stomach is easily damaged.

Despite the importance of this fight, the rituals of training were unaltered. For a man who enjoyed his creature comforts as much as many and more than most, it was the usual grind; he was only able to talk to his wife on the phone. 'Obviously, if there was anything wrong at home, or a kiddie was sick, I couldn't tell him anything about it, it would only make him worry,' she recalls. 'If Henry Marco had whooping cough or something else, I'd just have to cope with it.'

Henry's experience was very different of course: 'Training camps are supposed to make you mean, by keeping you away from your wife. It's not to do with the sex or anything like that, that never did anyone any harm, it's just that away from the wife and family, you get mean.'

Wicks's deliberate policy, honed to perfection over the years, of dropping deliberately irritating remarks that were purely designed to nark, was another method of raising the volatile temperature, as Henry remembers only too well: 'They would prod me on one or two little things to see me snap and lose my temper. Then they knew I was coming to my peak. I'm a very easy-going guy normally, but after four or five weeks of training Jim didn't have to say much, just be a little argumentative, perhaps, and I'd bite his head off.'

The opposing camp was much less vociferous than they had been three years before. The Muhammad Ali he was about to face was no longer the comical but likeable braggart – by contrast Ali was now a rather serious and tense young man (although still very handsome). Thanks to the attentions and priorities of the Nation of Islam he had, lost much of the bounce that had previously made him such a tolerated figure of fun. Under its tenets, he was supposed to behave himself. Of course, he had proved much – two defeats of Liston, despite the controversy of the second one, had made him a hero – but much of that glory had been offset by a truly brutal and unnecessary humiliation (entirely at the behest of the Nation) of Floyd Patterson the previous November, which had done much to drop his popularity quite off the chart. Patterson, who was widely liked by the establishment, had been unwise enough to ridicule his name change and Ali had punished him cruelly for it, torturing the insecure veteran (but without knocking him out) for 12 rounds, until the scandalized referee finally stopped the fight. It was a stunt Muhammad Ali would pull again within the year against Ernie Terrell, again under instructions from his new church. Ali, against a black opponent, could call upon vast reserves of subliminal malice via the Nation of Islam, but against Henry Cooper, Catholic nice guy, this was worth less than dust. Despite the fact that Ali was accompanied almost everywhere by a coterie of sinister-looking Black Muslims, the movement held little credibility in London.

And Henry already knew, instinctively, how to defuse this vaguely threatening situation. At midday, the time of the weigh-in at the Odeon, Leicester Square, the two men faced each other. This time Henry wore no boots containing any ballast but decided to adopt a trick taught him by Max Baer, who had lightened his weigh-in before he fought Primo Carnera in 1934 by plucking hairs from the Italian giant's chest while intoning 'He loves me – he loves me not.'

Unfortunately, Ali was not particularly hirsute, as Henry remembers: 'I said, "Oh, look, he's a man all right, he's got a hair on his chest." And I gave it a tweak. It brought the house down.' Ali himself remained unusually impassive.

Ali's long-suffering white Louisville backers, the same syndicate that had supported him since he turned professional, were genuinely lowered at the prospect of the end of their relationship with him. The men could merely look on with nervous resignation. All this would end soon enough in any case; they sincerely prayed now that it would not end at Highbury. Despite his adopted (and clearly feigned) radicalism, they all rather liked him.

On the evening of the fight, the quiet sober routines of the previous five weeks' training were clearly over. A Rolls-Royce, theirs for the day, and which had taken him to the weigh-in, was courtesy of a local car hire firm. It arrived at the *Duchess of Edinburgh* to convey Henry, George, Holland and Wicks up to Highbury. The firm had been generous: no bill if he won, a 50 per cent discount if he didn't. There was no plan for an option C – all involved knew full well that this fight would be most unlikely to end in a draw.

The police escort which accompanied the Rolls into the stadium car park was something new as well. This was clearly building into quite an emotional occasion as the giant collective sympathy of the crowd started to build. Henry takes up the story of the most significant night of his career:

I was in the main Arsenal dressing room and Ali was in the bum's room. I hadn't seen anything of him or his entourage and hadn't even seen the arena. But I could hear the roar of the crowd, and Jim and George went out to have a dekko. 'Looks marvellous,' they reported, 'a wonderful crowd.'

While I started to change, Jim Wicks opened the telegrams. There were all the regulars, all the restaurants I visited regularly, like Simpson's and Sheekey's. Richard Burton and Elizabeth Taylor, Donald Houston, they were all wishing me well. Jim would never let me open the telegrams or letters on the night because you do get the cranks.

… Danny meanwhile cut the tapes provided by the Board of Control steward. We would need nine three and a half inch strips to go across the hand, then a long piece of about eight inches which he would cut into three to go between the fingers. No two boxers tape the same way. Taping is not to make your hand any harder so that you can knock your opponent out more easily, but to protect your hand …That night, in the

Highbury dressing room, I taped as I had always done – I put the plaster against my skin in cross fashion, three slanting across the knuckles one way and three the other. Then I band- aged around the thumb and hand just below the knuckle. I put three strips through the fingers and the tape I had left I bound around to keep it all in and cover the knuckles. The steward stamped the hands with an ink stamp, and after that you couldn't add any more.

This was a ritual Henry had been through 44 times before and he performed it exactly as he had always done. But this was a big fight, with his wife in the audience for the first time:

Taped in my left boot were religious medallions which people who meant a lot had given me. One was from Albina. Another was from her aunt, Maria Rizzi. I would always put them under the tapes which I put under the bootlaces to stop them coming undone. Last of all, I put my shorts on, and then I started warming up.

I always said a little prayer before I left the dressing room, and made the sign of the cross. I didn't say, 'Please let me win,' it was just asking God to watch over me and keep me safe, thinking really of the family. And you asked that you would be able to do your best and put up a good performance.

As the warm-up fights came and went outside, the tension built, and the last well-wishers and visitors came and went – old schoolfriends, Harry Levene, Onslow Fane, Teddy Waltham. Finally, the referee, George Smith: it was a familiar litany, elements of which would be repeated in the ring before the opening bell:

I want a clean fight. When I say break, I want a clean break. I want both of you to take a step backwards. I want no rabbit- punching. You must punch correctly with the knuckle of the glove. I won't be giving points if you're slapping. If one man goes down the other must go into a neutral corner, and I won't start counting until you're there. All the best, and may the best man win.

It had been almost exactly a century since the Queensberry Rules had been written by Chambers and those few words uttered by Smith that evening say more about the long-term objectives which had been behind them than any essay on the subject ever could. It was time ...

The first thing that struck Henry, apart from the size of the crowd, was the size of the ring. Ali had wisely insisted upon the largest allowable, twenty feet square, which Levene had grudgingly financed as a one-off. It was huge. 'It seemed to take ten minutes just to arrive at the centre of it,' says Henry. 'You could have had three fights in there at the same time.' And if the huge emotional tug generated by the collective goodwill of the crowd hadn't quite unmanned him, then the National Anthem nearly did: 'As I stood there, for the first time I can remember in the ring, I could feel a lump in my throat.'

His three biggest fans, the Welsh musketeers, Richard Burton, Donald Houston and Stanley Baker were all ringside, along with half the West End underworld and, of course, his family, including a quite terrified Albina. She had not been looking forward to this and was only present as an act of solidarity. 'I didn't really see any of it,' she says. 'I had my face buried in the programme for the whole time; I just couldn't bear to watch.'

It would not be a pretty sight, in fact. It was not entirely a rerun of the previous encounter – if anything, Henry looked stronger than he had before, whereas Ali, no doubt remembering his near humiliation in 1963, appeared reluctant to engage. He used the giant space available to him to dance away from Henry, who pursued his man relentlessly, trying to set Ali up for the left hook, and Ali clearly knew it. At the first sign of trouble when he closed in, though, Henry found himself enveloped in a vice-like bear hug, which allowed little rough and ready 'inside work'. As soon as Smith called for the break, Ali would leap back to avoid the left he clearly feared would pursue him like a sidewinder. By the end of round five, Henry was marginally ahead on points but he also realized that Ali, or at least Dundee, had learned a thing or two. The danger remained, though, from those long flicking jabs which could do enormous damage to Henry's eyebrows. He had, for five rounds, managed more or less to control his territory and avoid trouble. He had hit more than he had been hit and yet neither boxer had really inflicted any damage on the other.

Then, early in the sixth, the bad thing happened – 'the disappointment of my life' as Henry later recalled it. Ali let go a right hand punch, which he shortened into a slashing, chopping blow, which landed above Henry's left eyebrow. Immediately, Henry realized he was in trouble. There was no pain, merely a stinging sensation followed by numbness, but he could feel the blood pouring down the entire left side of his body. It would not be long before he would be unable to see. Tommy Smith, who had stood by, quite amazed, when Henry had demolished Jefferson Davis so comprehensively, and may well have been looking for more of the same here, called a halt for a quick inspection then dubiously said, 'box on'. But after another frenetic assault by Ali on the eye, he finally stopped the fight.

This was a huge deep cut, worse than he had ever experienced, and right down to the bone. So bad was it that the Board of Control doctor counselled no immediate treatment but suggested plastic surgery as soon as possible. He wrote down the telephone number of Guy's Hospital and gave it to Wicks. After the unique build-up to this fight, with all the emotional goodwill that had drenched Henry as thoroughly as the cut had, there was very little left to say. He had done his best, and had, in the opinion of many, out-boxed and even out-psyched his man, but against those damaging jabs, relatively painless though they were, he had little defence once he was cut.

The surgery took place the very next day, after Henry had spent a quiet and gloomy night at home. The objective was to excise old, encysted scar tissue, which had developed under the surface, and then repair both the outer and inner layers of the cut, the inner layer being treated with tiny, almost invisible stitches, which would dissolve of their own accord. In this way the eyebrow would in all probability be stronger even than when it was new; certainly, that world championship fight was the last encounter that Henry would lose to a cut eye, which made him regret that he had not sought this course of action before, although his next fight would provide an experience of rather deeper impact.

CHAPTER TEN

Finally, Floyd Patterson

'To travel hopefully is a better thing than to arrive...'
ROBERT LOUIS STEVENSON, *Virginibus Pueresque*, (1881).

FLOYD PATTERSON was by any measure an unusual and interesting man. He was the first heavyweight champion to lose a world title and then win it back. He was also the youngest heavyweight champion ever, until the arrival of Mike Tyson more than 25 years later. Patterson had first wrested the title from a doddering Archie Moore in 1956, a fight that was only possible upon the retirement of Rocky Marciano, and he won it with no particular difficulty: Patterson knocked Moore out in the fifth round. It was and is said that Moore had 'taken a dive' against Marciano in their last fight together but Moore's loss to Patterson triggered the end of his heavyweight career, although he remained light heavyweight champion, his proper weight, until 1961.

It was almost as if Patterson could scarcely believe his own luck. Always a man short on self-confidence, he had been discovered and trained by that Svengali of the boxing world, Cus d'Amato, who would, many years later, also discover little Mike Tyson as a confused, abused and tearful teenager. Patterson had, embarrassingly, lost his title to Ingemar Johansson, who had stopped him quite luckily in June 1959, and he had recovered it a year later by knocking Johansson out. He had defended it twice more, once more against Johansson and then against Tom McNeeley, before being destroyed twice in quick succession by Liston.

Those two defeats by Liston, which were followed by that brutal humiliation at the hands of Ali in November 1965, which had ruined any popular following enjoyed by the champ, had not done anything to assist his already atrophied sense of self-regard. Essential pieces of kit for Patterson as he prepared for a fight included a hat, as well as dark glasses and a false beard. One of the first details he always needed to know – really needed to know – at any venue which was new to him was the direction of the exit, so total was his sense of humiliation at even the prospect of defeat. Patterson was a man with the foetid breath of his Bedford–Stuyvesant origins forever blowing on the back of his neck. Failure, for Patterson, would consign him back from whence he had come, just another young black man from a crowded cold-water walk-up and cursed forever by a criminal record. Such was Patterson's innate humility that the prospect of loss clearly terrified him. Such insecure fighters were as putty in the hands of subtle motivators like d'Amato, and under certain circumstances they would pay a price for that, not least a financial one. In Patterson's case, so badly did he even take the prospect of defeat that, as we have seen, d'Amato had been, even by the extreme standards of the heavyweight division, ludicrously over-protective of his fighter, and not merely to keep him out of the clutches of the forces of darkness as he identified them.

But despite his psychological handicaps and nervous disposition, Floyd Patterson had at his disposal a bewildering arsenal of punches, manoeuvres and combinations thereof – a great coffer of imaginative alternatives to which only he and d'Amato had the keys. They all had codes, too; d'Amato would shout them out from the corner and Patterson would obediently deliver them. One of his most dangerous weapons, if only because of its weird unpredictability, was the 'kanga-roo', a whirling, leaping confection, really rather more African than Australian, which surprised his opponents as often as it stunned them. The Cooper left hook was a relatively simple and straightforward thing by comparison. But Patterson also had extraordinarily fast hands, very much faster than Muhammad Ali's, although Ali's speed around the ring, his main means of defence, was quicker. Patterson seemed to still be operating at the same extraordinary fast-forward rate that had made him stand out at Helsinki in 1952, over a dozen years before. Henry remembers, with feeling: 'God, he was quick; he didn't move around as fast as Ali did, but his hand speed was just ridiculous. He was a fantas-tic puncher, hard and fast. He and Cus d'Amato worked by numbers, and you just didn't know which one was coming up next.'

Jim Wicks was a little wary of matching Patterson with Henry, the main reason being not that Patterson was particularly dangerous, but that Henry's left elbow was giving him more and more trouble now. Because Henry had a slight height advantage, he would have to punch downwards, which would put an unnatural strain on the elbow joint – every seriously good punch has something of the uppercut about it, otherwise the strength in a fighter's legs becomes irrelevant. The elbow problem remained a well-kept secret as there were plenty of boxers who knew very well indeed how to take advantage of such a weakness (not that Patterson would be one of them – he was simply too polite) but this was also the reason why Henry's virtually pristine right had also started to come more to the fore. Pleasingly, it was rather better than he thought it was, although the sudden shift in polarity went quite against all his instincts. God forbid he should ever contemplate actually leading with it: the inexperienced spectator might even mistake him for a southpaw.

The fight was generally forecast to be a trade-off between two potential weaknesses: Henry's eyebrows against Patterson's rather suspect jaw, a target that Johansson had first identified. Donald Saunders said: 'This is a fight that should have taken place seven years ago,' forgetting perhaps that in 1959, while defeating Patterson may have yielded the world championship to the winner, had anyone been able to get to him, the price to pay for that would be facing Sonny Liston, the most feared heavyweight ever.

The Patterson fight – actually the American's British ring debut – was arranged for 20 September 1966 at the Empire Pool, Wembley, and initially it seemed as if Henry might even be in the ascendant. For two rounds he attacked with remarkable aggression, trying hard to connect with Patterson's only known (physically at least) weak point, his jaw. But by the third round, Patterson had found his pace and started to retaliate with his famous combination punch flurries. He caught Henry full in the face at the end of the round and put him down for a short count but appeared to have done no serious damage. Henry recalled later: 'I tried to fight him as I did Ali. Patterson was a counter-puncher … Like a fool I took the fight to him, and though I did hurt him once or twice to the body, I didn't connect to the chin.'

And in round four, Henry was on the receiving end of what he still claims was the finest punch he ever took. It came after a dazzling left/right combination to the face put him down again, and he wisely took a count of nine, giving a confident nod to his corner, but when he rose, Patterson let rip with another with right/left, which Henry, still according to some observers not fully recovered from the knock-down, simply didn't see coming. 'Suddenly, the lights went out,' says Henry. 'He had a hell of a good punch, Patterson.'

Typically, Floyd Patterson helped a dazed Henry to his feet and cradled him back to his corner, all the while consoling the loser. Spectators were moved: 'Floyd wanted to help him to his feet and later cuddled him, and tried to console him,' wrote the *Boxing News*, sadly. Joe Louis, seated ringside, quietly nodded his approval as Henry dropped, briefly but totally disconnected from the world. This was complete anaesthesia. There was no pain.

And no ignominy, either. There was no shame in losing to a fighter of the quality of Floyd Patterson; indeed, Henry almost looked upon it as a privilege and, despite the murmur of unease, that perhaps he was carrying on a little past his sell-by date, he was and is unrepentant:

> If Ali and Patterson had been mugs, then I wouldn't have needed the press to tell me to go. But one was a world champion and the other an ex-world champion, and there was no disgrace in losing to either. I had the know-how and the knowledge to beat any of the youngsters in this country or Europe, so what was wrong in employing it?

There was another little matter, of course, that of the prospect of a third permanent Lonsdale belt, which, if it was not necessarily as important as a world, or even European title, would only require two more defences of his British one after his win against Prescott. One owned belt was a fine thing, two were remarkable, but three would be unique. He properly felt that he could deal with the obvious contenders for the British title (and he was right) and so retirement at this stage would have been both unnecessary and even hasty. More importantly, he wanted to take this decision himself. Henry liked the press but he was fully aware of their need to build a story, and Wicks, his conduit with Fleet Street, was frankly running out of them.

Henry was certainly to prove his point against Jack Bodell in June but only after he had delivered a curiously lacklustre performance against another American, Boston Jacobs, in April, shortly after his old opponent Zora Folley finally had his long awaited crack at the world title and Ali had knocked him out. Jacobs gave a good account of himself on the night and appeared to be completely unmoved by Henry's reputation as a puncher. Henry won on points but it was a fight he should have won inside the distance. One reason may have been that he was well above his fighting weight again and nudging 14 stone, which always made him sluggish, and might have betrayed the long layoff he'd had, but whatever, it was certainly an off day. The news that Albina was expecting another child was a morale-booster, though, but on the other hand, it might well have been a natural distraction.

Jack Bodell, who enjoyed the very nineteenth-century soubriquet of the 'Swanlicote Swineherd', challenged Henry Cooper for his British and Empire titles at Wolverhampton Wanderers' home ground, Molyneaux, on 13 June 1967. Possibly the most ungainly boxer these islands have ever produced, he was also potentially a man who might cause the odd upset, mainly because he was a southpaw, which for a conventional boxer is rather like fighting a mirror image of oneself – right foot forward, leading with the right. Bodell was not at all a dirty fighter but on occasion he could look it, as if he was simply wired up differently from other men. An almost entirely left-handed man like Henry, when facing a southpaw, often has to resignedly rethink his game and either use the right hand or await opportunities if he wishes to avoid embarrassing accidents. Henry's philosophy, as we shall see, was to try to finish them quickly, but first size them up to avoid trouble. There was no question of even trying to look at ease. 'They always bring you down to their level,' says Henry, with rare derision. For a left-side boxer like Henry, southpaws were always hard work: 'You could never look good against them.'

Bodell plunged in during the opening round, using his weight advantage to work Henry onto the ropes, and even inflicting a modest measure of damage upon him. At 27, he had the advantage of age and weight but not, alas for him, subtlety. Henry spotted his weaknesses very quickly and saw the opportunity to use his left hook, over the top of Bodell's right, but only when the challenger swung it; it was a rare occasion of Henry Cooper uneconomically accepting two punches in order to land one but, he reasoned, if that is what is necessary, then so be it.

Nearly two minutes into the second round, he saw his chance and launched one of the longest left hooks of his career. It was of necessity a compromise of a punch, a hybrid; it sailed over the top of Bodell's right arm and shoulder and hit him on the jaw, after which point the whole matter became quite academic. Henry went after the dazed challenger, thumping him onto the ropes and chasing him around the ring. Obeying the received wisdom about facing southpaws, he even hit with the right a few times, at which point the referee, Ike Powell, saw that the game was clearly up. He stopped the fight, giving Henry his fastest yet championship victory.

Henry and Albina's second son, John Pietro, arrived on 5 August 1967, closely followed by yet another challenge for the British and Empire title, this time from Billy Walker, whose home turf was very close to the Cooper clan's first London base over a century before, in West Ham. Walker's brother George had fought (and fought very well) as a professional and Billy was an extremely promising, if rather inexperienced prospect. He had both youth and strength on his side but, as he later admitted with beguiling modesty, 'You need three things to be a great fighter: heart, a good chin and boxing ability. Unfortunately, I only had two out of three.'

*

In many ways Billy Walker was a product of the times. He was extremely telegenic and the thought persists that his career was pushed too far too fast for the sake of his appeal to a television audience. It was exactly the policy of so many unscrupulous managers over time, although this time the culprit was not Billy's manager (actually his brother George) but rather Harry Levene and his ally Jarvis Astaire, who had made a large investment in offering a contract to Walker and were quite keen to recover it as quickly as possible, which is why the encounter between Billy Walker and Henry Cooper was in reality something of a mismatch in Henry's favour (which takes nothing away from Walker's bravery). The fight took place at the Empire Pool, Wembley, on 7 November 1967. Billy Walker quipped a revealing aside before the fight: 'I reckon even my friends will be rooting for Henry.' They weren't, in fact.

Henry, having seen Walker in action as an amateur, knew that he was extremely tough and planned for a long fight. He was unlikely to knock his man down quickly – 'Billy had a very hard head.' – and so assumed that he would have to soften him up somewhat before producing the hammer. This is more or less what happened, although Walker gave an extremely good account of himself for the first three rounds, despite which he absorbed some serious punishment in the opener, and it was at the end of round five that a cut appeared on the challenger's eye. In the interval it was plain what was required: the faintly distasteful task of opening up the cut. 'You know what to do,' said Wicks, and Henry went in and did it; George Smith stepped in towards the end of round six and stopped the fight, to Walker's intense and visible disappointment. Henry's grip on his third Lonsdale belt was now complete and unassailable.

No one had ever done this before at any weight and Henry was starting to cost the Board of Control, who paid for the belts, rather a lot of money. Immediately, he announced that he would now challenge Karl Mildenberger for the European championship, which he had been forced to resign in September 1964. If he won, he would be back exactly where he had been four years before, albeit with an extra belt for his groaning trophy cabinet.

Harry Levene, perhaps having seen his investment in Billy Walker depreciate somewhat, overcame his scruples and agreed rather reluctantly to promote the fight at Wembley on 18 September 1968, which gave Henry fairly light duties in the ring that year; it was to be his only fight in 1968. Challengers were actually becoming few and far between, for the simple reason that he had beaten all the rated British heavyweights and many of his old adversaries were retiring. He was in the no-man's land between generations.

But he was busy. Wicks was in constant receipt of requests for Henry to make appearances, in television commercials, on chat shows and radio and TV commentary slots, and some of the sums of money involved were quite startling and, when all was said and done, less than arduous. It was perhaps the inevitable rehearsal for retirement, calls for which had rather receded with his defeat of the young and strong Billy Walker.

So, in between all these novel engagements, he maintained his fitness regime and enjoyed his new baby. He was relaxed, he had nothing to prove and he looked forward to taking back the title he felt was rightfully his. Mildenberger, of course, was the boxer he would have fought previously had he not been incapacitated and it became clear on the night that he had not necessarily improved as an opponent with the passing of time.

This was not a particularly inspiring fight, being characterized mainly by rule infringements, both in the ring and in Mildenberger's corner. It was a fight of clinches; after ten months out of the ring, Henry took a round and a half to settle down before belting Mildenberger hard 'on the break', while coming out of a clinch, which clearly troubled the champion, for while Henry was being warned for this sneakiness by the indignant Italian referee, Nello Barroveccio, poor Mildenberger simply fell over.

Unwisely, Mildenberger's seconds applied smelling salts quite liberally during the second interval, which suggests that Henry had actually hit him rather hard and that the champion might no longer be quite the master of his subject, but the use of the ammonia created a rare storm of protest from the BBBC officials, which rather begs the question: where they had been looking on the evening of the fight with Clay in 1963? There was indeed some uncertainty as to whether this fight was being held under British rules or European ones – it was a European title fight, but it was being held in London – and further confusion arose later on.

Mildenberger was in turn warned for 'careless use of the head' several times but Henry seemed untroubled; he put the champion down again in round seven and arguably the fight should have ended there, but just before the closing bell of round eight, Barroveccio stopped it, not because Mildenberger was unable to continue, but because he had clearly butted Henry, causing a rather nasty cut. Without hesitation, Mildenberger was disqualified. It was a stout piece of refereeing.

At first it had been assumed that Henry's victory was as a result of being injured while clearly in the lead, according to a new and rather baroque EBU regulation, but no great commotion erupted upon Mildenberger's disqualification. Obviously to win a fight in this way is not as satisfying as doing so in the traditional manner, but Henry was now British, Empire and European heavyweight champion again. He would be called upon to defend it within six months, and that process would not be a pleasant experience.

But, despite the pleasure of the European title, there was another nagging commercial worry. The grocery business had done rather well for some time but it was starting to take up an inordinate amount of time, almost to the exclusion of all else, yet it was now losing money. Henry had discovered that his partner, Harry Cooper, while a perfectly pleasant fellow, seemed quite happy for Henry to be doing the lion's share of the work. During some periods Henry would be in the shop all week, which made training and PR work almost impossible. Not only were the losses mounting, but he was also forced to forgo some lucrative television and promotional work, which made things infinitely worse. As he explains, he was reinforcing failure:

> I'd introduced Harry to the boxing crowd, which might have been a mistake, because frankly he started to behave a bit like Jack the lad; the business wasn't going well, and the creditors always seemed to be calling me about it rather than him. It cost me a lot of sleep. I paid some of the company's losses from my own account, but around Christmas 1968, I just decided to call it a day. I paid off the staff and pulled the shutters down. That was that."

The venture had cost him in the region of £10,000; in reality, given that he was putting tax-paid cash into it, it was considerably more. Couple that with the opportunity costs created by simply being there, and the little venture had proved to be a very costly exercise indeed.

But there was good news, too: Henry was awarded an OBE in the New Year's honours list. It was a signal honour and, while it was the cause of several butterflies in the Cooper household, an experience to cherish. Henry, dressed perfectly, courtesy of Moss Bros., describes it:

> It was marvellous … The Queen looked round straight away as my name was called and she smiled a wonderful smile as I walked towards her. She knew about my boxing, because at the time I'd been having the knee trouble and she asked me about it. I told her it was a lot better and that I was back in training and she said, 'It's marvellous to see you again.'

He would need the morale boost of his investiture, for scarcely a month later he was due to defend his newly won European title against the new challenger. It would be an evening to remember, and not at all for the right reasons.

CHAPTER ELEVEN

Endgames

'Southpaws should all be strangled at birth.'
SIR HENRY COOPER, K.S.G., O.B.E., (2002).

SIGNOR RINO TOMASI was an extremely successful promoter. Aged 35, 'handsome and personable', he was in many ways Italy's equivalent of Harry Levene, apart from the fact, of course, that he was both handsome and personable. Tomasi was particularly proud of his favoured venue, the *Palazzo dello Sport* in Rome; of the 23 European title fights, whether challenges or eliminators, that he had staged there at all weights, no Italian fighter had actually lost any of them. It was a trend he was committed to continue. Naturally, he had help.

The traditions of the Roman Colosseum were alive and well at the *Palazzo*; the place was virtually ruled by the heaving, braying mob of up to 18,000 Romans whose noise output was so intimidating that even the most determined of boxing referees could easily quail under its onslaught. The fact that so many of the Italian fighters who triumphed there would go on to humiliation at other more neutral venues was lost on no one. It was generally held that any Italian midget stood at least a chance of a title win in this place. It was a major asset to Italian boxing in a way that the Wembley Arena could never be.

It was at this highly partisan location, on the eve of the Ides of March 1969, that Henry Cooper, buoyed by his New Year's honours list OBE, was booked to defend his European title against the 'Axeman of Manerbio', Piero Tomasoni, a match to be refereed by Dutchman Ben Bril. This was to be a fight distinguished only by the minimalist elegance of the poster that announced it.

An overgrown welterweight, Tomasoni was a rough and dangerous southpaw fighter with a useful right hand but little finesse. He came from farming stock near Brescia. He was not a boxer in the sense that Henry was – he was a scrapper. He had beaten an unlucky Jack Bodell in three rounds, in one of the most inelegant fights that anyone could remember, and gone the distance with Karl Mildenberger, even knocking him over in the process. He had only been stopped twice in 44 fights, in fact, but, as we have seen, that can be a mere statistic. His style, as a relatively short man, was to fight from a crouching position, throwing out hard, swinging right hands with no particular concern as to their destination. In short, he was a little less than classy.

As a mildly concerned Donald Saunders, clearly familiar with the venue, pointed out: 'Although Mr. Bril is the most experienced, accomplished and impartial of Continental referees, I think Cooper would be wise not to waste time in settling the issue.'

Others agreed, including John Rodda, the boxing writer, who wrote two days before the fight:

No one, not even the promoter ... is putting this match forward as a classic. In fact, with a man of 6ft 2in who does almost all his fighting off the left flank against an opponent four inches shorter who relies on big swings, then all kinds of disasters could be imagined. But unravelling every possibility the strongest one is that after six or seven rounds, Italian courage, enthusiasm, perhaps even wildness will have been dampened by the Cooper left jab, and then the left hook should bring Cooper victory No. 38.

The relative size of the fighters' purses rather said it all; Henry was to receive £20,000, and Tomasoni £3,000. I remember watching the fight on television and being utterly appalled by it; it had the truly ghastly fascination of the road accident.

Despite the intimidating atmosphere, Henry was calm, chatting to his little entourage. When the time came to go into the ring, he simply nodded, saying, 'I got to go to work.' He slipped in his gumshield (which he would not need in this fight) and climbed up into the spotlights.

The Italian press were well aware that Henry was married to an Italian, and when she was interviewed by several of them at home,

Albina broke her habit of not commenting on what her husband did for a living and trenchantly expressed her hope that Henry would 'knock over Tomasoni in ten seconds', which he nearly did, catching him with a near perfect left hook late in the first round. The 'Axeman of Manerbio' took a count of eight, and clearly needed it. Commenting shortly after the fight, Henry remarked very charitably: '...in fairness to him, he may not have known too much of what happened later.'

The rest of the fight, only four more rounds, in fact (but I recall it seemed much longer), involved some of the most blatant fouls and rule infringements ever seen in the post-war ring at this level. The thuggish Tomasoni, squat, plodding, clearly outclassed and hunched like some grotesque *Nibelung* of mythology, launched a panicked flurry of the crudest body punches. Craftily waiting until Ben Bril was unsighted, he threw out a desperate right in the second round that caught Henry full in the balls; he collapsed in outraged agony and Bril blithely started the count, to the clearly audible delight of the crowd. Henry dragged himself to his feet at nine. It was only at the end of the third round that an enraged Jack Solomons, seated ringside, loudly pointed out to Bril what was going on. Bril promptly but nervously warned the Tomasoni corner during the break, to the clear disgust of the crowd. It is perhaps hard to believe it, but worse was to come.

In round four, Henry let rip with a honking left, which dropped his opponent again, but not until he had grabbed Henry and pulled him down to the canvas with him. As they scrambled up, Tomasoni lashed out with another low blow. This was not boxing, it bordered more on sexual assault. As Henry said: 'The fairground wasn't in it!'

This time a justifiably nervous but finally alert Bril saw the foul blow and issued a formal warning to the local hero, which was when the oranges started to rain down …

It was 9.15 in the evening and the crowd, aggressive and well lubricated, made their feelings quite clear. Fruit, paper cups, bread rolls, half-eaten salami – it all came cascading down into the ring, as Henry recalls: 'I wasn't so much worried by the food. I was just waiting for the backs of the seats to follow! In an arena like the *Palazzo*, with a balcony fifty feet up, they could knock you sparko. I was ready for a quick dive under the ring.'

He had already seen a distressed Peter Wilson of the *Daily Mirror* clobbered by a badly aimed blood orange the size of a grapefruit and nearly KO'd by it. Henry already knew rather more than he had ever wanted to about fruit and vegetables; disgustedly, he stepped gingerly around the ring, his bruised undercarriage aching, and kicked the debris back out under the bottom ropes. Round five was coming up; it was time to finish this nonsense and put an end to Signor Tomasi's proud record as a promoter as well as Tomasoni's challenge hopes. Without a clean knockout it was quite conceivable that if the farce continued he might even end up with a points loss or, even worse, a cut, not that Tomasoni had seriously attempted to even hit him in the face, being apparently more concerned at assuring that the Cooper family would not get any larger.

It didn't take Henry long, in fact; early in the fifth, he used his usually quiescent right for a short, extremely pissed-off uppercut to the Axeman's chin, which travelled, as I recall, a matter of four or five inches. This novelty punch, a complete surprise, set the dazed Tomasoni up for the ritual execution with the left. It was a mighty blow when it came. Henry hit him with every ounce of force he could muster and Tomasoni's feet left the floor and he slumped, his arms around Henry, probably unaware even of his own name. As Henry disdainfully shrugged him off and made for a neutral corner (if the *Palazzo* possessed such a thing), Tomasoni collapsed. He briefly struggled up on all fours before slumping down again and a relieved Bril counted him out. 'God, the so-and-so must have got my middle stump three or four times,' says Henry. 'It was a pleasure to see him drop.'

Having now seen at least some humiliation, the crowd calmed down a little and a decent cheer went up for Henry. Even the most partisan of them swiftly calculated that this was not a total loss for at least the winner had an Italian wife, and anyway, two other British boxers, Vic Andreeti and Brian Cartwright, were beaten by Italians that night. Other spectators, it must be said, had probably been embarrassed and disgusted by Tomasoni's tactics but they threw their assorted missiles just the same, in protest at his foul play. Of course, the effect on those below was indistinguishable.

Bril, attempting to claw back some shred of objective dignity, later stated proudly: 'Don't worry, Henry, if you hadn't got up in the fourth, I'd have disqualified him.' Perhaps justifiably, Henry was (and remains) sceptical.

Some of the press, ringside though they were, had been a little uncertain as to what they had seen of the foul punches. Wilson was probably still dazed but Neil Allen of *The Times* reported:

> As Cooper stood in the ring surrounded by photographers afterwards, I asked him how low the blows had been which had put him down …
>
> The European champion invited me to come to his dressing room and examine the protective cup which every boxer wears under his trunks. In the dressing room there was a horrified grasp as Cooper showed that a normally convex piece of sports equipment had become concave.

So cross was Henry that, no doubt egged on by the reporters, he took the bold step of holding up this usually extremely private boxer's appurtenance for the inspection of the television viewers back home in Blighty. I vividly recall that the sight of the still-steaming accessory certainly raised my grandmother's eyebrows (indeed, possibly her pulse and temperature) very high indeed, as Henry brandished the faintly disturbing and clearly unfamiliar object in front of the fascinated cameras. Energized, he pointed to the clear and obvious damage, while announcing to Europe: 'I don't care what anybody says – that was bloody low.' It was a seminal moment in television sporting history.

There was some flak here for Albina, though. Almost as soon as the fight was over (Lily had given her a slightly wincing blow by blow commentary) the Italian press were on the phone. When asked her opinion of what had taken place, she stated categorically: 'Piero Tomasoni should be ashamed to be an Italian.'

Unsurprisingly, her remarks were spun somewhat: 'Henry Cooper's wife ashamed to be born Italian,' raged back the headlines, which created some trouble in the village of Boccacci, near Parma, where her parents lived and farmed. It created trouble with Wicks, too, and he reiterated the importance of his previous message: 'I received another phone call from him, telling me to mind my business,' she recalled.

This had been an exhausting, painful and, despite its championship status, trivial fight, and it would be Henry's only one that year, as 1969 was the year of further controversy; the year when the British Board of Boxing Control proved that, although it was competent (most of the time), it was also politically naive and in thrall to other interests rather than being truly independent. It was to be a lowering experience for Henry, Jim Wicks and the millions of Cooper fans who, irrespective of their opinion of boxing, were coming to adore him.

At 34, Henry knew full well that his time was running out for another crack at the Big One, the world title. Since Muhammad Ali had been stripped of his own world title in April 1967, over his refusal to accept being drafted for the Vietnam War, the American heavyweight division had undergone yet another unseemly spasm over who should replace him. Naturally, because of the vast amount of money involved, there were several attempts to manage a result, the most persuasive having been the WBA, an organization that enjoyed the widest support (45 out of 50 US states), who announced their roster of eliminators. It did not include Sonny Liston, but perhaps that was fair enough – he had already by then been knocked out by his sparring partner, Leotis Martin, who was definitely not highly rated. Further, Joe Frazier refused to take part in The WBA contest, preferring to line up alongside the New York Athletic Commission, Norris's old fiefdom and their version of the title as represented by the World Boxing Council.

*

The WBA champion was announced to be Jimmy Ellis, Muhammad Ali's old friend and sparring partner. Of the two men, Ellis was clearly going to be the better match, and Henry challenged him, only to be told that the BBBC would not sanction the fight as a championship bout but merely an eliminator; they were firmly lined up behind the WBC.

Rather impulsively, Henry resigned his British heavyweight title in protest but the BBBC were quite unmoved. They had in all probability expected his retirement soon anyway and seemed not to care less.

A cynic might say that the BBBC had earned as much out of Henry as they were going to and there were other fighters on the way up. Joe Bugner, a strapping lad of 15 stone and only 19 years of age, had just won his fifteenth fight, for example, and was clearly being groomed for a crack at Henry's titles.

But there were intimations of age for Henry and the wear and tear that went with that. One of Henry's party pieces at ringside and in the gym was Cossack dancing – it was good exercise and pleased his fans. While demonstrating the trick at a well-attended training session, though, he managed to wreck the cartilage in his right knee. He had encountered trouble with it before but that had been seen off with painful but necessary cortisone jabs. This was much more serious. Even worse was the condition of his left elbow by now; the wear in the joint was potentially handicapping and the seizures after a fight were becoming both more painful and lasting longer. Few but insiders were aware that for up to a week after a fight the left arm was almost useless. Given that he barely ever used his right hand, in the ring or out of it, unless he had to, then it was clear that the clock was ticking, and loudly, and that both Henry and Wicks could hear it. Nothing was said and nor did it need to be. Wicks, at 75 years of age, had been through this depressing cycle many times before.

However, Henry reasoned that there were a few paydays left, hence the attempt to match Ellis. But unless the cartilage was attended to he was unlikely to match anyone. The operation, the one that footballers dread and with good reason, was swiftly arranged and went well, although two weeks of total immobility for the right leg were both frustrating and damaging. The 2-inch loss of circumference of the right thigh during recuperation illustrates very well the level of fitness enjoyed by a fighter.

Of course, footballers understand these matters very well indeed and their clubs have developed to a fine art the rehabilitation training necessary in order to recover. The nearest club to the Cooper household was Arsenal and so, after a fortnight of inactivity, it was to Highbury Stadium that Henry commuted, Monday to Friday, for weeks of the hardest training he had ever endured. To a boxer, strong legs are useful rather than vital, merely the means of delivery for the punch. To a footballer, they are everything and, after experiencing the rigours of the Arsenal circuit training programme, Henry developed a profound respect for the regime and an even greater respect for the club.

The level of training required to recover the status quo was huge, so much so that Henry was not in a position to defend his European title, which, under EBU rules he was obliged to do within six months of every defence of it. Very practically, he resigned it before the EBU took it away again, to concentrate on fitness. He was to discover that, even though he was only 35, the work rate required to gain back all that he had lost was now of a wholly different order.

But now there was some unpleasantness in the Cooper camp. Danny Holland, as Wicks's trainer of record, simply wanted more money. The convention, that a trainer receives a fee of ten per cent of a fighter's earnings, which comes from the manager's take, was quite a normal one. Unfortunately for Holland, he had always been signed up on salary and wanted to change the arrangement. In fact, he was already the highest paid trainer in the country, as Wicks was not an ungenerous man, and he was earning in the region of £4,000 a year. But with the large purses that Wicks was generating on Henry's behalf, he wanted more.

Holland, though never really trained Henry in the way that Angelo Dundee trained Ali, or Cus d'Amato trained Patterson; his responsibilities were by now chiefly to do with cuts, for Henry had really always trained himself, with George's assistance. There had been friction between Wicks and Holland over the arrangements for some time and they came to a head just as the team were preparing to take back the British and Commonwealth heavyweight titles, which Henry had surrendered. 'On the Friday before we were due to set up camp, Danny rang Jim to tell him that he wasn't going to go unless he was paid more money,' says Henry. 'Jim told him that if he wasn't satisfied he had better go somewhere else. Danny said, "All right, I will."' And that was how it ended after 14 years.

Obviously, a replacement had to be found, despite the fact that Henry had experienced very little eye trouble since the plastic surgeon had operated on him, but this was no time to take risks. Eddie Thomas, the ex-British welterweight champion, was happy to step forward and assume the role. As both a fighter and a manager Thomas was a figure who commanded enormous respect and also understood the importance of the big moment, which might unnerve a more junior corner man. Crucially, he was accomplished at dealing with cuts. But cuts were less important now than age was.

*

Henry found that he was not knocking over sparring partners with the same ease as before. Certainly, they were not knocking him over either, but it was another indication that he was, if realistic, looking at the end of his career. The objective now became simple: recover fitness, take back the titles, British and European, which he had surrendered, and aim to retire undefeated. The recognized world title, given that Joe Frazier now held it, was a most unlikely prospect, and anyway was not a match that Wicks would have sanctioned willingly.

But Jack Bodell, who had seized the title after Henry had surrendered it, was quite another matter. Henry had stopped him in two rounds in 1967 and saw no reason to imagine that anything had changed. Bodell, a southpaw and somewhat ungainly with it, was not a particularly easy man to fight, but Henry discovered, on the evening of 24 March 1970, that the new champion had matured somewhat. 'Having the title certainly gives a man something,' says Henry. 'Although he was still a clumsy sod, he took me the distance.'

Henry won this fight by a very large margin, in fact, but, as we have seen, a left-hooker opposing a southpaw is never a simple task; it was more a matter of awkward jabbing, although he managed to put Bodell on the canvas three times without knocking him out. So, a pleasing fight, not merely to recover the title, but the knowledge that he could, after such a long layoff, still box 15 rounds with a younger man and still win. But while Henry was clearly supremely fit, thanks to the ministrations of the Arsenal trainer, George Wright, his left elbow was now completely seized up for over a week. Knees, Arsenal could help with but elbows, alas, were off-limits for obvious professional reasons.

What Henry regarded as his European title was by now in the hands of Spain's José Urtain, a robust slugger from the Basque

Country, whose spare-time hobby was the minority sport of championship rock-lifting, so he was clearly a tough prospect, if perhaps a
little unrefined. Harry Levene paid an astonishing amount of money
to attract the reluctant Spaniard to London and in Henry's opinion
rather over-priced the fight but, after a burlesque of confusion and
uncertainty, Levene finally nailed his man. Quite possibly the promoter
thought that Urtain was trying to dodge this fight and he even considered applying to the EBU to strip him of the title, suggesting Henry
take on Jurgen Blin instead. Wicks was having none of it and sat back
to watch the fun as a panicked Levene tore all over Europe trying to
track the champion down. When he did, he was in no position to
haggle overmuch, and undertook to guarantee him £50,000, win or
lose – a great deal of money.

In the event, Henry stopped Urtain fairly easily, despite a cut eye
in the first round, a dangerous right swing, which gave him pause for
thought in the seventh and a succession of head butts throughout the
bout. Henry drew on his vast experiences to produce some of what are
euphemistically termed 'professional touches' himself. According to
The Times, one observer, an unnamed former manager, remarked
admiringly: "Enery was gettin' away wiv murder in there.'

The referee, Bernard Mascot, finally assented to stop the fight in
the ninth, after Urtain's corner had pleaded their case.

Having recovered both his titles, the prospect of retirement now
loomed. There was an unspoken assumption between Henry and
Wicks that the end was near, which would certainly relieve Albina,
who, while she hated the prospect of her husband being hurt, had
tactfully refrained from urging him to quit, apart from that one previous wince-inducing effort. It was hard for her, and Henry had
always realized this: 'I knew that at 36, when the tell-tale signs arrive,
when you take ten days to recover from an injury, when previously it
would have taken three, that the game was up. One day in the gym,
Jim looked at me and I looked at him, and that was that – this would
be the last.'

One more defence, then, and that would probably be that. The
challenger was Joe Bugner, the giant 21-year-old, originally from
Hungary, whose family had fled to Britain in the wake of the Soviet

repression of the 1956 uprising. Now a naturalized Brit, and therefore eligible to contend for the British, European and Commonwealth titles, Bugner was 6ft 4in and 15½ stone, one of the largest heavyweights on the planet. The match was made for 16 March 1971.

But Bugner was not 'reckoned' by the *cognoscenti*; big and strong though he undoubtedly was, the press corps viewed with some scepticism his extreme youth against a record of 33 victories out of 34 fights. It was pointed out that most of the opponents were well past their best; even phrases like 'manufactured fighter' were whispered. It was widely held that Bugner, a very telegenic young man, was essentially a media creation, the perfect 'golden boy'. He was certainly nice-looking and blessed with an impressive physique, but could he, would he, fight? The same question had, of course, been asked of another 'golden boy', Billy Walker, and Walker had answered, and eloquently; in doing so he had also demonstrated that, whatever his shortcomings as a boxer may have been, cowardice was not among them. Walker had shown, possibly unwisely, that he was prepared to take two or even three punches in order to land one. The same could not in all seriousness be said of Joe Bugner.

This criticism of Bugner was probably most hurtful to one so young, and indeed several commentators sprang to his defence, but always in the back of their mind was that in facing Henry, young Joe was taking on the most experienced tactician in the European ring, a ring-savvy survivor whose punch, although it had not been unlimbered overmuch, was still a truly frightening attribute.

Over the years, ''Enery's 'ammer', as Wicks had christened it all those years before, has almost developed a personality of its own – part of the man, certainly, but to some it was almost alongside him in the ring like a mentor rather than actually attached to his left shoulder. To those who admired Henry, and they were counted in their millions, there were many who detested boxing as a barbaric throwback. They could morally embrace Henry as a fine man but they almost preferred to think of his major asset as an entirely separate entity. They saw in Henry Cooper a model of probity, dignity and quiet pride. His punch, however, was still a truly terrifying thing. That truth was very straightforward, as the Institute of Aviation Medicine had revealed at around the time of the Urtain fight, which had possibly made the Spaniard so reluctant to engage.

Interested in the physics of boxing, the simple impact of that famous punch, the RAF team arrived at the room over the *Thomas à Becket* with a quite remarkable camera; it would shoot 1,000 frames per second and even then it could not really witness the speed of Henry's left hook. After a little bit of work with pencil and paper, it was calculated, with some disbelief, that from inception to delivery, over a distance of approximately six inches, Henry's left fist landed on target after an acceleration of over 30 times the force of gravity, with an impact of more than four tons per square inch. That entire process took $\Delta 7/100$ths of a second. Truly, it was a gift from God. A punch like this one, which would knock out a horse, simply cannot be developed. 'If it was that good then why didn't I knock them all over?' was Henry's predictable response.

Bearing in mind that Henry was at the end of his career when these observations were made, with an audible crepitus from the elbow behind that left fist, not to mention the pre-existing knuckle damage, then we can only speculate as to its quality when his career was at its peak and pity those men who had to endure its effects.

Training for what would be Henry's last fight was as rigorous as ever. The team stayed at the Clive Hotel, Hampstead, and training took place at the BBBC's own gymnasium on Haverstock Hill. Immediately, Henry realized that he was measurably slower than even a year before. Sprains, which were annoyingly frequent, took far longer to mend than before and one or two of the sparring partners were remaining obstinately vertical. Further, the speedballs were not disintegrating with the same pleasing regularity. Over the years Henry had gained a reputation for being rather hard on sparring partners, but he had rationalized this. 'Well, that's what they were for, ' he says. 'They were getting paid about £20 a round, which frankly is more than they could probably expect actually fighting.'

Now it was all a little different. A fortnight before the fight, his thoughts on retirement finally crystallized; he was chatting with Albina on the telephone one evening and he simply came out with it. He had already decided to retire should he by some unlikely misfortune actually lose this upcoming fight, but his performance in the gym had pointed out to him that he was simply getting too old for this. No, he would call it a day, come what may. It was as if a great weight had been lifted and, predictably, Albina was relieved and delighted. For the remaining fortnight of training after that telephone call he concentrated fully on the matter in hand. He had shared his thoughts – finally – with Wicks, who may have been relieved, but who also rationalized that there would be no shortage of work of a publicity nature. Henry could easily spend the rest of his working life doing something he already did superbly well – just being Henry Cooper.

So, by the time the eve of the fight arrived, confidence was high; the Cooper camp knew full well that Bugner had never fought a full 15-round contest before, that Henry was as fit as he could be and that there was certainly enough power in the excruciatingly painful left jab or hook to give a good account of himself. The betting odds rather reflected this: Henry was 5:2 to win on the evening before the fight. Donald Saunders commented:

> The enormity of Bugner's task can be gauged from the fact that, since winning the British and Commonwealth titles in January 1959, Cooper has beaten off the challenges of Erskine (three times), Dick Richardson, Brian London, Johnny Prescott and Billy Walker – without once being in serious danger of defeat.

Rather to Wicks's concern, the odds had rather changed by the morning of the fight, though too late to be reflected by the press coverage, which had been predictably extensive. Wicks was suddenly in receipt of a flurry of nervous telephone calls from mystified bookies, including Albert Dimes, as a tidal wave of bets was simultaneously placed up and down the country, the vast bulk of them in the London area and the vast bulk of them for Bugner to win. Was Henry ill? Had he hurt himself in training? The questions were asked. Calmly, Wicks denied that anything was wrong (which was entirely true) but this development may well have given him pause for thought. Of course, betting coups were nothing new to him – he could remember some memorable ones of his own, after all – but he was experienced enough to realize that they were usually unwelcome. He decided to keep quiet to Henry for this was not a matter of boxing, it was purely a matter of money. His own was firmly on Henry.

If Henry's first encounter with Clay had been the most famous fight of his career, and his second the most disappointing, then this one with Bugner was certainly to be the most controversial, the more so because it was also to be his last.

The referee was Harry Gibbs, from Bermondsey. Gibbs had been having a little trouble with the BBBC the previous year; he had felt, possibly accurately, that he had not been receiving his fair share of top division fights. But perhaps there was a reason for that, which he could not acknowledge. A semi-official rota existed within the Board of Control, the sort of Spanish practice with which Gibbs, as a docker, was entirely familiar, and he asserted his rights, as he saw them, regularly. He was also quite litigious. But he had also been responsible for some controversial decisions, once against Henry in the Amos Johnson fight, but more notably against Billy Walker when he fought Midlander Johnny Prescott and again (by some verdicts) Walker once more against Northerner Brian London a little later. Not all these verdicts necessarily sat well with other commentators and quite possibly had led to his joining the back of the queue with the Board of Control, which situation had, according to Gibbs's own memoirs, led to him to consider resigning. Perhaps he had a point to make.

No one, least of all in the Billy Walker camp, had ever complained about these potential lacunae, however much they may have disagreed with them, but the faint suspicion does rather emerge that Gibbs tended to overcompensate for his impeccably London origins when calling a tight decision in the favour of an 'outsider'. He also clearly relished being controversial as well as being in control; there was something of the loose cannon about him. Under the UK rules, of course, the referee enjoys total autonomy in coming to his decision and there is no element of external control. This was to be a fight that stretched the limits of that rule.

Gibbs's verdict in the Cooper/Bugner fight was and is quite inexplicable, even at this distance, and it still causes controversy to this day. He himself would also wince a little at its impact, both at the time and later. I recall this fight very well, especially as it was one of the first things I saw on a colour television. It was a great scandal at the time and I contend that it remains one today but not, of course, through any fault of the challenger. Even my late grandmother, admittedly no great expert (and a committed Cooper fan, it must be said, despite his defeat of her two favourite boxers, Erskine and Richardson), thought it grotesquely unfair.

*

It was an interesting fight, if relatively dull by comparison with certain others. Henry, conceding all that height, weight and reach to a man who was also 16 years his junior, gave a quite magnificent perform-ance. On the other hand, Bugner displayed an observable reluctance to risk damage, which made his efforts seem pedestrian by comparison and this was a tendency that rather typified his later career. If any-thing, he looked nervous. Perhaps he had read Neil Allen that morn-ing in *The Times*: 'If he gets too rattled this evening, young Bugner may find himself on the floor.'

Interestingly, Danny Holland was now in Bugner's corner as cut-man; he knew Harry Gibbs very well, having trained him in 1946, before joining Wicks, when Gibbs had actually fought briefly (but quite successfully) as a professional heavyweight.

Wicks, presiding over what he knew to be their final appearance – at least in the ring – announced: 'We are not hanging around. We have a commercial TV appointment after the fight so we might be in a hurry.'

This was not to be a fight characterized by knockdowns, dramas or even particularly heavy punches. Neither fighter seemed in any serious danger, it was merely 15 rounds of faintly repetitive boxing, and clearly hard work for both men. Peter Wilson reported:

> It was a good, sensible first round with both men feeling each other out and Cooper learning just how strong was this nearly 16 year-younger man, weighing 15st. 2 lbs. to his 13st. 7lbs. No one could claim any real advantage in the first three minutes.
>
> But Cooper must have realized that it was going to take a long time to chop down the young giant whom he could not

move around, as he would have liked to, in the clinches.

After four rounds, in which no really serious damage had been caused, Cooper was slightly ahead.

On Gibbs's card, Bugner was a half point ahead. Wilson continued:

In the fifth and sixth, despite Bugner's occasional big, single blast, usually to the body, we saw the older man going further ahead. Indeed, in the sixth, the 21 year-old began to look thoroughly 'moithered' as though things were going too fast for him. And one left hook from Cooper nearly drove the Hungarian born boy's nose through the back of his head.

Gibbs scored round five to Henry and round six to Bugner. Wilson takes up the story:

Bugner rallied in the seventh. He started Cooper bleeding again slightly from the left eye and he also registered a graze under the Champion's right eye. The eighth round was the fulcrum of the seesaw. They had arrived at the half-way stage.

For Gibbs, round seven was even. Wilson continues:

[Henry] was moving nicely, not in-and-out like a tram on rails, but breaking up the pattern of Bugner's straightforward advance by switching from side to side. In the eighth, he gave Bugner a boxing lesson.

But for Harry Gibbs, round eight was a draw as well. Wilson's infuriated comments continue:

Bugner took the ninth, really hurting Cooper with a body blow and shaking him with two of the most uninhibited punches he had so far let go. The tenth seemed to give the inevitable march to victory for Cooper. He brought off one of his more effective ploys when he pushed Bugner back into the ropes and then, timing then, timing the rebound perfectly, caught him as he bounced off. From then on … Cooper went further and further ahead. His best round of all – some good judges gave it to him by half-a-point, was the thirteenth. In the fourteenth, Cooper toyed with his man, mostly with the left, but using one overhand right.

Gibbs allowed Henry a quarter point win in the thirteenth. By now most observers felt that Henry was comfortably ahead. Peter Wilson had him 9–4 up and Donald Saunders agreed, with Henry 'several rounds ahead'.(It must have been one of the few occasions on which the *Daily Mirror* and the *Daily Telegraph* have ever agreed about anything.) Desmond Hackett of the *Daily Express* rather concurred, indeed he made Henry 10–4 up going into the last round.

But on Gibbs's card the fighters were exactly even going into the last and it is probably safe to say that the last round was Bugner's, although even the *Guardian* disagreed about that. But, when Henry confidently offered his hand to Gibbs, he was startled when the referee showed him his back and stalked over to Joe Bugner. Raising the clearly surprised blond giant's hand, Gibbs gave him the verdict.

There were perhaps three heartbeats of disbelieving silence – and then followed complete uproar. Henry's corner had not witnessed anything like this since the near riotous conditions of the Piero Tomasoni fight. Debris poured into the ring as the stunned crowd gave vent to a vast collective roar of outrage.

Henry predictably behaved with great dignity. He sighed and tousled Bugner's hair almost affectionately. However unfair he thought the decision, it was clearly no fault of Bugner's, who had done his best, however modest his efforts had been according to the crowd. Henry recalls:

All my friends and family were there, with Albert's [Dimes] crew sitting ringside. The situation was getting quite ugly and the last thing I wanted was to have a fight break out – I'd already been through one, after all. If they started throwing bottles, I have no idea what would have happened.

George Cooper and Jim Wicks cast concerned looks as Henry takes up training again after his cartilage injury in 1969.

Top: 16 February 1966. First round knock outs are rare in the Heavyweight division but this victory over Jefferson Davies was a personal best for Henry at 100 seconds.
Bottom: 24 March 1970. When Henry challenged Jack Bodell to recover his British and Commonwealth title the match went the distance, although it is hard to see why as here we see Henry smack another left jab into the champion's face. Henry won on points.

Left: Second time around and Henry starts as he means to go on when he fights Muhammad Ali for the World title on 21 May 1966. The referee stopped the fight in round six and it's not hard to see why *(below)*.

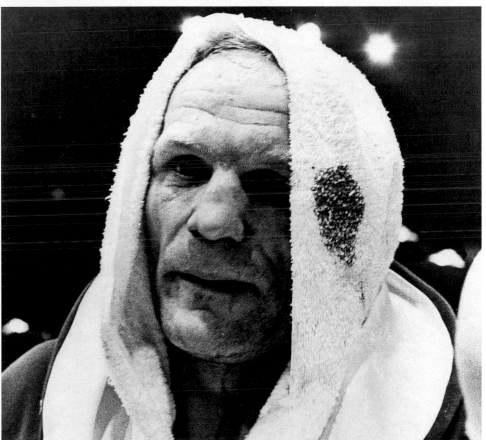

Left: 7 November 1967. A brave Billy Walker challenged Henry to the British and Empire titles, and fought with great courage. Unhappily for Walker, Henry opened a cut early on and the fight was stopped in round six.

Right: The victory over Billy Walker gave Henry the freehold on a third Lonsdale belt. This had never happened before and can never again (due to a change in the rules).

Below: 18 September 1968 Henry, arms aloft, has just taken the European title from Karl Mildenberger.

Above: Down but not out from a low blow delivered by the 'Axeman of Manerbio', Piero Tomasoni. 13 March 1969.

Top right: The best hooks often travel the shortest distance. Here Henry beds one in José Urtain's liver. The fight is stopped in the ninth round and *(bottom right)* Henry delivers a benediction to the appreciative crowd. 10 November 1970.

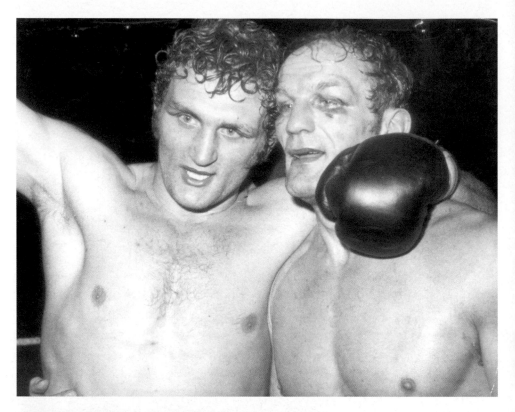

Above: Whatever his opinion
of the verdict in his last fight
Henry bears Bugner no
grudge. Here he congratulates
the new British Commonwealth
and European champion who
appears to be rather more
surprised than Henry is.
Left: Henry immediately after
the fight. 16 March 1971.

Naturally, it is very easy to confuse a profound sense of dismay with mere sentimentality, an emotion with which the boxing ring has always been liberally drenched. Henry was inordinately popular with the London crowd but there were other, more neutral observers, such as Joe Frazier's manager, Yancy Durham, who felt that Henry had won quite comfortably. On the other hand, both *Boxing News* and *The Times* scored the fight exactly the same way that Gibbs had. Seldom had a fight been scored so differently by such a range of experienced observers. A discreet file of policemen gathered to escort Gibbs down from the ring (and out of the reach of Jim Wicks) and out into the limelight of British boxing history.

For Henry's fans in the press corps, his next words, to the saddened assembly in the dressing room after the fight, were lowering but inevitable: 'Well, gentlemen, that's my lot. It's a choker having to go out like this. It was close, but I thought I did enough to clinch it. I want to thank the public and everyone else for all the wonderful years. I don't regret one moment of it. I'd do it all over again.' He meant it, too.

Wicks, completely empurpled with indignation, was rather more forthright, if inaccurate: 'It was a diabolical decision. Henry Cooper retires today – Harry Gibbs retires tomorrow.'

He, of course, did not retire. The two men, Wicks and Gibbs, who had never been particularly close in the first place, never spoke again. For Albina, though, the final announcement of Henry's retirement was a godsend: 'It was lovely – one of the greatest gifts ever bestowed on me, like a great weight lifted. When he retired, it was wonderful; I started to feel like a different person.'

British boxing rapidly felt rather different, too. Suddenly it seemed that Henry had been around for ever and his retirement, however inevitable, was to create a huge void in the heavyweight division, even in the wider sport as a whole. For his friends and allies in the sport, it came as a blessed relief that he had finally decided to stop. All who knew him closely realized that the sheer work involved in achieving and main-taining the levels of fitness required to shine against younger men was taking a lot out of him. Between the Tomasoni fight in 1969, and this last fight with Bugner, he seemed to have aged rapidly – he was suddenly looking much older than 36. The last thing anyone wanted was the ignominious spectacle of a public decline. The loss to Bugner, was, they reckoned, as good a reason to stop as he had ever had.

But if Albina Cooper thought that retirement from the ring meant that she would start to see as much of her husband as other wives saw of theirs, she was to be mistaken, for the groundwork undertaken by the Wicks organization prior to Henry's retirement had prepared him for a life in the public eye the like of which no British sportsman had ever experienced before. While his training schedule was sharply curtailed (he found it hard to give it up completely) he still kept in shape, not because he ever seriously contemplated a comeback but because the sudden cessation of training for a man as fit as he was could be extremely dangerous; ask any befatted ex-swimmer. Instead, Henry the Ninth, as some of the press now referred to him, had rediscovered golf.

It had been 30 years before, on the wartime Beckenham course, that the brothers Cooper had first dealt in 'rescued' golf balls, but Henry did not take up the game until 1970, when he joined Ealing Golf Club. He became as hooked as any unwary fish as he started to discover the pleasures and torments of this unique game. It would start to redefine him in his boxing retirement and would become a vehicle for some of his best work.

Of course, his temperament was perfect and he recalled being pleased at having taken it up so relatively late in life because he came to it without any particular preconceptions – no baggage. His previous career had been one of a series of 10 or 15 violent and tiring rounds, with communication with his opponents being defined by a series of unrepeatable grunts punctuated by heavy punching. Now, over 18 holes and a pleasant chat, he could finally allow his innate personality to actually complement his new sport, as opposed to act against it, as it had done for 17 years as a professional fighter.

Further, because it would not be his living, he was able to pace himself. He was pleased to learn that the unfairness of life, that some are athletes and some are not, is a natural opposition for which the game of golf has a ready answer. The handicapping system, he realized quickly, meant that he would not be condemned to playing only with rabbits.

But, passionate about it though he would become, it was not a living. That, he would have to do in other ways.

PART THREE

WHAT ON EARTH DOES A RETIRED BOXER DO?

CHAPTER TWELVE

Celeb

EDITH SUMMERSKILL: Mr. Cooper, have you looked in
the mirror and seen the state of your nose?
HENRY COOPER: Well, have you? Boxing is my excuse –
what's yours?

WITH THAT SLIGHTLY UNGALLANT and, it must be said, rather untypical riposte, Henry made his new role, as Britain's leading apologist for
boxing, quite clear. I asked him if he thought he had been rude. He
replied: 'Well, I thought it was fair enough really; I'd been a very good
boy all the way through the discussion, even agreeing with her, and
then she just turned round and ambushed me. Bless her, she was no
oil painting anyway.'

The occasion on which this *lèse-majesté* took place was a television
debate on the sport in 1972. Henry recalled it as a 'points win'. In truth,
this was not a new debate as boxing had been mocked even in ancient
times, and the nature of the previous Whig position on the sport of
prizefighting had been rather focused on the harm it did to the fighters.
The approach of Baroness Summerskill and her cohorts was rather more
holistic, if only in the sense that fighting was not only bad for the fighters, it was bad for the audience, too; she felt free to wag her finger at all
involved. But to a generation of fightgoers and other citizenry hardened
by their experiences in wartime, her view seemed quite ridiculous. To
those architects of the nanny state, many of whom sat on her side in the
House of Lords, it was not a campaign that was considered politically
viable, given the number of potentially useful votes that would be lost if
a ban was imposed. The man who had done more than most to make
boxing so inordinately popular in Britain was now clearly the implaca-
ble opponent of the highly vocal campaign to ban it.

For the politically motivated anti-boxing lobby, Henry was a formidable bundle of contradictions; he was a working-class hero, he was highly intelligent, he was honoured with an OBE, he had been a lunch guest of the Queen and, most difficult, he was clearly quite undamaged by his experiences. He was therefore a truly dangerous and highly popular opponent, as the exchange quoted above suggests. For the purely medical lobby, the situation was different, as the British Medical Association was attacking the sport not on a moral or ethical platform but simply on a physiological one. Edith Summerskill, polymath as she was, had a foot in both camps, which fact could, from time to time, appear to confuse her argument. Did she oppose boxing because it was medically dangerous and therefore immoral or was there a sinister Stalinist agenda at work? The British public, ever suspicious of politicians' motives, affected not to care, but that public was by now also completely in love with Henry, which made for an even more uphill struggle for the anti lobby. It was all very well for Edith Summerskill to win a debate with Jack Solomons, who was both inarticulate as well as astonishingly rude (which rather served to belie his carefully constructed cheeky chappie image), as his motivations were merely and obviously financial, but Henry was a radically different prospect. Not only had he prospered as a boxer, but also, outrageously, he had even dared to enjoy it and was never bashful about saying so. And everybody loved him.

The issue over the morality, if not the legality of boxing was, of course, something of a press bandwagon, which was wheeled out after every disaster that befell a fighter. Regrettably, there were several, one of the most tragic being the fate of Gerald McClennan after he lost to Nigel Benn in February 1995. The fight had been broadcast to a TV audience of 15 million, and all who were able to bear to watch the whole event knew that McClennan was, on the morning after the fight, locked in the iron dark of a deep coma. Naturally, the mediafest contained the usual paradox of mawkish headlines, predictably illustrated by the most prurient of pictures available to them. Henry told the *Daily Mirror*: 'Nobody makes men box – all boxers do it because they want to fight. We all know the possible tragic consequences, but we all pray its not going to be you. There are thousands of fights every year and it's only occasionally where there is an unfortunate tragedy of this nature.'

The debate will go on; the simple fact, that boxing is a blood sport, the only activity whose purpose is for one man physically to hurt another, is clear. What is more blurred is the morality that allows it to take place at all. The libertarian right would argue that if two men wish to train hard, climb into a boxing ring and seek to knock each other out, and millions of people will pay, in one form or another to watch that take place, then that is entirely their business and nobody else's. The opposing view, that boxing falls into the same category as dog-fighting, perhaps misses the point made by Henry, that because the sport of boxing is a voluntary one then the issue is really one of civil liberty. Essentially, then, it becomes basically a political matter. The lentil-eating tendency will always oppose fighting, whereas libertarians will always prefer to allow it even if they do not follow it particularly closely. In Henry, the libertarian view has a powerful spokesman. The dice are clearly loaded in their favour because of that. Henry has survived and prospered and he is who he is primarily because of what he did for a living until 1971. But there was rather more to him than that, as the successive decades were to show.

Initially, he recalls, his first impulse upon retiring was to become a trainer/manager. He had hoped to find a young heavyweight hopeful and bring him on in the way that he had himself been managed but to his regret, even now, there were few prospects. He had no particular hostility to Joe Bugner (although he never particularly reckoned him), indeed he offered his services only a few days after that fight to the Bugner corner when they were due to challenge Ali. But elsewhere it was a fruitless task. 'There just didn't seem to anyone around,' he told me, still slightly regretfully. 'I wanted to find a decent heavyweight – the bigger men think differently – and really bring him on, but I couldn't really see anyone suitable.' It was almost as if he had seen through the fog of hype that surrounded American boxing and understood that there were some unalterable fundamentals that a clever tactician could exploit. A singular and mighty punch, coupled with some plain old-world common sense, could perhaps drill down through the hype?

*

There was some serious unpleasantness quite shortly after his retirement. He produced, in 1972, an extremely tactful autobiography, which rather walked on eggs, with the skilled assistance of John Samuel of the *Guardian*. That journal has, over the years, built up a well-earned reputation for the occasional misprint (the *Grauniad*, as it is known), but the error which was contained in Henry's book was nothing to do with that. It was more a matter of an overenthusiastic sub-editor at the book's publishers, Cassell. The issue was to do with the addition on Harry Gibbs's' scoring card during and after the Bugner fight. What Henry and Samuel finally produced, concerning the final assessment and scoring of the fight, read like this: 'On Peter Wilson's [of the *Daily Mirror*] score card I had won nine of the fifteen rounds, but Harry Gibbs had me losing by a quarter of a point.'

Not a particularly sensitive matter, one might think, but when the book came out the passage read: 'On Harry Gibbs' scorecard I had won nine of the fifteen rounds but he had me losing by a quarter of a point.'

Whoops. This well illustrates some of the perils that can be encountered as a result of sloppy proof-reading but Harry Gibbs sued Henry and the publisher for libel, and won. Damages were modest at £1,000 (Cassell quite properly paid them) but Henry was forced to make a slightly humiliating apology in open court for something that was in truth not his fault.

Henry did have a grievance against Gibbs but the issue over the passage in the book did not express it; that was merely a simple publisher's slip-up. Perhaps the fact that Gibbs sued so promptly was significant but unfortunately the laws of libel permit me to go no further. Gibbs is no longer with us, but others are. It was an unpleasant episode, which was clearly irreconcilable without recourse to a major investigation by the Board of Control, which never took place.

The controversy over the Bugner fight actually served an unforeseen purpose, which was to add an edge to Henry's popularity. He and Gibbs would not speak for 15 years, in fact, and only did so when Henry, goaded by the offer of a large donation to charity, agreed finally to shake Gibbs's hand at a charity boxing evening at the London Hilton: 'Well, I was told that if I shook his hand, then at least £2,000 would go into the pot, and probably £20 each from all those present, so I did it,' says Henry. ' I didn't have to sleep with the bloke, or anything after all, I just had to shake his hand, so I did it. For charity.'

*

I can well recall a rather bored, mainly student audience, slumped on a wet Saturday night in the dismal fleapit that passed as the local cinema in that jewel of Dyfed, Aberystwyth. It was 1975. A group of us had decided to inspect *Royal Flash*, the promising adaptation of George MacDonald Fraser's reworking of *The Prisoner of Zenda* theme. It had been a first-rate book but the early stages of the movie were disappointing, despite the presence of Oliver Reed, whom we all rather admired. Then suddenly a scene arrived that called upon Reed, who played Otto Bismarck, to receive a boxing lesson from the retired prizefighter John Gully. When the audience saw who played Gully, as Henry Cooper turned to face the camera, a loud cheer erupted, which was an unusual event in that dismal little theatre, to say the least.

Actually, Henry was probably the best thing in the film, and probably because in reality he was playing himself; we were not to know it but *Royal Flash*, in most other ways a disappointment, marked the start of a good friendship between Henry and Reed, but Henry told me that he learned quite fast to be rather wary of his new mate: 'Ollie was a lovely bloke, but really dangerous. God, he drank!'

Reed's ability to get himself into alcohol-fuelled scrapes was legendary and he also sailed very close to the wind in terms of matters sexual. He had started his relationship with his second wife, Josephine, when she was suspiciously young; Henry and Albina encountered them on holiday in 1980:

Oh dear. I told Albina I'd just go and have a quick drink with him before lunch, it was about 11.30, I think. One of his minders said, 'Careful Henry, he's been on tequilas since four this morning.' Ollie then told his girlfriend exactly what he would do with her that night, right there in the bar! Well, I left as soon as I could, but when I got back to the room there was a phone call from the *Mirror* asking – was it true that Oliver

Reed was there with his under-age girlfriend? 'No, don't be silly,' I said, 'I've just seen him…'

Reed admired Henry tremendously, as he admired most red-blooded males, but he could take his expression of this to toe-curling extremes. His habit of appearing on television when roaring drunk was an unfortunate one and invariably embarrassing for all concerned, no more so than when appearing with his hero Henry on a disastrous episode of Michael Aspel's chat show. Reed had decided, clearly under the influence, that the most appropriate way to pay tribute to his hero would be don shorts and gloves, ketchupped eyes and all, and simply punch his way through the studio scenery in order to reach the sofa. Needless to say, the show had to be cut, which was perhaps rather a pity. Reed would attempt a similar stunt when sharing a line-up with Billy Beaumont, with truly embarrassing results.

Even without *Royal Flash*, which did relatively poorly, Henry's place in the public eye was assured, if only as a result of his myriad television appearances. It seemed that not a week went by without him popping up somewhere. He had been an inaugural panellist on BBC's *A Question of Sport* since 1969 and had starred in an extraordinary array of commercials, for Crown Paints, Shredded Wheat and, most famously, Brut aftershave, so his public profile was always going to be high. Only recently, as one of Britain's favourite OAPs, he fronted the flu jab campaign. Another important job, though, had been to step into the BBC radio slot vacated by Barrington Dalby , who had retired from the role just before Henry had retired from his. Henry had to provide authoritative assessments of the state of various broadcast boxing matches between the rounds. He did this expertly with all the authority that only a 17-year career can provide. He had started working for the BBC before he had retired from the ring, in fact. The journalistic challenge was quite formidable – to provide a 30-second running commentary of how the last round had gone, an assessment that called for an extremely quick brain indeed, for the view of a fight from the ringside is a radically different thing from the perception offered elsewhere, particularly to a radio audience.

Evidence of the speed with which boxers have to think is to be found in conversations held with them. Albina describes for me some of the frustrations of conversing, particularly about a topic in which Henry has a special interest: 'He will keep interrupting! He won't let someone finish their sentence before he butts in.'

Clear evidence, in my opinion, that he probably already knows where the conversation is going; time to move on, but his speed of conversational riposte, as Edith Summerskill had discovered, is astonishing, both witty and well timed. The latter we should expect from a boxer, and Henry's commentaries for BBC radio were a rich seam of swift, accurate and pithy inputs. Even if his assessments of the relative merits of the fighters to each other, or to people whom he had fought himself, were low, he was never rude about them, however scathing his inner view may have been. That would change, though, as he found himself more and more disconnected from boxing. An encounter with the singular Christopher Livingston Eubank illustrates this:

EUBANK: Mister Cooper, I've heard you don't like me.
HENRY: No, I don't; I think you're bloody weird.

*

As the game of boxing changed, with the arrival of Eubank, Naseem Hamed, Frank Bruno *et al,* he was distressed by the deterioration of his beloved sport into what he viewed as an unseemly and undignified three-ring circus. He hid his frustration well, until 1996, when so exasperated was he at the sheer vulgarity of what was going on, he resigned from the BBC. He told Frank Keating of the *Guardian*:

Since they've allowed all this crazy hype, to be honest with you, the whole scene has been getting on my nerves for the last couple of years. I've always disliked with a passion those American wrestling shows on television with rivals threatening, shouting and mouthing off at each other. And I'm sad to say that's what boxing here has become in many ways. It's crazy. In their fight, it took Bruno and McCall 45minutes just to arrive in the ring before they could start to fight.

They had fireworks – the whole place was covered in smoke

– they had singers, a band, dancers, coloured laser beams. To me, that's not boxing. Other times, they have fighters come down on Harley Davidson motorbikes [Eubank] or on cranes. It's like a circus. Some fellow will soon come in on an elephant. I'm just disillusioned with it.

He further thinks that the ritual abuse, which had become the norm, was distasteful in the extreme, and drew a very fair comparison with Ali:

Ali was different. He did it with some wit for a start. And he knew that you knew that his antics were just a way of scoring a psychological point. He always did it with a twinkle in his eye. You could always see his tongue in his cheek and he meant you to.

But now fighters actually mean their nastiness. It's much more than a bit of growling to sell tickets. It's so distasteful, as a former boxer, to see current fighters personally deriding opponents, even having scraps outside the ring.

But, given the astonishing volume of ticket sales and the resultant huge purses, it seems that few agreed with him. But his point was well made and well taken, at least by those who respected his right to have a developed view.

Politically, boxing politics and ability aside, he is quiet. He is a man mildly of the libertarian right but does not make a particular issue of it; politics to Henry is a private thing, rather like religion, which is probably best left alone. He becomes rather more animated when discussing sports, though. He has a quite encyclopaedic knowledge of sport and, of course, understands its motivations intimately. Interestingly, he feels that professional boxing has a very limited future and he thinks it may simply wither on the vine:

When you think about it, boxing's roots are basically economic; it's a sport of poor people. The more prosperity there is the less men will need to box. If you look now in America, most of the up and coming fighters are Hispanic and Mexican;

the gyms are full of them, and I also hear that there are plenty of Russians who are quite useful … You wouldn't want to have economic decline just to save boxing, now, would you?

Well, I know one or two people who probably would, but he makes a fair point, even though, if he had his time over again, there is very little he would seek to change because he also realizes that had he been born into more affluent circumstances he would have been most unlikely to have boxed, and would, upon reflection, probably feel the lack of that unique experience. He knows that it is boxing, as well as his attitude to it, characterized by a realistic but slightly sardonic humility, that has made him so popular. In that sense, he remains our senior link to the Colosseum and is clearly as popular as any gladiator.

But a high public profile is no guarantee of popularity, as generations of third-rate comedians and politicians can testify; the public saw (and see) in Henry something rather different from other, rather run-of-the-mill manufactured celebrities. They see a fundamental decency – 'a kindness', as Albina calls it – about him, which they find irresistibly attractive, whatever they may think about boxing – assuming even that they have an opinion on it at all, for many are completely agnostic about the subject now. To a British public his appeal is, in my view at least, very much a nineteenth-century one, as if the public can make a direct connection with the prizefighters of the past, Caunt, Cribb and all the others. If he stood for parliament like John Gully had he would probably win, for example although it must be said that Gully, who was not the gentle giant portrayed by Henry in *Royal Flash*, simply bought his seat according to the custom of the day.

But it is for his charitable activities, many of them invisible, that he received his OBE, and a later, perhaps even more singular honour, which, while it means relatively little outside the Catholic Church, was nonetheless important. In June 1978 he was awarded the Papal Knighthood of St Gregory, which was bestowed upon him by the late, great Cardinal, Basil Hume. It must have given Hume a particular pleasure, as he was a keen follower of the fistic sport, another apparent inconsistency in what we must really start to regard as the mystery of boxing.

If any proof were needed that boxing's hasty exit, pursued by the law, into the music halls all those years before, an event which probably ensured its survival, then Henry's role in the Variety Club of Great Britain offers it. He has been involved with it for nearly 30 years, and the now established charity golf tournaments to which he puts his name (he chairs the Variety Club Golfing committee) have raised millions, both for the Variety Club itself as well as other charities. His devotion to this cause is total. Every boxer must imagine what it must be like to be handicapped, and many of them, including Henry, know exactly what it is like to be poor. Despite his rather survivalist take on life, his efforts on behalf of the underprivileged are legendary and he remains a stalwart of many other charities. In short, he has put back into life far more than he has taken out of it. 'When you've got healthy kids of your own, and you see all those physically and mentally handicapped children at a Sunshine coach presentation, well, I just knew I had to get involved,' he said in 2000.

And get involved he certainly did. He offers a living link between boxing, which is the most violent sport on the planet, show business, and one of the best-hearted and hardworking charity networks there is. Neither he nor anyone else sees any particular inconsistency in that; he draws the line at pantomime, though. Boxing and show business may be intimately connected, but there are limits, and he found them quite easily. Henry Cooper may be many things but he was never going to be a pantomime dame.

In between our chats, I notice two still-life paintings, which are more than competent, hanging on his kitchen wall. They are signed 'HC' and I asked him whether he had painted them. 'Well, I was a bit idle for a while,' he says, 'so I just bought a book, you know, *How to Paint*, or something, and knocked them out. They're not very good.'

Well, there is one of a trout, which does look rather *surprised*, but I have to say that I have seen much worse. But he doesn't paint any more; there is perhaps something of the 'been there, done that' attitude of a man who seeks an experience but feels, internally, that he knows his limitations, even has a slight sense of insecurity. He took some serious risks in the ring, and is not averse to taking some now, but is swift to call a halt if the process seems to lead nowhere, rather like the Wembley grocery enterprise.

Weather and reptiles permitting, golf is still his main hobby. 'I like golf a lot, because you can happily play at your level for as long as you like,' he says. 'There aren't may sports which let you do that.'

A quite remarkable aspect of the Cooper phenomenon is the way he unconsciously engages people's attention. Quite simply, total strangers think they know him. I recall, as this book was in the early stages of preparation, we were walking together down Shaftesbury Avenue; I was startled at the number of people who simply and cheerfully greeted him, 'Morning, Henry'. I had never seen this before – dozens of, I am sure, perfectly intelligent people who had convinced themselves that this was quite normal behaviour. Whether they were surprised when he calmly greeted them back, treating this as an everyday occurrence, which it clearly is, I cannot tell, but I imagine they were not. It is as if he physically exudes an aura of accessible amiability, very similar to that perceived to radiate from the late Queen Elizabeth the Queen Mother, who was apparently an avid Henry Cooper fan.

It is a matter of record that once he retired from the prize ring; the audience figures for British boxing simply fell off the edge of a cliff. He still gets fan mail from fightgoers who gave up on the sport when he did and who have never returned to it; his presence had been the only reason for their being there, or even watching it on television. A similar phenomenon applied to Stirling Moss when he had retired nine years before Henry, but Stirling's following was mainly among motor racing fans and was based much more on vast respect for his phenomenal talents than anything else; they did not feel as if they really knew Stirling, whereas they just knew that they knew Henry, and they knew they also liked him. It was another example of British enthusiasts not necessarily demanding world championship status for their idols – British champion is quite enough, thank you; this also enables us to hang on to our heroes and not have to share them with the rest of the world.

Very few men, and certainly very few boxers, accomplish this; the public does not appreciate the obsessive/compulsive disorder symptoms frequently exhibited by sports personalities, nor do they particularly like braggarts. In a sense, there is an innate disdain for the ethos of professional sport, which is why the only three men who spring to mind who might fit into the same category as Henry are Mike Hawthorn, who died in 1959, Denis Compton, who passed away in 1997 and Bobby Charlton, who is happily still with us. George Best we all like, particularly if we ever saw him play, but while we are distressed over his state of health, we tut-tut at his lack of discipline. We want it all.

Sports stars make it look easy and in doing so they unconsciously remind us of our own shortcomings. When we discover, however, that what can make them outstanding competitors can also flaw them as men, we turn away. We are cruel to our heroes in many ways; we seek a perfection that cannot exist, an ideal that is both impractical and ephemeral. Actually, we might be said to prefer them to be dead so that the myths we weave around them can remain unchallenged by their subject. When it was realized that Nigel Mansell was a whinger, or that Jackie Stewart had his left jacket cuff made shorter than his right, in order to show off his Rolex, a company of which he is a (tax-exiled) director, or even that Lester Piggott had been economical with matters fiscal, we pause. Any single element, even unconnected with what they did for a living, can serve to make us forget those sublime moments those men offered up to us; the sheer balls-out courage of Mansell against Senna, or the sheer artistry with which Stewart triumphed, or Piggott's astonishing record of over 4,500 wins. Really, we don't deserve these people.

Henry, of course never made it look easy, but the gory sight he frequently presented was quickly offset by his unfeigned chirpiness only a few days after one gruelling encounter or another. In defeat he was gracious and in victory, modest, and invariably generous to his opponent. We like that, if only because that is almost certainly not how we would ourselves behave in the same circumstances.

So, Henry Cooper, who had won his audience and following the hardest way, now found himself attracting a bigger one than he had enjoyed in the ring, for despite the fact that boxing has always been a minority sport when compared to football or motor racing, Henry's appeal has always been wider than the orbit of his occupation, and all agree that he is very good indeed at simply being Henry Cooper.

It is a full-time job, and he is seldom at a loose end, but there is one sport that he is pleased he took up; if there is one activity apart from boxing about which he is passionate it is the ancient one of golf. 'I think that without golf, Henry wouldn't be the man he is today,' says Albina. 'It really gave him a new lease of life.'

But the combination of golf and his happy-go-lucky, optimistic attitude was nearly the undoing of him three years ago. He was playing golf in Buckinghamshire in the late spring. While looking for someone else's lost ball ('of course', sighs Albina), he failed to observe an aggressive and healthy specimen of *Vipera beris* lurking in the rough and the adder bit him on the ankle.

Jim Wicks had been the man who had taken care so effectively of most of the multifarious other reptiles to have crossed Henry's path in his previous career, so perhaps his reaction was both understandable and forgivable, if perhaps, in the light of hindsight, a little bit unwise. Typically, he made little of it and simply carried on playing, slapped a Band-Aid on the oozing puncture in the clubhouse and drove himself home. He explained that he had been scratched by a thorn when Albina asked him about the plaster. 'Well, I didn't want to worry anyone,' he says now. 'Everybody knows they can't kill you.'

They can, actually; an adder bite is no small thing, depending on the time of year. Unhappily, he was bitten in May, during the nesting season, when adders are at their most defensive and aggressive. Even when the bite refused to heal he was not overly concerned, and only seven months later, when a lump of medically interesting and clearly mortified tissue the size of a small walnut simply dropped out of his ankle, did he realize that something was seriously amiss, and he reluctantly revealed the truth, caught in the harmless fib. Albina resignedly sums it up: 'There you are, that's my Henry. I asked him if he'd killed it – "No," he said. "She ran away ..."'

So, that rather says it all: Henry Cooper, one time British, Empire and European heavyweight champion, the destroyer of Erskine, London, Richardson and Tomasoni, the owner and deliverer of perhaps the finest punch – God-given – ever to grace the British ring, couldn't even bring himself to kill the snake that bit him. There is, I maintain, a great symbolic truth in this little anecdote.

Although he will still be the first man to volunteer to find a lost golf ball, he does so rather more carefully now, particularly because the Kent countryside where he lives is fairly liberally stocked with 'narrow strangers' as Emily Dickinson memorably christened them.

At this stage I am trying to work out if there is anything that will actually make him cross, apart from his professional disdain for awkward southpaws, particularly those who attempt to rearrange his dangly bits. I am certainly very clear now how hard his team must have had to work to bring him to the appropriate emotional match fitness, but what actually enrages him?

Others, with much more reason to be confused about this than I am, have, over the years, asked the same question. In October 1958, Max Baer, world heavyweight champion for a year less a day after he demolished Primo Carnera in June 1934, was visiting London as a guest of Jack Solomons at the Harringay Arena. Jolly Jack had been told that the owners of the arena saw a greater future for the site as a warehouse and he therefore knew that the game would shortly be up. It was a gathering of the great and the good, all in black tie, and given that it was also the occasion of Henry's celebrated defeat of Zora Folley, Baer was rather interested to meet him. Danny Cornell introduced them and Henry was his usual sunny self. As Henry wandered off, Cornell takes up the tale:

> 'Tell me,' demanded Max Baer, staring morosely at the departing back of Henry Cooper, 'doesn't that guy ever get mean?'
> I wagged my head in a negative sort of way.
> 'Well, you can get just so far by being a nice guy,' continued Mr. Baer, 'but no further. To go all the way to the top in this game, you need to be a nasty egotistical character like me. Don't you agree?'

It was actually quite difficult for Cornell to give a useful answer, as you might imagine. But Max Baer, the Clown Prince of Boxing, as he was known, was himself something of a comedian, but clearly grasped, as his remarks reveal, that there must be an element of schizophrenia in every boxer. Marciano had it, for example, and so did Joe Louis; that the memory of their actions in the ring are a blur when compared to anything else that they do. Marciano could never believe his aggression in the ring, when watching film of himself, but he apparently accepted the contradiction willingly. So, to rephrase Baer's question – What makes him mean? Albina tells me: 'We were watching the news; an old lady had been beaten up by some thugs and they showed her picture on the TV. I glanced over at him; his face had suddenly gone quite grey. He said, "If I could get hold of them, I'd feed them some of their own medicine."'

Well, Lloyd's riled him, too. He had been an underwriting member since his retirement, introduced to it by his friend Charles St George. Lloyd's was perceived to be the ideal business for anyone affluent enough who was too busy to manage their own affairs. The principle is simple enough: 'names', as the underwriting members are known, sign a commitment of unlimited liability and put up their wealth as collateral in exchange for joining syndicates, which receive insurance premiums. Their share of those premiums constitutes their income. Over time, Lloyd's had become known as a profitable but undemanding way of achieving respectably high returns; it had paid the school fees of several generations of that section of Britain that has always had assets but not necessarily any cash.

But, of course, nothing is for nothing. It was also known, in the City at least, that while there was clearly no great trick to this, Lloyd's was not an institution that was necessarily blessed by a high frequency of PhDs among its workers. Nice people, some of them, but not necessarily *la crème de la crème* in the IQ department. It was held that it was the employer of last resort for someone who desired a career 'in the City'. The last examination that many of them had passed, the standard joke went as I recall, was probably the cycling proficiency test. On a re-take. As an institution, it was also astonishingly lax, a fact well hidden behind a resolutely stuffy facade. Small minds and loose fiscal morals are dangerous, particularly in a place that works on the basis of unlimited liability and is – ahem – self-regulated. When one observer opined that the new stainless-steel building rather resembled a huge dairy, one who overheard drawled elegantly: 'Yes, it does; those ****s inside it have been milking it for years.'

The punters were not to know that all was not well, of course, because no one told them; informed insiders (very few of whom actually suffered any serious financial loss) knew, however, that they were riding the tiger. Legions of glib salesmen were dispatched to the shires, with a simple purpose: to tap in to the emerging housing boom in order to top up the dwindling internal reserves of cash and assets that were being destroyed by a succession of disasters, particularly from America, as a series of class actions on behalf of victims of asbestosis started to have their impact. Lloyd's was, in the parlance of the industry, 'under-reserved'– functionally broke, in fact.

The recruitment drive had started in the middle of the 1970s as the potential horror of the asbestosis crisis made itself clear. There was no public discussion of the matter; it simply became a tightly guarded secret, the One Big Thing which was fully understood by the uniquely under-qualified stewards of this looming disaster. The level of liability as defined by the ever-generous American courts was astonishing; clearly something had to be done. When Henry joined Lloyd's the organization had around 6,000 members; it had been growing modestly at around 200 or so per year since the war. From 1975, though, the rate of growth was startling, culminating in a peak membership of 32,400 in 1988. That arithmetic is self-explanatory. In truth, though, there was no big secret about asbestos, as the following anecdote suggests.

One friend of mine, an engineer by profession (we shall call him Brian, as that is his name) and a man a little older than Henry, returned from his National Service in the Royal Air Force in 1949. He went to work as an apprentice in the family firm and, full of enthusiasm, threw himself into a relatively simple task, the re-commissioning of an ancient asbestos-lined crucible. As he started to take it apart, the foreman, aged *circa* three score years and five, rapped sternly: 'Don't you touch that, Master Brian, that ****er will kill 'e.'

Brian queried, not the (permissible) over-familiarity, but the simple accuracy of the statement: 'That there is asbestos, young Brian; it's ****ing deadly.'

'Who told you that?' replied my friend.

'My grandfather,' replied the old sage shortly, suggesting that this intelligence had originated at around the time of the Great War (if not before), when the majority of these financially deadly (and perpetual) policies were being written.*

So, there was no great secret about asbestos; it was a matter of shop-floor, if not public record.

It was held, as uncertainty grew, that these vast claims would dwindle eventually and the new money coming in would balance the overcooked books. In short, Lloyd's of London became a giant Ponzi scheme, a task made easier by the fact that it had been permitted, ten years into its secret crisis, to remain self-regulating in the wake of 'Big Bang'. Henry recalls, slightly agitated now: 'As soon as those people signed on the dotted line, they were all completely broke, but they just didn't know it; all their money was gone – all of it – before they even walked out of the door. It was outrageous.'

It certainly was. As the claims multiplied, the syndicate salesmen worked even harder, and with some success, as upwardly mobile punters, completely sold on the sheer respectability, the grandness of the place, were sucked in, and indeed persuaded their friends to join. As the crisis deepened and the news started to leak, the scandal finally broke, with expected results. A whole swathe of the population were financially wiped out as their assets were put under the hammer in an already uncertain economy battered by the delayed action effects of the 1987 stock market crash. The liquidation of so much real estate certainly contributed to the collapse of the housing market. Some investors were so badly clobbered that they were unable even to buy newspapers.

Of course, this being Britain, there was no particular public sympathy for this new underclass, which had been so instantly created, perhaps, indeed, until the news came that Henry Cooper himself had fallen victim to this unique fraud, one of the longest-running and cynical in history.

---

* With great irony, this same friend was later invited to join an insurance syndicate (when it became clear that after half a century of hard graft he was clearly worth a few bob). His response was logical, if somewhat brutal 'Why the hell am I going to hand over my hard-earned cash to some twit with no 'O' levels? Bugger off.'

He was clobbered, but not as hard as some. He had, in his first career, been hit far harder than that and recovered. As he had been an active (if slightly nervous) member for over 20 years, he had learned the value of 'stop-losses', which can be used to put a floor under the level of liability, but there was still a huge hole in his finances. Friends, notably Jimmy Tarbuck, were quick to offer financial assistance, but his boxer's pride asserted itself and he declined.

The original purpose behind Lord Lonsdale's belts had in fact been primarily an economic one. If a fighter won a belt outright, he had not only a trophy but also an object that was a genuine store of value against hard times or the breadline. Henry famously owned the freehold on three of them and, despite an ardent lobbying by friends and family, he decided to sell them. 'It was either that or risk losing the house, and I wasn't going to do that,' he told me.

I well recall the giant collective sigh of dismay that this announcement triggered, whether from those who realized full well how hard he had worked to achieve this unique accomplishment, or from what we can happily refer to now as his 'general fans'; it was a huge wrench, and when the belts went under the hammer at a country auction in June 1993, they realized a modest £42,000, against an estimate of £100,000, which was the cause of further sympathy. But their sale provided a necessary stopgap, saving him from the unwelcome clutches of the stone-faced hardship committee at Lloyd's, a body which had already made a reputation for itself as one which took few prisoners, despite the essential rottenness of the institution which it represented. He was also pleased that the three belts had stayed together, a unique memento of a unique career, whoever it was who now owned them. It was the sad result of one well-known British institution cynically ripping off another.

Unsurprisingly, his knighthood, announced in the 2000 New Year's honours list, pleased him hugely. Rather as Buckingham Palace had come to the rescue after his controversial loss to Amos Johnson with a decent lunch, now here they were again after the embarrassing snakebite episode. It was, he told merecalled to me, his pride in his family aside, the highlight of his life: 'I was a bit sad that Mum and Dad couldn't have seen it, but the old heart gets thumping and the adrenaline gets going.' Rather like the old days, in fact …

What was particularly pleasing for Henry was the fact that although both his OBE and his papal knighthood had been for services to charity, his KSG was for services to boxing, which in these politically correct days was extraordinary, and therefore all the more to be appreciated, not the least by him. He was the first English boxing knight, although remember poor old Daniel Donnelly, who had been rather impulsively dubbed at the behest of the Prince of Wales the year before he became George IV. Donnelly had of course at the time been a subject of the Crown, but, having died a year later, in circumstances already described, was rather forgotten, except apparently in Co. Kildare. So, Henry Cooper was not the first boxing knight, rather that honour had fallen to the man whose heroics, passed down to him in song, had so inspired little George Cooper in the 1870s. The connection is pleasing.

*

So, after an Odyssey through this fighter's life, it is a relief but, I confess, no particularly great surprise, to discover that the public Henry Cooper is also the private one. There is no spin there; he is the natural inheritor of the mantle of all those other great British champions, and the British public, which can so often be entirely correct in their collective assessment of a person, have maintained their respect and regard for him for two generations, ever since that evening in London in 1963, which has passed into history, for the general public at least, as the most memorable fight in British heavyweight history. He lost it, but nobody cared then, and they certainly don't care now. They can easily forget his successors, and probably will.

As this book was being finished, we suffered a family tragedy when my wife's poor mother lost her battle with cancer. I was sitting with the nurse as the shifts changed. We were in the kitchen, drinking some of my execrable coffee, as her colleague started work upstairs. She asked me what I was up to; I told her that I was finishing the biography of Henry Cooper. Her tired face lit up a little and she smiled: 'Ah, my son will look forward to that; so will I, actually.'

Pleased, I asked her how old her son was.

'He's ten,' she replied, 'he's a great fan of Henry's.'

*

As the sport of boxing has re-invented itself in Britain after its slump in the wake of Henry's retirement, many things about it changed. The *Thomas à Becket* is still there in the Old Kent Road, and it is still a pub, but its once-famous upper room, with the gym, the skipping ropes, the punch bags, the speedballs, the whole place redolent of sweat, pain effort and liniment, not to mention Jim Wicks's ratty little office where so much business was done, is no longer. It is now an art gallery, which some might find entirely appropriate.

Peter Mario's restaurant, along with Jack Isow's, closed some time ago, and Sheekey's is now re-invented and relocated – still excellent, though – but you can still go to Simpson's in the Strand to eat; they will serve you, with impeccable courtesy, from a very similar menu to the one from which Jim Wicks chose so gravely all those years ago, ensconced in his usual stall in the first-floor dining room.

Jim Wicks died, nine years a widower, on 10 December 1980 and until he fell ill with the cancer that would plague him for the last 18 months of his life, he and Henry would continue their traditional culinary progression around the West end. Towards the end, Henry asked him why on earth he had never written down his life history: 'Well, son, it's simple,' the old man had wheezed, in his unique Bermondsey patois. 'The bigger the truth, the bigger the libel suit.'

And Wicks was entirely right. Jim Wicks had, through the course of his extraordinary life, seen changes in the sport of prizefighting which would have been unimaginable when he fought his one and only professional fight all those years before. Boxing had moved from being on the margins of the law to being respectable, to being immensely popular and, in the period when Henry fought, to becoming almost a national obsession.

Wicks's influence on this sport, mainly subliminal, it must be said, had been huge; he had, along the way, worked at every level of it, from fighter to promoter, manager and fixer. He had over his long career observed a great many sadnesses and glories, errors, tragedies and triumphs and he had paid Henry Cooper out with the full coin of those experiences. Henry is in no doubt that Wicks was, professionally, the best thing that ever happened to him; he still feels a profound sense of honour that by the time he retired he was the only boxer left in Wicks' organization, such as it was by then; indeed that Wicks had gone on in the fight game longer than he had to purely to work with him.

A cynic might say that Henry was actually the best thing to happen to Wicks, and it is hard to disagree, but in reality the relationship between these two men was a quite unique symbiosis, based upon a rare blend of mutual self-interest, but fully balanced by great affection. For Wicks, his approach to life was reflected by that plain statement that might well have served as his epitaph: 'The game, son, must be played.' For Henry, there was a more important aspect to the role that Wicks played in his life, as Albina related his own words to me: 'He always told me, "All my life, I wanted to be somebody."'

Well, I am pleased to be able to report – he is.

PROFESSIONAL
FIGHT HISTORY

Key to abbreviations:

KO – Knockout   RSF – Referee Stopped Fight   W – HC Wins   L – HC Loses   DW – Draw
PTS, Henry Cooper Wins or Loses on points decision   DISQ – fight decided on disqualification
RET – Loser retired (corner or throws in towel)

Date of Fight	Opponent	Venue	WLD	Verdict	Rounds	Titles
14/09/1954	Harry Painter, GB	Harringay Arena	W	KO	1	
09/10/1954	Dinny Powell, GB	Harringay Arena	W	RSF	4	
23/11/1954	Eddie Keith, GB	Manor Place Baths	W	RSF	1	
12/07/1954	Denny Ball, GB	Harringay Arena	W	KO	3	
01/27/1955	Colin Strauch, GB	Royal Albert Hall	W	RSF	1	
08/02/1955	Cliff Purnell, GB	Harringay Arena	W	PTS	6	
08/03/1955	Hugh Fearns, GB	Earl's Court	W	DIS	2	
29/03/1955	Joe Crickmar, GB	Empress Hall	W	RET	5	
18/04/1955	Joe Bygraves, JA	Manor Place Baths	W	PTS	8	
26/04/1955	Uber Bacilieri, I	Harringay Arena	L	RSF	2	
06/06/1955	Ron Harman, GB	Nottingham	W	RSF	7	
13/09/1955	Uber Bacilieri, I	White City	W	KO	7	

Date	Opponent	Venue	Result	Method	Round	Notes
15/11/1955	Joe Erskine, JA	Harringay Arena	L	PTS	10	British Heavyweight title eliminator
28/02/1956	Maurice Mols, F	Royal Albert Hall	W	RSF	4	
01/05/1956	Brian London, GB	Empress Hall	W	RSF	1	
26/06/1956	Giannino Luise, 1	Wembley Arena	W	RSF	7	
07/09/1956	Peter Bates, GB	Manchester	L	RTD	5	
19/02/1957	Joe Bygraves, JA	Earl's Court	L	KO	9	British Empire Heavyweight title
19/05/1957	Ingemar Johansson, S	Stockholm	L	KO	5	European Heavyweight title
17/09/1957	Joe Erskine, GB	Harringay Arena	L	PTS	15	British Heavyweight title
16/11/1957	Hans Kalbfell, D	Dortmund	W	PTS	10	
11/01/1958	Heinz Neuhaus, D	Dortmund	DW	–	10	
19/04/1958	Erich Schoeppner, D	Frankfurt	L	DIS	6	
03/09/1958	Dick Richardson, GB	Porthcawl	W	RSF	5	
14/10/1958	Zora Folley, USA	Wembley Arena	W	PTS	10	
12/01/1959	Brian London, GB	Earl's Court	W	PTS	15	British & Empire Heavyweight titles
26/08/1959	Gawie de Klerk, SA	Porthcawl	W	RSF	5	British Empire Heavyweight title
17/11/1959	Joe Erskine, GB	Earl's Court	W	RSF	12	British & Empire Heavyweight titles

Date of Fight	Opponent	Venue	WLD	Verdict	Rounds	Titles
13/09/1960	Roy Harris, USA	Wembley Arena	W	PTS	10	
06/12/1960	Alex Miteff, ARG	Wembley Arena	W	PTS	10	
21/03/1961	Joe Erskine, GB	Wembley Arena	W	RTD	5	British & Empire Heavyweight titles
05/12/1961	Zora Folley, USA	Wembley Arena	L	KO	2	
23/01/1962	Tony Hughes, USA	Wembley Arena	W	RTD	5	
26/02/1962	Wayne Bethea, USA	Manchester	W	PTS	10	
02/04/1962	Joe Erskine, GB	Nottingham	W	RSF	9	British & Empire Heavyweight titles
26/03/1963	Dick Richardson, GB	Wembley Arena	W	KO	5	British & Empire Heavyweight titles
18/06/1963	Cassius Clay, USA	Wembley Arena	L	RSF	5	World Heavyweight title eliminator
24/02/1964	Brian London, GB	Manchester	L	PTS	15	British, Empire & Heavyweight titles
16/11/1964	Roger Rischer, USA	Royal Albert Hall	L	PTS	10	
12/01/1965	Dick Wipperman, USA	Royal Albert Hall	W	RSF	5	
20/04/1965	Chip Johnson, USA	Wolverhampton	W	KO	1	
15/06/1965	Johnny Prescott, GB	Birmingham	W	RTD	10	British & Empire Heavyweight titles
19/10/1965	Amos Johnson, USA	Wembley Arena	L	PTS	10	

Date	Opponent	Venue				Title
25/01/1966	Hubert Hilton, USA	Olympia Circus	W	RSF	2	
16/02/1966	Jefferson Davis, USA	Wolverhampton	W	KO	1	
21/05/1966	Muhammad Ali, USA	Arsenal F.C.	L	RSF	6	World Heavyweight title
20/09//1966	Floyd Patterson, USA	Wembley Arena	L	KO	4	
17/04/1967	Boston Jacobs, USA	Leicester	W	PTS	10	
13/06/1967	Jack Bodell, GB	Wolverhampton	W	RSF	2	British & Empire Heavyweight titles
07/11/1967	Billy Walker, GB	Wembley Arena	W	RSF	6	British & Empire Heavyweight titles
18/09/1968	Karl Mildenberger, D	Wembley Arena	W	DIS	8	European Heavyweight title
13/03/1969	Piero Tomasoni, I	Rome	W	KO	5	European Heavyweight title
24/03/1970	Jack Bodell, GB	Wembley Arena	W	PTS	15	British & Commonwealth & Heavyweight titles
1/11/1970	José Urtain, ES	Wembley Arena	W	RSF	8	European Heavyweight title
16/03/1971	Joe Bugner, GB	Wembley Arena	L	PTS	15	British, Commonwealth & European Heavyweight titles

Index